THE KAIZEN
BLITZ

National Association of Manufacturers Series

Published titles in this series are:

Pathways to Agility: Mass Customization in Action
0471-19175-2
by John D. Oleson

Time Out: Using Visible Pull Systems to Drive Process Improvement
0471-19214-7
by Wayne Smith

THE KAIZEN
BLITZ

ACCELERATING BREAKTHROUGHS
IN PRODUCTIVITY AND PERFORMANCE

**ANTHONY C. LARAIA,
PATRICIA E. MOODY,
AND ROBERT W. HALL**
of the Association for
Manufacturing Excellence

John Wiley & Sons, Inc.
New York ➤ Chichester ➤ Weinheim ➤ Brisbane ➤ Singapore ➤ Toronto

Copyright © 1999 by The Association for Manufacturing Excellence. All rights reserved.

Published simultaneously in Canada.

This publication is designed to provide accurate and authoritative information in regard to the subject matter covered. It is sold with the understanding that the publisher is not engaged in rendering legal, accounting, or other professional services. If legal advice or other expert assistance is required, the services of a competent professional person should be sought.

Library of Congress Cataloging-in-Publication Data

Laraia, Anthony C., 1947–
    The Kaizen Blitz[SM]: accelerating breakthroughs in productivity and performance / Anthony C. Laraia, Patricia E. Moody, and Robert W. Hall.
        p.   cm.—(National Association of Manufacturers series)
    Includes index.
    ISBN 0-471-24648-4 (cloth : alk. paper)
    1. Production management.   2. Manufacturing industries—Management.   I. Moody, Patricia E. II. Hall, Robert W.
III. Title.   IV. Series.
TS155.L257 1999
658.5—dc21   98-41478
                                                                     CIP

Printed in the United States of America.
10 9 8 7 6 5 4 3 2 1

Contents

Acknowledgments

Sometimes a group will have an idea, and the more the idea circulates, the more it takes on the character of the hands that touch it. The Association for Manufacturing Excellence's (AME) Kaizen Blitz[SM] is an idea that grew in the hands of some eager and energetic shop floor people, the *real* experts. We have tried to remain true to their spirit and to well convey the work of their hands. We are happy to recognize their many valuable contributions to U.S. manufacturing, and we are indeed proud to have the opportunity to name their many names:

Jon Brodeur, President, Surplus Direct
Jon Brodeur created AME's Kaizen Blitz concept, and as a member of the Board of Directors of AME's Northeast Region, he championed and organized the first AME Kaizen Blitz event held in September of 1994. The first event was an outstanding success, and it was followed by a second, also organized by Jon, in May of 1995. Since then, events have been held across the country introducing hundreds of attendees to this powerful new concept.

James P. Womack, founder, The Lean Enterprise Institute, member of AME's *Target* magazine Editorial Board
Jim Womack's keynote address to AME's 1994 International Conference in Boston on November 18, 1994, "From Lean Production to Lean Enterprise," inspired us. His subsequent book (with Daniel T. Jones), *Lean Thinking: Banish Waste and Create Wealth in*

Your Corporation (Simon & Schuster, 1996), focused our attention on the need for companies to look at their businesses in a new way and to employ tools of radical change like kaizen, to realize their potential. We hope the work of our hands will approach Jim's high standards.

Masaaki Imai, Chairman, The Kaizen Institute
Imai's book *Kaizen, The Key to Japan's Competitive Success* (Mc-Graw Hill, 1986) called attention to the effectiveness and potential of kaizen as a tool for improvement. He has long been a leading advocate for its adoption throughout industry.

Richard Schonberger, author of *Creating a Chain of Customers, and World Class Manufacturing* (Simon & Schuster), and a member of AME's *Target* magazine Editorial Board
Dick was around at the beginning of the manufacturing revolution in the United States and every contribution he has since made to showing people the way has helped to return the United States to its hard-earned, globally competitive level. Thank you, Dick.

Anand Sharma, President, TBM Consulting
Every new thought has a *sensei*, a great teacher who opens minds. Anand understands the potential of his students and continues to offer them new challenges. Thank you, Anand.

Teruyuki Maruo, Honda's great *sensei*, believed in the power of kaizen in the hands of thousands of small suppliers, and he taught his followers how to find that power. Terry calls his approach BP, and as a cousin to the Kaizen Blitz in the family of kaizen, it too has changed the way suppliers work. Thank you, Terry.

Dozens of other hands have worked, clapped, written, and rested, and we thank them all:
Art Byrne, Wiremold Company, Hartford, CT; Pat Lancaster, Chairman, Lantech; Ralph Todd, AME Educational Events Coordinator; Ray Cheser, Boston University, formerly of Critikon; JoAnn Weitzenfeld, AME Production Manager; Cheryl Tanner, Johnson & Johnson; and Ken McGuire, president of MEAC.

Introduction:
The Creation
of AME's Kaizen Blitz^{SM}

The word Kaizen is a Japanese term meaning "to make better." Building on this concept, AME developed a series of educational events known as AME's Kaizen Blitz^{SM}, which AME has been doing since 1994. This book grew out of the interest shown in these seminars.

In 1984 I began working for the Emhart Corporation, headquartered in Farmington, Connecticut, a $2 billion manufacturing conglomerate with over 150 manufacturing operations in 30 different countries. Emhart was profitable and growing at a healthy pace, primarily through acquisition of synergistic businesses. Emhart's strategy was to be the number-one or number-two manufacturer for targeted markets.

Emhart was truly a diverse group of businesses producing anything from machines that make glass bottles or shoes, to golf shafts, electric motors and timers for washers and dryers, commercial and residential hardware for doors, glues, adhesives, footware material, and automotive components. Manufacturing names such as Corbin and Russwin, Mallory Timers and Capacitors, True Temper, Kwikset, Pop Fasteners, Dynapert, United Shoe Machinery (USM), Price Pfister, Hill Refrigeration, Bostick and others made up the family of divisions and product groups within Emhart Corporation.

In 1983, before I joined the company, Emhart upper management decided that, to accelerate the process of business acquisitions, existing businesses had to become more efficient and throw off more cash. They mandated a hybrid corporate department that would be responsible for accomplishing two primary goals during visits to the field—first, to conduct necessary compliance work required for internal audit purposes and second, to perform operational reviews for the purpose of identifying cost savings through efficiency improvement ideas. These visits lasted for eight weeks and typically resulted in an audit report covering compliance and internal control weaknesses, as well as an operational review identifying opportunities for efficiency improvement.

Management decided that the teams sent out to the 150 manufacturing operations would have diverse backgrounds from operations, finance, strategic planning, marketing, and so forth. In a relatively short time the company hired 40 professionals to build up the department domestically and internationally. I was one of the new people hired, and I enjoyed the eight-week stints that took me to parts of the United States I had never seen.

■ AN AWAKENING

About a year after this effort was launched, a senior manager within the group who had over 25 years extensive manufacturing line experience began to read about "just-in-time" and some of the truly remarkable results it yielded to committed companies in Japan and elsewhere. The results being achieved by many Japanese companies and some European and U.S. companies appeared to be everything Emhart was striving to achieve. His name was Dick "Sledgehammer" Reed.

It wasn't long before Reed was able to convince Emhart executive management that Just-in-Time was the formula for success at Emhart. Shortly thereafter, Dick was promoted to director and asked to assemble a team that would learn as much as possible about just-in-time (JIT), package it, and spread the "JIT gospel" far and wide to Emhart's many manufacturing facilities. I joined the six-member team to help the information gathering process and subsequently spread the JIT gospel.

■ GETTING UP TO SPEED

Our team split up and visited some of the best Japanese, European, and U.S. factories. We bought the General Electric (GE) JIT Training program, a package of slides, videos, and simulation games covering the concepts and practical applications of JIT. We supplemented the GE program with additional real world applications of JIT in such factories as Toyota, Kawasaki, Harley-Davidson, Citizen Watch, Yamaha, Hyster, John Deere, Black & Decker, and others.

Our team reassembled to build a new JIT training program that we called World Class Manufacturing. It included as major elements flow, setup time reduction, work cells, pull signals, total quality, cooperative vendor relationships, and management by sight.

■ HIT THE ROAD AGAIN

After putting together the interactive training program, the six-member team dispersed again to sign up converts. We conducted one- to three-day World Class Manufacturing training at approximately half of the 150 manufacturing divisions over the next three to four years. During the training we split the trainees into cross-functional teams of five to eight people; with the help of a facilitator, the teams used overhead transparencies to work out their image of how particular World Class JIT concepts and techniques could be applied to improve a particular process in their business.

We offered longer-term facilitation services to those divisions interested in applying what they had learned to their real-world processes within their company. In many cases this involved working with cross-functional teams one to two hours per week to accomplish specific goals—setup reduction, product quality improvement, or lead-time reduction. We distributed reading materials and developed a corporate newsletter to continue communicating the concepts, as well as promote success stories within sections of Emhart.

Feedback on the training and facilitation was quite positive. We thought we were home free and we "knew" it was only a matter of time before the new converts were well on their way to World Class.

■ THE REVOLUTION THAT DIDN'T COME

For the next four to five years our team split up and traveled almost every week to one of 150 different divisions in 30 different countries. Sure, we learned a lot during our training and facilitation, but this was not the hoped-for revolution we had envisioned. We witnessed isolated incursions and flare-ups, but never did we see a company-wide movement that would generate 10, 20, or 30 percent savings.

■ STEPPING INTO THE GAP

But few of our divisions "got it," and we fell into a big gap between the theory and thought processes and the actual execution. Although we were hired as internal consultants to conduct over 100 projects and to train the trainers, the conversion ratio was less than 10 percent.

I attributed the gap to lack of management understanding and commitment, combined with what I would find out later was our own failure to learn the truly effective application of these techniques. Most of the executives heading up our divisions had not been grounded in the new manufacturing ideas; they usually found themselves on the outside looking in at projects done by other people in their organizations. If management couldn't fully understand the challenge and the expected benefits, without a doubt the project and the philosophy behind it would die.

■ CONNECTICUT SPRING AND STAMPING

After four-and-a-half years at Emhart my career took me to KPMG Peat Marwick for five years, where I continued to travel to manufacturing plants in great need of complete makeovers. One of our clients, Connecticut Spring and Stamping (CSS) offered me the position of chief operating officer, and for two years I enjoyed the opportunity to work with a highly complex operation. Connecticut Spring and Stamping was a large job shop fabricating high-precision components for companies such as Canon, GE, Xerox, Jacobs Manufacturing, Pratt & Whitney, and Johnson & Johnson. We had over 1,000 different routings for approximately 7,000 individual and unique fabricated part numbers. The number of operations in a routing for any given part ranged from 1 to 40, with an average of about 8. We had changeovers averaging 3 hours, although some changeovers lasted more than 24 hours. Manufacturing lead times averaged five weeks.

After about one year on the job, it was clear that just talking about JIT or World Class Manufacturing wasn't going to get it done. I found I was no different from the unsuccessful general managers and plant managers with whom I had consulted through the years who couldn't find the time to get the key stuff done.

Thankfully, in 1993 I heard about a few Connecticut manufacturing pioneers, some our customers, who were doing "kaizen stuff"; I decided to take a look. Wiremold, led by Art Byrne and Al Blake; and Jacobs Manufacturing's Dan Kirby and Steve Brochetti; as well as Art Soucie, Tom Tanner, and Gary Temple at Hamilton Standard; Tom Voss and Ed Kantor at Pratt & Whitney; and Cheryl Tanner, Ron Roncardi, and Jeff Madsen at Critikon had all been heavily involved in kaizen over a one- to three-year period. Each one had learned this approach from Shingajitsu (a group of Japanese consultants who, as employees of Toyota, had implemented these kaizen techniques personally over a number of years).

■ THE ASSOCIATION FOR MANUFACTURING EXCELLENCE

Fortunately, all these companies were within a 10-mile radius of our Hartford facility. I visited each one and came back energized. Coincidentally, the same time I needed some real help in jump starting the World Class Manufacturing process at CSS, the Association for Manufacturing Excellence (AME) was exploring new ways to help member companies improve their manufacturing processes. Up until this point AME workshops had been primarily "show and tell," but these companies doing kaizen presented the great opportunity to actually get something done, on the shop floor, very quickly, in real time.

■ THE BIRTH OF THE BLITZ

We sought help from the key kaizen practitioners at Wiremold, Critikon, Hamilton Standard, Jacobs Manufacturing, and Pratt & Whitney. The blitz was born! The plan was to put some kaizen teams at each one of the pioneering companies; the AME event would host AME members who would actually join teams at Wiremold, Hamilton Standard, Critikon, and Pratt while simultaneously hitting the floor.

But a planning meeting held at Critikon in early 1994 sent us down a different path. At the end of the second meeting our volunteer group of kaizen practitioners decided that it would be more eye opening to hold the kaizen events at five or six companies who *wanted* to do kaizen. The kaizen practitioners had learned that, in the beginning of their process-improvement journey, there were big opportunities to "pick the low-hanging fruit," but as time passed improvements came in smaller incremental steps that were also less exciting and visible.

We thought that each company could support two to three kaizen teams; in total we expected to run about 15 teams at six different plants, all working on a variety of different processes requiring a Kaizen Blitz^{SM} to make significant improvement. Simplifying and streamlining processes such as machine changeovers, material flow, and processes within the office area were identified.

We decided to use as facilitators key practitioners from Critikon, Jacobs Manufacturing, Wiremold, Hamilton Standard, and Pratt & Whitney; they had learned kaizen directly from the consultants at Shingajitsu, and they wanted to help their own eager suppliers learn how to apply kaizen at their operations. Connecticut Spring and Stamping, a supplier to Jacobs Manufacturing, Hamilton Standard, and Pratt & Whitney, signed up for three teams; Plastic Design, Inc., a local plastic injection molder, sponsored two; Jackson Corrugated, a supplier of boxes to Wiremold, provided two teams, along with a supplier to Hamilton Standard and several suppliers to Pratt & Whitney. Each of the 15 teams had 8 members. Other outside attendees and employees from host companies, a combination that would blend internal with external knowledge and experience, brought the total participants to about 80.

■ WHY THREE DAYS?

Most manufacturing personnel have little or no time for improvement junkets. Our decision to structure the Kaizen Blitz as a three-day event came down to economics; three days was the right amount of time people could spend away from their companies and still get a good taste of the approach. Three days would not magically transform the organization, but a three-day blitz would give management and people at all levels a good idea of what could happen in a concentrated effort driven by human creativity. We had heard that most kaizen events being held at any one of the experienced kaizen companies lasted one to two weeks.

■ CONCENTRATED EFFORT

Incremental improvement was not what we were after. We felt, and we proved, that concentrated effort—go in, hit hard, blitz the area, pick up the pieces and put them back together in a new way (with fewer pieces)—rather than a one-hour-per-week session strung out for months, was what stalled companies needed. One of our members described it as "blow it up, start all over, measure the starting point, and reassemble the pieces."

■ THREE-DAY BLITZ

➤ Day One

Dan Kirby, vice president of Operations from Jacobs Manufacturing, probably the first company in the United States to use the Shingajitsu consultants and adopt kaizen, directed training and reviewed high-level concepts. Team members reviewed improvement concepts: definitions of waste, takt time, one-piece flow, the use of a few forms, and so on. They were to immediately put them into practice. After four hours of training, teams piled on buses to their assigned companies, not returning until 7 P.M. The *blitzkrieg* pace kicked in quickly as team members, assigned to do preliminary presentations on day one, with overheads, prepared for dawn-patrol reviews.

➤ Day Two

After the dawn reviews, members got back on the buses, worked all day, and returned at 7 P.M. for a working dinner of presentations to cover the day's progress, critique the results, measure the gains, and get ready for another round.

➤ Day Three

Teams hurried to complete their projects and return by noon. Each team used its video camera to record and measure each step of the project, such as distance traveled; amount of raw material, work in progress, and finished goods inventory existing in the process being kaizened; walking distance for operators; travel distance for parts within the process; and setup times. After the final project presentations, the blitz was over.

◼ WHAT DID I LEARN?

After participating in many of these Kaizen Blitzes, I found that there is absolutely no substitute for getting out on the manufacturing floor and applying in a methodical way the kaizen tools and concepts. What is interesting is that the JIT concepts I had learned 10 years before were still as sound as ever. What I found new and different was how these concepts are applied using a kaizen template for improvement. I found there were a few new tools that made up the kaizen template, such at takt time, standard work, one-piece flow, and cycle time. These tools are used religiously and methodically. The interesting part is that these tools are not only used in the kaizen improvement process but also in maintaining and institutionalizing gains. Proper and consistent usage of the tools ultimately separates those companies that make a short-term, unsustainable improvement from those that institutionalize their new improved process until the process is kaizen-blitzed again.

I visited Jacobs Manufacturing, one of the early U.S. kaizen pioneers, and found certain processes had been blitzed nine times over a three-year period. Each time improved efficiencies were obtained and sustained, work-in-process inventory was reduced, cycle times and lead times were shortened, and the "visual factory" was enhanced. It has come as no surprise to Jacobs Manufacturing, Wiremold, and Critikon management that improved profitability and growth across their respective companies have followed their dedicated kaizen efforts.

◼ WHAT'S NEXT FOR KAIZEN BLITZ

We think non-consultant-driven events—training and on-the-floor work by the experts, the hands-on employees who have experienced the power of the Kaizen Blitz—will continue to be a welcome addition to any organization's arsenal of improvement approaches. Small- and medium-sized companies can do it as well as larger ones and they may have an advantage if operations are small enough in scope to get their arms around. Experienced facilitators are invaluable to get you going. After that, your own core group of experienced Kaizen Blitz leaders is as valuable a human asset as you can have. Becoming a Kaizen Blitz leader is learned by doing and by consistent practice, so the talent has to be kept sharp.

The Association for Manufacturing Excellence will continue to urge companies to take this course of action—and will continue to hold events that introduce people to the power of Kaizen Blitz. This book is written for senior managers who intend to be serious. It is not a prescription for a magic potion. Diving in is the only way to learn to swim. Check the water first, but don't spend a lifetime doing it.

All processes in all operating areas can benefit from this powerful improvement approach. Lantech, a Louisville, Kentucky, manufacturer, has used its kaizen approach to redesign products and power their new product introductions. Overall, proven efficiency improvements range from 20 to 50 percent; inventory reductions are drastic and immediate, from 20 to 80 percent; distance traveled is typically cut in half with some reductions up to 90 percent; suggestions from involved employees increase overnight and build enthusiasm; setup times drop by 50 to 80 percent; productivity improves by 10 to 50 percent. The Kaizen Blitz is everything your company is looking for to improve the bottom line and improve customer service and product quality.

Jon Brodeur

The Power of AME's Kaizen Blitz

Learning by Doing

The Kaizen Blitz[SM] approach has resulted in 90 percent reductions in setup time in one week, 20 to 60 percent improvements in productivity in four days, and inventories cut in half in only a few days![1] These are truly impressive results, if you can hold them, and they weren't achieved by professionals with unlimited budgets. Indeed, they were delivered by teams of typical employees and ad hoc groups of outsiders gathered from a wide variety of companies and disciplines. They all learned how to achieve these remarkable results by participating in Association for Manufacturing Excellence (AME) Kaizen Blitz events hosted by companies ready to test the principles and benefits of kaizen in their own companies and attended by people eager to experience this powerful improvement technique first-hand, making real changes on processes in real factories.

Since 1994 over 60 companies have hosted hundreds of participants on AME Kaizen Blitz teams applying kaizen concepts to a

---

[1] Kaizen Blitz[SM]—"A rapid improvement of a limited process area, for example, a production cell. Part of the improvement team consists of workers in that area. The objectives are to use innovative thinking to eliminate non-value-added work. Ownership of the improvement by the area work team and the development of the team's problem-solving skills are additional benefits." From the *APICS Dictionary,* Ninth Edition, edited by Cox and Blackstone, © 1998, American Production and Inventory Control Society, Falls Church, Va.

wide spectrum of processes in a broad range of industries. Results have been consistently impressive, whether improving productivity in forming metal for jet engines, building cells to assemble precise medical products, or reducing setup times on many different kinds of equipment in dozens of plants; these results are all the more impressive because they were all achieved by first-timers, neophytes learning this powerful process for the first time in unfamiliar businesses and surroundings. For many companies, AME's Kaizen Blitz represents their first big step into Lean Manufacturing.

The Kaizen Blitz is about experienced practitioners sharing knowledge and skills in learn-by-doing exercises—not *just* exercises, but projects that change the way people do their work in real companies, yielding results that really make a difference. People learning about kaizen—what it is, how it works, and how they can bring this powerful new tool to their own companies.

There are many reasons for wanting to begin or explore the Kaizen Blitz process; results such as these have been the reward for many companies hosting AME Kaizen Blitz events.

■ KAIZEN: CONTINUOUS IMPROVEMENT

Kaizen can be simply translated as "continuous improvement," but in what sense?[2] Businesses in the United States have pursued continuous improvement for years under various "Total Quality" or "World Class Manufacturing" banners. Progress is most often incremental, delivering small improvements over prolonged periods. Focus is broad, often across the whole organization; breakthroughs are rare. Risks can most often be characterized as sins of omission—too little change, too late. But kaizen is a different, more powerful approach to continuous improvement.

Kaizen is a highly focused improvement process aimed at producing step function performance improvements—20, 50, 90 percent—in a short time, in narrowly targeted areas.

---

[2] Kaizen—"The Japanese term for improvement; continuing improvement involving everyone—managers and workers. In manufacturing, kaizen relates to finding and eliminating waste in machinery, labor, or production methods. See: continuous process improvement." From the *APICS Dictionary*, Ninth Edition, edited by Cox and Blackstone, © 1998, American Production and Inventory Control Society, Falls Church, Va.

TYPICAL RESULTS ACHIEVED BY AME KAIZEN BLITZ TEAMS

Setup time reduction	70–90%
Productivity improvement	20–60%
Process time reduction	40–80%
Inventory reduction	30–70%
Walking distance reduction	40–90%

Results taken from Kaizen Blitz projects conducted at the following companies:

Connecticut Spring and Stamping, Farmington, Conn.

Critikon (a Johnson and Johnson Company), Southington, Conn.

Hamilton Standard, Windsor Locks, Conn.

Jacobs Manufacturing, Bloomfield, Conn.

Meriden Manufacturing, Meriden, Conn.

Plastic Design, Inc., Middletown, Conn.

Pratt & Whitney, West Hartford, East Hartford, and Farmington, Conn.

United Tool & Die, West Hartford, Conn.

Wiremold, West Hartford, Conn.

Dell Manufacturing, Farmington, Conn.

Gros-Ite Manufacturing, Farmington, Conn.

Marion Metals, Southington, Conn.

Rand-Whitney, Montville, Conn.

Seitz Corporation, Torrington, Conn.

AMS Schneider, Minneapolis, Minn.

Hoffman Engineering, Anoka, Minn.

Intek Weatherseal, Hastings, Minn.

Northwest Airline Overhaul Facility, St. Paul, Minn.

Pfizer, Minnetonka, Minn.

Fel-Pro, Skokie, Ill.

HydraForce, Lincolnshire, Ill.

(continued)

TYPICAL RESULTS ACHIEVED BY AME KAIZEN BLITZ TEAMS

(continued)

White Cap, Chicago, Ill.

Century Mold, Rochester, N.Y.

Diamond Packaging, Rochester, N.Y.

ENBI Corporation, West Henrietta, N.Y.

EG & G Sealol, Warwick, R.I.

Liquid Metronics, Acton, Mass.

MicroTouch, Methuen, Mass.

Nyman Manufacturing, East Providence, R.I.

Nypro, Inc., Clinton, Mass.

Bird Packaging Limited, Guelph, Ontario

Hammond Manufacturing Company Limited, Guelph, Ontario

Kenhar Products, Inc., Guelph, Ontario

Boston Scientific Corporation, Redmond, Wash.

Genie Industries, Redmond, Wash.

MicroSurgical, Redmond, Wash.

Junkunc Bros., Crete, Ill.

US Robotics, Mt. Prospect and Morton Grove, Ill.

Keene Manufacturing, Warwick, R.I.

Tech Industries, Inc., Woonsocket, R.I.

Uvex Safety, Inc., Smithfield, R.I.

Barrday, Inc., Cambridge, Ontario

Keene-Widelite, Cambridge, Ontario

Rockwell Automation Allen-Bradley, Cambridge, Ontario

ACCO North America, Wheeling, Ill.

Flexible Steel Lacing Co., Downers Grove, Ill.

Atlas Copco, Holyoke, Mass.

Greenfield Industries, South Deerfield, Mass.

(continued)

TYPICAL RESULTS ACHIEVED BY AME KAIZEN BLITZ TEAMS

(continued)

Human Resources Unlimited, Springfield, Mass.

Palmer-Goodell Insurance Agency, Springfield, Mass.

Springfield Institute for Savings, Springfield, Mass.

Springfield Wire, Springfield, Mass.

Tubed Products, Division of McCormick, East Hampton, Mass.

There are several types of kaizen activities, ranging from those that focus on developing solutions to problems on the factory floor, to implementing a predetermined plan for change, to streamlining the flow of paperwork. The most familiar and common type, the factory kaizen, provides a good example of the technique.

In a typical Kaizen Blitz project, a cross-functional multilevel team of 6 to 12 members work intensely, 12 to 14 hours a day, to rapidly develop, test, and refine solutions to problems and leave a new process in place in just a few days. They don't plan, they don't propose, they *do*. This focus on doing is what sets kaizen apart from other improvement tools, but in order for it to work effectively, we need to recognize that it has other similarly unique characteristics.

➤ Kaizen Is a Top-Down Process

The kaizen process must begin with the process owner, the individual with real ownership and responsibility who has the authority to change the process and be answerable for the consequences. He or she may be the general manager, president, or in some cases plant manager, but *always* the person in charge. Kaizen cannot be successful without strong support and direction from the top.

➤ Kaizen Is a Team Process

A team of individuals is selected from a range of functional disciplines, with a core of members from the area attacked, the real people who do the work. These are often the true experts who can, with real management support, make change stick. The team's work involves the intense application of a few simple tools in a straightforward, commonsense approach to bringing about real and profound change.

The team is brought together prior to, or at the beginning of, the project period and given basic education in the principles of lean manufacturing and training by experienced experts in the kaizen tools required to do the work.

The team then spends three to five days defining and carrying out the actions necessary to change the process and bring about the needed improvement. Several 12- to 16-hour days are spent developing, testing, and implementing their ideas. Kaizen experts also facilitate during the project itself, working with teams and management to ensure success.

■ KAIZEN PRINCIPLES

The kaizen process is based on several rules that may vary in detail from company to company. But the underlying concepts are the same:

Be open minded.

Maintain a positive attitude.

Reject excuses, seek solutions.

Ask Why? Why? Why? Why? Why? There are *no* stupid questions.

Take action. Implement ideas immediately, don't seek perfection. That is, do what can be done *now*, with the resources at hand.

Use all of the team's knowledge. The experts are frequently found on the factory floor.

Disregard rank. All team members are equal and everyone has something to contribute.

Just do it!!

➤ Kaizen Is Doing, Not Proposing

Kaizen fundamentally differs from traditional continuous improvement processes because it is almost entirely action-based.

Teams are charged with both developing and implementing their solutions; they create processes or change existing processes, leaving a *new* process in place.

➤ Getting Dirty Together

Kaizen is very much a *hands-on* process. Team participants not only plan, they clean equipment, sort tools, move machinery (within the bounds of safety), assemble, build, and run the process. They get tired, they get frustrated, and they *get dirty together*. Rank is not recognized—factory managers and company officers work side by side with machine operators to find and implement the best of their ideas. The team's job is to make change happen. To create and leave in place a *new way of doing things*.

➤ Kaizen Is a Low-Budget Process

As a tool for bringing about improvement in a rapid and targeted manner, a Kaizen Blitz is a low-cost process. When teams are charged with demonstrating and implementing changes to live processes in three to five days, there is no time to spend money on new capital equipment, complex and expensive tooling, or elaborate systems solutions.

Setup time reduction projects are good examples. When asked to reduce changeover time for a machine by 90 percent, say, from one hour to six minutes, the engineering solution may be a new machine, programmable controller, or sophisticated (read *complex*) new tooling. A Kaizen Blitz team has *at most* five days to complete its work—that means to demonstrate new methods and to start to make them the new standard way of doing the work.

Even if unlimited funds were available, the money couldn't be spent and the goods received in the time allowed. The team must make do, for the most part, with what is already at hand and concentrate on eliminating waste to achieve its goals.

Most teams work with a very modest budget ($300 to $400 is typical to support their projects), the kind of challenge that leads to the most creative solutions. The kaizen technique itself teaches that eliminating waste and developing creative solutions using the equipment and tools at hand are the preferred methods for achieving improvement goals.

■ CUTTING TO THE CORE OF VALUE

Many companies that have adopted kaizen improvement techniques as part of overall lean manufacturing or lean enterprise initiatives report that their more effective application of the means already at hand has resulted in significant reductions in their new capital equipment costs.

Certainly, many opportunities exist for companies to sample the process, but in reality, the biggest payoff comes to those willing to commit the resources required to do it right—to choose, train, and follow up.

Kaizen is not a process easily mastered. Although the principles can be simply defined, learning their effective application through cross-functional kaizen teams requires study, commitment and perseverance.

Guidance by experienced practitioners, often on a prolonged basis, is cited time after time as an underlying fundamental of success, and as with most business improvement processes, the rewards are commensurate with the investment.

Although the range of projects that a kaizen team might be asked to carry out is large, the scope and focus must be narrowly defined, clearly bounded (for example, improve a press or cell, not a stamping plant). In a factory environment, a team might be assigned to build a manufacturing cell from individual functionally applied machines, another might attack changeover times on a key bottleneck machine, yet another might create a pull system to regulate a part or all of a process. Results must be unambiguously measured—parts per shift or man-hour, minutes per setup, setups per day, and so on.

From Pratt & Whitney's jet engines to Wiremold's wiring devices to Johnson & Johnson's medical products, from metal stamping to turning to cost accounting systems to product distribution, kaizen has proven its worth in cutting to the core of value in what we do and how we do it.

■ FOCUS AND COMMITMENT

One of the keys to kaizen's success is the close focus that this method brings to the process.

Management is often unwilling or unable to authorize, or to give full authority, to those charged with bringing about a change. Problems range from the possible impact on other parts of the operation to the real risks, the unforeseen impacts, of dramatically changing too large a part of the business. The larger the area affected, the larger the potential risks. Intended actions become "recommendations" as the fruits of change are watered down in endless studies. Risk avoidance outweighs the opportunity for gain.

In kaizen, a more narrowly defined focus is established along with clear, measurable improvement goals.

The team's target might be a machine, a cell, perhaps a department, but the scope is generally such that the risks of unforeseen consequences are minimized. An authorization to "do what needs to be done" becomes feasible. Furthermore, because kaizen is a short-term change process, typically spanning no more than several days (an AME Kaizen Blitz lasts three to four days), whatever is changed can be changed back.

➤ Commitment Is Key

Management *must* be ready to make a real commitment to change—not only to acquiesce or agree to the need for change but to lead the process.

A kaizen team should be directed to *"do what needs to be done."* If you're not ready to see a new process in place by next Monday, not just proposed, but in place and functioning as the new way of doing business, then don't start—kaizen just isn't for you.

■ IN THE LONG RUN, ONLY THE SIMPLE STUFF WORKS

Kaizen is a simple process. Like the game of golf, the rules are simple but mastery takes practice and above all, commitment. The results kaizen brings come from the application of simple, commonsense principles in an organized and disciplined fashion in an environment of real commitment to continuous improvement. Kaizen stresses linkages of simple steps that build on each other to reach a goal, rather than developing complicated, broadly focused systems.

Complex solutions are hard to maintain and harder to monitor. Most organizations lack the energy and attention span required to make them work. The simple, easy-to-follow solutions, the kind that kaizen delivers, are the ones that last.

The Kaizen Blitz process offers outstanding benefits at many levels. If you are interested in kaizen as part of an overall commitment to adopting lean manufacturing, to achieving results like these on a broad scale, for the whole enterprise, if you want a tool for addressing specific problems or opportunities, if you need a remarkably effective tool for demonstrating that *radical change can happen,* that it's safe to *try,* to do it *fast* and do it *now,* then you may find that kaizen is the way to *do it.*

■ KAIZEN: FOUR DAYS TO BLITZ

➤ The Story of a Typical Kaizen Blitz Team

Monday 7 A.M. At Universal Valve's largest plant, an hour from Nashville, Tennessee, the team—machine operators, assemblers, an engineer, a tool designer, a salesman, a local supplier, an executive from corporate—assembled in the cramped conference room for the kickoff meeting.[3]

The team's objective was to build a manufacturing cell that would incorporate all of the necessary equipment and people to machine, clean, assemble, and package parts to customer order in the same day.

The Valve Cell Team

Frank Harris, team leader	Supervisor, machining
Bill Walsh	Machine operator
Sally Ford	Machine operator
"Doc" Moore	Assembler/Setup, second shift
Mary Romano	Assembler
Sammy Garcia	Tool designer

---

[3] Universal Valve, the site of the Kaizen Blitz in our story, isn't a real company, but the experiences of the team are an accurate composite of real teams in real companies that have hosted AME Kaizen Blitz events. The principles behind the story are what's important, what counts.

Learning	Hit the ground running	Build it	Change it again	Refine it	
Planning		Try it	Try it again and again	Test it	THE NEW WAY
Preparing	Do it *now!*	Change it		Prove it	
Prework	Day 1	Day 2	Day 3	Day 4	

Figure 1.1. Four Days to Blitz

Scott Olsen	Product engineer
Marty Ross	Lake Metals Foundry (supplier)
Mike Werner	Sales, Philadelphia office
Tom Nichols	Corporate materials manager

The team leader, Frank Harris, the machining department supervisor, introduced each member and presented their objective. They were to solve a chronic problem—build a manufacturing cell that cuts the process time for completed valves in half—by Friday! Along with a process time target, the team had goals to meet in productivity and work-in-process inventory reduction as well. Two other teams were introduced, each with equally challenging goals.

Larry Wilson, the plant manager, and Steve Sandusky, the team's facilitator, an experienced kaizen veteran, added their exhortations, and the work began.

➤ How It Began

Larry and Steve had talked for several months about the plant's first projects, choosing them carefully for maximum impact. They wanted to find highly visible opportunities that would showcase the power of a kaizen team and allow Larry to demonstrate convincingly his commitment to change and to the teams themselves. The cell-building project represented a radical departure from the traditional batch and queue concepts the plant had followed for its entire 20-year history. Its process time reduction goal would highlight improvement in lead time, a chronic problem area for the plant. The productivity improvement goal was set to address the skepticism of much of the staff with regard to multiple-operation cells versus traditional dedicated operations.

At one time the plant had been one of the most profitable plants in the company, but domestic and foreign competition had taken its toll. Now Larry and his peers were under increasing pressure from corporate to increase productivity, reduce costs, slash inventories, and improve return on assets. The old remedies just didn't work any more. New capital equipment meant more investment—not less—and potential for payback was harder and harder to justify. Technical or engineered process solutions just couldn't deliver the kind of rapid improvement needed. The problem was how to do more with what was already in hand.

Larry had visited several other plants undergoing a lean conversion using kaizen improvement techniques with some real success. He'd even had the chance to be a team member in a nearby facility in another company. He was anxious to try what looked to him like a breakthrough technique.

➤ A Typical Facilitator

Steve worked in a corporate process improvement group and had helped several other plants begin their kaizen projects. He'd had his first kaizen experience on a Kaizen Blitz team in another company. When Universal began its own program, he'd been mentored by an outside consultant who had many years of experience with the kaizen process in a stamping company. Steve had been a member of several teams and served in some team-leader assignments before formally beginning to develop his facilitation skills. Several successful cofacilitation and training assignments led to independent project development and facilitation assignments. He'd developed a number of technical skills along the way, but his most important role was guiding the team, particularly the team leader, through the stress, pressures, and pitfalls of their kaizen week.

➤ The Team Leader

Frank had been as supervisor at Universal for several years. He had a reputation as a hard worker and someone who wasn't afraid of new ideas. He also was seen as someone trusted by his people;

"tough but fair" was a typical description. Steve and Larry had chosen him to be team leader for these reasons and because he'd ultimately be responsible for the new valve cell. They hoped he'd be able to make the changes stick.

➤ Day One: The Work Begins

Much of the morning was spent cleaning the workplace: scrubbing machines, washing the floor, cleaning out cabinets, and discarding unneeded items. Cleaning and organizing would be part of each day's routine for the rest of the week. The team was a little slow getting started, a bit tentative with each other. They had first met as group only last week. They'd attended a half-day class in lean manufacturing, learning the key principles of the Toyota Production System and specific techniques they would need to use during their kaizen project. Now that they had a chance to work together—and work hard—the tentativeness soon wore off.

By late morning the team was hard at work designing their cell. Up to now, it had taken six weeks to get a valve through Universal because the plant was functionally organized, with machines set up to perform individual operations, more or less one step at a time. Batches of work, usually consisting of several wire baskets holding hundreds of housings or pistons, were moved from operation to operation until they were completed. The parts then went to a central stockroom before being issued to assembly to fill customer or stocking orders. The problem was that the process typically took up to six weeks to complete and customer service was mediocre at best despite huge raw-material, in-process, and finished-goods inventories.

Just Chalk Marks on the Floor

By early afternoon the team had decided on an initial configuration for the new cell, and they, along with several maintenance tradespeople, had begun the process of disconnecting and relocating equipment. No precise engineering drawings were needed—as a matter of fact, they weren't allowed—just some chalk marks on the floor following a familiar U-shaped pattern. No hard wiring or plumbing either—after a few trials they'd probably be moving things around again, anyway. (It took a few kaizen projects for the plant engineer to get used to the idea, but eventually quick-connect devices became the standard for machine hookups.)

At the late-afternoon review meeting with Larry, his staff and Steve, Frank, and the other team leaders presented progress reports and plans for the evening and next day.

The plant was under a lot of pressure; a key customer was in the middle of a seasonal ramp up. Sales called asking for yet another schedule move up. Larry, the plant manager, anxiously questioned Frank on how long it would be before production was resumed.

They were walking a tight line; he had spent a lot of energy in emphasizing the importance of the team's goals to the whole organization. It would be a mistake to signal that he was backing off to meet another expedite. Frank and his team were already aware of the need, however, and he arranged for the first-shift maintenance crew to stay on late into the evening to make sure they could start up again by noon the next day.

After the update meeting, Steve, the facilitator, advised Frank that the team should consider breaking up into subteams to focus on their many remaining tasks. There just wouldn't be enough time for everything to be discussed by the whole group before taking action. Frank was a little uncomfortable. He felt that as team leader he had to okay any major new ideas. Steve pointed out that there was a lot of talent and experience on the team and that he needed to rely on and take advantage of their abilities. He emphasized, as he almost always did, that kaizen teams need to *make mistakes quickly* and then correct and move on, not deliberate. The subteams would just have to use their best judgment and get things done on their own. Frequent progress checks would point out sticking points or false starts before they got out of hand.

The teams had a quick dinner together in the cafeteria. Afterward, Frank's team converged in their conference room. Each team had its own small meeting area with a blackboard and easel; Steve did his best to make sure they spent very little time there— the problems and opportunities were out on the floor!

They broke up into three subteams: One continued with the move; a second sorted out needed tooling and came up with a point-of-use storage system; the third designed a kanban system to regulate the flow of work to and from the new cell (see box on p. 15).

By late evening it was apparent that the move was a larger undertaking than they had expected, so the first-shift maintenance

KANBAN

For our purposes the term *kanban* refers to a pull system whereby product is made only to a signal. The signal is typically a visual cue: a card, an empty container, an empty space. In addition, work-in-process stock for any item in the system should not exceed a fixed upper limit. This definition is a little simplistic; a better sense of its broader meaning is in the following excerpt from *Zero Inventories,* by Robert W. Hall, (Irwin, 1983):

> The Toyota Motor Company assembled ideas from many sources and combined them with their own thinking to create stockless production. . . . Kanban is the corporate name of the version of the system pioneered by Toyota and companies of the Toyota group. It is a Japanese word meaning card, a definition which conveys very little of the total scope of the system. Later Toyota sometimes referred to it as a "just-in-time" system, but that implies only that transfers of material are made prior to being needed; there is no suggestion that many improvements in all phases of production are necessary to do that. (The strict definition of *just-in-time* is to have *only* the necessary part at the necessary place at the necessary time, or, as an American worker would say, "Don't have anything you aren't working on.")

crew stayed on to work with the second shift. But it looked as though the move still couldn't be completed before late Tuesday afternoon. The team called it quits at 10 A.M. and agreed to assemble at 6:30 the next morning.

➤ Day Two

The next day was more of the same, but more intense. The pull-system team had diagrammed the flow of materials and selected locations for kanban "squares" (see Figure 1.2). Because several valve versions required different sequences of operations, they were also preparing work instruction kanban cards to accompany these parts through the process. The team had identified all of the

Red 100 pieces	Yellow 100 pieces	Green 100 pieces
Red 100 pieces	Yellow 100 pieces	Green 100 pieces

Figure 1.2. Kanban Squares

tools they needed to set up and run the milling and turning equipment in the cell and were building shadow boards with painted outlines of the tools for mounting on the machines. Under pressure from Larry and Steve to step up the pace, the team finished the machine moves and began running some test parts in time for the 4:00 status meeting.

Larry was relieved to hear that production was starting up again, but his relief didn't last. By early evening it was clear that the cell configuration needed to change. The cell couldn't meet takt time (the seconds per piece needed to meet customer demand). Frank and several of his team were frustrated with the problem. They worried that they'd gotten off on the wrong track and wouldn't have time to recover. They'd be to blame for missing shipments!

Steve could see that Frank was starting to feel some of the pressure that comes with the team leader's role and took him aside for some coaching. He shared his experience with past teams that suffered similar frustrations, and he talked about some approaches Frank could take to move the team ahead. He was careful not to offer what were, to him, obvious solutions. The team still had enough time to get the job done, and helping them to learn ways to solve their own problems was one of the key goals of the exercise.

Frank called the whole team back together to work on the problem. They discussed and argued about several ideas before they chose an approach. By moving a drill press into the cell, they could take some of the load off of the CNC (computer numerically controlled) mill and meet their target. Unfortunately, they would need to relocate three other machines to do so. Convincing the plant engineer to relocate the machines wasn't easy for Frank, especially because he had to depend heavily on him for support in his regular job. The plant engineer wasn't happy: His crew had worked late last night to get the job done and now they had to do it again—life was a lot easier when engineering spent weeks doing formal layouts before any move was approved. (With experience, he eventually agreed that the new kaizen process gave better results in the long run than the traditional technically driven, deliberative approach; it just made life a bit more hectic for a time.)

The team again worked until 10 P.M. to get the job done and planned an early morning trial.

➤ Day Three

On Wednesday morning the team began running the new cell in earnest, changing from one product to another to develop and refine the new process and ensure that it would work on all required parts. The equipment operators and assemblers were the keys to this part of the process; they brought real skill and experience to the team. They had come up with several ideas for fixtures and quick-change work holders that were being put together by the machine shop.

For the machine operators in particular this was a new and satisfying experience. They'd spent years running and setting up machines, but their opinions had never been considered in the design of the tools and equipment they used. Now they had a real chance to put their own ideas into practice. They'd been hesitant at first, but working with the tool designer on the team had helped; his skills and confidence had encouraged them and drawn them out. Frank, their team leader, had also helped by letting them know he was depending on them to work out the needed solutions.

One of the team members had found a hydraulic clamp they wanted to try at a distributor about an hour away; he'd driven off early that morning to pick it up. The assembly operators were working together with two other members to set up an assembly bench and storage area for packing materials so that they could begin assembly in the cell. This was a difficult concept for them to accept after years of working on large batches one step at a time.

One-Piece Flow

Steve coached and coaxed them through the change. One-piece flow, he felt, was the key to success here, but he knew it would be hard for the plant to accept until they'd seen it work on their own products. Experience told him that it would probably be a long time, if ever, before most of the organization recognized the real value of the one-piece flow cellular concept. The business was still being driven by the old measures. Sales wanted plenty of inventory available to ship at a moment's notice. The plant's mediocre delivery performance over the years had made them skeptical that they could trust the new short-cycle, lean concepts. They'd wait and see.

Most of the manufacturing staff had grown up in an environment in which idle machines were considered a mortal sin—better to produce an extra batch of parts that won't be needed for a while than to have expensive equipment not running. The idea of a cell running at the pace of the slowest operation just didn't make sense. It would take strong personal support from Larry and his staff to make this team's new operation a long-term success.

Managing cash flow was another hard concept to grasp for a plant that had been remotely driven to produce to schedule with little or no direct contact with customers. The realities of global competition were changing all of that to be sure, but change would mean struggle and a real risk of failure.

Following up on the Kaizen Blitz team's work—standardizing the process to get everyone to do the work in the same way—*every time*—would be the real key to long-term success. The kind of diligent, committed, relentless support and follow-up required to reach this goal would be an ongoing challenge to the whole organization.

The New Pull System

The new pull system was beginning to come together; taped squares on the floor would be painted once the team was satisfied. Castings, control rods, assembly hardware, packing material, and piston blanks would flow to the cell along the pull system and be replenished only as they were consumed.

Tools: In the Right Place at the Right Time

As the tooling subteam's work began to come together, tooling was moved from a central crib to new point-of-use locations in the cell,

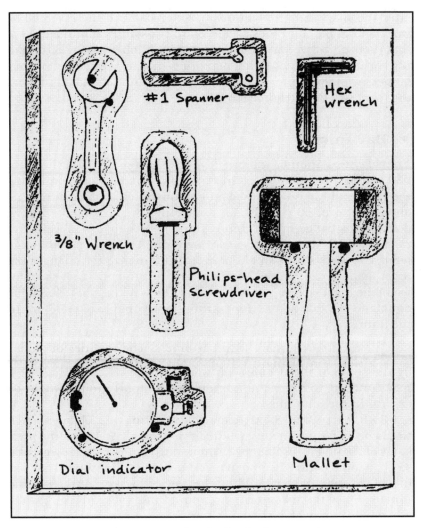

Figure 1.3. Sketch of a Shadow Board

and individual shadow boards with outlines of individual hand tools were being made for each machine (see Figure 1.3).

At the 4:00 P.M. status meeting, Frank was able to report that their goals were in sight. They'd successfully demonstrated that they could meet the output targets, although assembly was still a little clumsy. That evening they were going to change the work flow after the machining operation to better balance the assemblers' work and make their jobs easier; Steve constantly reminded them that their objective was to make everyone's job *easier* by eliminating waste—non-value-adding activities—not to get people to work *harder*. Another dinner in the cafeteria and another late night, and the team was on the home stretch.

➤ Day Four

Thursday was another intense day, just shorter. By 5 P.M. the team had run and refined procedures for all of the part configurations the cell would handle. The team demonstrated a process-time reduction of over 90 percent, far exceeding its goal. Standard work documents that described simply the step-by-step flow of work and rates at which it should be performed were being prepared by the team; the work sheets would help institutionalize the changes the team had made. These hand-written documents and sketches would be displayed in the cell to show the way the work should be done and provide a basis for training everyone assigned there in the future.

The team hoped that new disciplines would be better maintained and accepted because they were being prepared and owned by the some of the people who would do the work. Selling these new concepts to all of the workers and support groups would be critical in the long run.

Both Larry and Steve knew that making the changes stick would be by far the greatest challenge for the plant. Under the pressures of day-to-day problems, customer expedites, breakdowns, and so on, people naturally tend to revert to old familiar ways. That was one of the reasons that building the new cell was an attractive first project: Once the machines were moved into place, the old batch-and-queue approach just couldn't work.

Standard Work

Another difficult concept would be "standard work," a well-documented process followed religiously by everyone doing the work. At Universal things were often done "because that's the way we've always done them." Of course, there were formal routing instructions and process controls, but considerable latitude was always allowed to let individuals perform the work in ways they found comfortable. The concept of everyone following the same steps *in detail*—for example, in setting up a machine—would require a new set of disciplines that would take a long time and many projects to work out.

Finishing touches were going into the shadow boards, tool racks, and kanban squares. After three days of fast food at the plant, the team enjoyed a celebratory dinner at a local pub. By now the team had really gelled. They were comfortable working together and had worked through some tough problems, although not without some strong disagreements. Above all, they'd accomplished something of real value to the plant and the business.

➤ Day Five

On Friday the team did a final cleanup, did some touch-up painting, and prepared their final report. At about 11 A.M. Larry toured each of the kaizen project sites and chose the one he felt had done the best job in cleaning up and effectively organizing its workplace. He would present a plaque to the winning team at the final presentation.

At noon the teams and plant staff gathered in the cafeteria for final presentations. Each team delivered a 20-minute presentation on its objectives and accomplishments, including recommendations for follow-up improvements to be accomplished over the coming month. No star performers here—all of the team members were expected to play a part. By noon it was over. In five days another kaizen team had met its targets, leaving behind a new dramatically improved process.

VALVE CELL TEAM RESULTS

Process Time reduced *93 percent,* from 15 days to less than 1 day.

Productivity increased *43 percent,* from 2.3 units/man-hour to 3.3 units/man-hour.

Inventory reduced *95 percent,* from 4,200 pieces to 218 pieces.

➤ Following Up

Although the project was complete, its consequences for the organization, and especially for the people whose jobs were directly affected, had really only begun. In the weeks that followed many adjustments were needed. Most affected, of course, were the people assigned to work in the cell. Some were members of the Kaizen Blitz team that built the cell. Others, particularly most of those on the second shift, were not. Training in the new procedures, especially cross-training on all of the operations now together in the cell consumed considerable time and effort. Some of the original team members helped out, but it took almost three months to select and fully train the second shift staff.

Some of the assigned operators did not adapt well to their new positions. The staffing concept that the team had developed called for operators to rotate through different positions twice each shift, but several people strongly preferred to stick to one function as they had in their prior assignments. Others were uncomfortable with the more obvious pacing of the work through the cell, with everyone's output directly pacing the output of the cell.

Support groups were affected as well. Because the whole cell would stop whenever a machine breakdown occurred, normal maintenance response and repair procedures were found to be inadequate. A priority response system had to be worked out to ensure prompt attention to problems. The plant needed procedures for ensuring that repairs continued through shift changes and into the off-hours without interruption. Later, improved preventive maintenance practices had to be adopted, and formal selection criteria for equipment to be used in cells were established. Equipment reliability and support were found to be far more critical for cellular manufacturing than for a traditional functional environment.

These problems are typical of those encountered in the early stages of an implementation. The challenge for management is one of stamina, the ability to stay the course. Considerable energy is required to sustain the attention, support, and emphasis needed and to work through the often-frustrating first steps of changing how individuals and organizations work.

The AME Kaizen Blitz was designed to give companies—especially small- and medium-sized ones—a powerful opportunity to make breakthrough change, to show through their own experience that change is achievable. The Kaizen Blitz approach is a good first step toward Lean Manufacturing.

■ BIBLIOGRAPHY

Target is a publication of the Association for Manufacturing Excellence.

Byrne, Art, "How Wiremold Reinvented Itself with Kaizen," *Target* 11 (January–February 1995).

Cheser, Ray, and Cheryl Tanner, "Critikon Declares War on Waste, Launches Kaizen Drive," *Target* 9 (July–August 1993).

Coltman, John, "Event Report: Unleashing the Power of Kaizen at NUMMI," *Target* 7 (Fall 1991).

Cook, Ian, "AME's Kaizen Blitz[SM] Goes Down Under, Making a Difference in Sydney and Melbourne, Austrailia," *Target* 13 (September–October 1997).

Ford, Sherrie, "High Velocity Change: Energized for Excellence at Mitsubishi Consumer Electronics—America," *Target* 13 (September–October 1997).

Galsworth, Gwendolyn D., and Lea A. P. Tonkin, "Invasion of the Kaizen Blitzers," *Target* 11 (March–April, 1995).

Lancaster, Pat, and Ron Hicks, "Using Kaizen to Improve Designs and to Speed Development: How Lantech Kaizened a Problem Product," *Target* 11 (September–October 1995).

Moody, Patricia E., "The Power of Kaizen," *Target* 13 (June–August 1997): 44–45.

Russo, Stephen J., "Five-Company AME Kaizen Blitz[SM] in Rhode Island," *Target* 13 (November–December 1997).

Tonkin, Lea A. P., "Event Report: Kaizen Projects, Lean Systems at Freudenberg-NOK," *Target* 10 (November–December 1994).

Tonkin, Lea A. P., "Kaizen Blitz[SM] 3: Making Improvements in Minnesota," *Target* 12 (January–March 1996).

Tonkin, Lea A. P., "Kaizen Blitz[SM] 4 Makes Its Mark," *Target* 12 (April–May 1996).

Tonkin, Lea A. P., "Kaizen Blitz[SM] 5: Bottleneck-Busting Comes to Rochester, NY," *Target* 12 (September–October 1996).

Tonkin, Lea A. P., "Kaizen Blitz[SM] 6 in Westborough, MA: Fresh Ideas, Fast Results," *Target* 12 (November–December 1996).

Tonkin, Lea A. P., "Kaizen Blitz[SM] 7: Building the Capability to Make Changes Quickly," *Target* 13 (January–March 1997).

Tonkin, Lea A. P., "AME's Kaizen Blitz[SM] Strikes Again!" *Target* 13 (June–August 1997).

Tonkin, Lea A. P., "Simple Process, Great Results: Illinois AME Kaizen Blitz[SM]," *Target* 13 (September–October 1997).

Chapter 2

The Roots of Kaizen

Kaizen is a Japanese word that means small-step improvement, or continuous improvement. Companies in the United States began to use the term following publication of the book, *Kaizen,* by Masaaki Imai in 1985.[1]

In Japan, or anywhere, kaizen—or continuous improvement— means whatever the speaker wants it to mean. Almost any effort to improve processes can be labeled *kaizen,* and antecedent practices have a long history. For example, early in the century all successful automobile companies had major programs in which engineers— some degreed, some not—developed better and better methods and machines to keep auto production flowing, but worker involvement was not a conspicuous part of the effort.

During World War II many of the methods used previously to develop industry were concentrated on defense production. An example is Ford's famed Willow Run bomber plant. Almost every issue of the plant newsletter, published once a week or so, had a few paragraphs describing changes to improve the flow of bomber production. Some were major efforts, such as the development and refinement of the fixtures to build center wings. Some changes were minor, but notable, such as the Rube Goldberg machine built to

---

[1] Imai's latest book on this subject is *Gemba Kaizen* (New York: McGraw-Hill, 1997). *Gemba* means workplace, and *Gemba Kaizen* means simple, low-tech problem solving.

sort by size the rivets swept up from the floor for return to the lines.[2]

The plant symbolized the development of manufacturing flow processes at the time. Where the work plugged up, experienced engineers were cut loose to solve problems on the spot. A group of experienced engineers assigned to quality control reviewed the squawks of the army test pilots; then they tracked down the source of each squawk in the process and fixed it—no big managerial reviews. The United Automobile Workers contributed several thousand suggestions, many of which were implemented, but those commanded less room in the paper than contests to install a record number of rivets in an hour. Many of the antecedants of today's buzzword improvement processes were present at Willow Run, but for the most part the action people of the time just did it without talking much about it.

Today, a kaizen program may go by many names: Continuous improvement, just-in-time production implementation, or plain, simple process improvement. Most programs attempt to engage the participation of workers in the improvement, with varied results. To be successful, the people need the power and ability to actually effect process change. In a factory, that takes increased worker skill plus support from those who can build or modify tools, fixtures, and equipment. A sort of electromechanical playground group dedicated to process improvement is now occasionally referred to as a "kaizen department." Most people in those playgrounds get paid to do work they enjoy.

Thus, the term *kaizen* designates a range of improvement approaches. At one end are staff-dominated projects with limited involvement from people working the process. At the other end are initiatives that emphasize participation through suggestions or team improvement projects. If these are limited to implementing simple, minor changes, they are mostly "human resource" programs. Outcomes are more substantive if technicians, programmers, and operators form high-skill process-change teams. In any case, for truly remarkable results some form of teamwork is important, and senior management has to push it with a passion.

---

[2] From the Collections of the Research Center, Henry Ford Museum and Greenfield Village, Dearborn, Mich., Accession 435, Box 40.

■ AME'S KAIZEN BLITZ

Kaizen Blitz is a short-term, intensive effort to dramatically improve the performance of a limited-scope process. A common example is the development of a production cell in a factory, as described in Chapter 1. The objective is to analyze the process, use innovative thinking to convert it to a cell, and try it out, all within a week or less—a dramatic hit on a limited target to show what can be done. Follow-up action to solidify the gains may persist for weeks, maybe months.

A Kaizen Blitz project is relatively low-tech, fixing simple, obvious stuff. The most common objective is to improve process flow by eliminating time-consuming waste, but blitzes are undertaken for other objectives too. Often teams hear that old battle cry, KISS (keep it simple, stupid), but keeping it simple takes dedicated effort.

There are three phases to a full improvement process using the Kaizen Blitz:

1. *Preparation.* Decide who will be on the blitz team. Inform people in the process area and those who support it that a blitz will occur, what they should expect, and what should be the aftermath.

2. *Kaizen Blitz event.* The core event ends in a demonstration of an altered process.

3. *Follow-up.* Standardize the gains and make them part of ongoing operations.

The intensive part of a Kaizen Blitz employs a team of people, at least some of whom work with the process being improved. Other team members are those who can technically take action to make the changes, including programmers, maintenance people, or "kaizen department" members. Others may come from seemingly unrelated process responsibilities: for example, a field sales representative bringing a different and valuable perspective to a factory cell development team. Some teams include representatives from suppliers or customers.

Often, a few people are included just to learn about Kaizen Blitz so that they can transport the practice elsewhere. For long-term progress, the development of process improvement capability in all the people on the team may be the most important outcome.

From time to time the Association for Manufacturing Excellence (AME) produces Kaizen Blitz events. These usually last four days. A number of people from outside the host organization are added to a Kaizen Blitz team dedicated to the substantial improvement of a real process in the host company. The outsiders bring fresh thought to the project, but the real purpose is to propagate the ability to make dramatic process improvement to many different organizations.

Most people find an intensive Kaizen Blitz experience to be both a lot of work and a lot of fun. However, the core Kaizen Blitz event is only the most visible activity. If long-term effects are to be achieved, if the adventure is to become more than an exploration party, both the preparation and the follow-up are important.

Kaizen Blitz participants need a general concept, or vision, of what improvement means. Otherwise, it's easy to have a series of projects that make improvements according to conflicting goals. After three or four iterations, the process is back to almost the state in which it started. The most common objective of a Kaizen Blitz is to reduce the time duration of a process by eliminating the waste, but that isn't always true, and time compression should not be done at the expense of other vital process characteristics. To keep from going in circles, one must measure results from several different viewpoints.

■ AVOID FUTILE IMPROVEMENT

Unfortunately, futile process improvement has a long history. Efficiency experts visit a process, make a flowchart, pick off a few obvious waste steps to eliminate, execute changes *for* the people running the process, and leave. If the experts (internal as well as external) are paid on the basis of savings, they can demonstrate results and collect their bonuses.

The improvements may or may not stick. If people running the process don't understand, or are filled with resentment, the new process will start to unravel. If support processes to maintain the gains (such as training, scheduling, or maintenance) are not addressed, reversion to the prior state will be quicker.

Kaizen Blitz needs long-term direction. Like any changes that will have substantial impact, senior management must set the direction and Lead with a capital L.

■ KAIZEN BLITZ IN CONTEXT

In most companies that employ it, Kaizen Blitz is not the only improvement activity taking place. Most also have suggestion programs, staff-led projects, quality improvement teams, and other change activities, but the Kaizen Blitz is a method to generate about as much change as work groups can stand at one time and keep going.

Staff-led projects, such as adopting hexapod machine tools or implementing a major software package, are more likely to be big-budget, technology-centered programs planned by technical experts. Many such projects involve commercial suppliers that have a product, package, or service to sell. Workers are minimally involved until they are trained as a part of implementation.

Some breakthroughs are major strategic innovations—novel ideas that change the rules of the game in both internal processes and in the market. A classic case is the xerographic copier that so changed printing and copying processes that life was never the same afterward. That's a home run. By contrast, Kaizen Blitz is a series of singles.

Kaizen Blitz simplifies existing processes with minimum money and maximum use of the people who daily make them work. It doesn't strive for a radical change in technology, but rather for changes in the basic process flow and methodology. However, the accumulation of many kaizen improvements, subprocess by subprocess, adds up to major-league results.

Participants in Kaizen Blitz are usually enthusiastic at the time, but the business press is not as likely to trumpet the improvement of current processes nearly as much as breakthrough innovations, sales booms, or financial restructuring. There, the bottom-line payoff is quicker and easier to see than that which comes from eliminating waste.

So far, the majority of experiences with kaizen in the United States have been with production processes. These make easy-to-understand examples. However, the power of kaizen extends to all processes, from sales order taking to customer after-sales service to service industry processes such as a realtor's preparation of a house for listing. With no major technical breakthroughs, but with an aggressive business improvement strategy, sustained kaizen can force competitors on the defensive—at least until they too catch on.

In itself, Kaizen Blitz is not a strategy. It is not miraculous. It does not strive for technical breakthoughs. It is a methodology to rapidly develop processes, provided that a strategic direction and the organizational climate for it are established.

■ THE KAIZEN BLITZ EQUALS ACTION

Make something happen! That's the idea of the Kaizen Blitz. It's a means to execute a strategy of process improvement. True, if equipment is huge and expensive, or complex and delicate, trying major ideas by simulation beats tearing up a work area only to find that a plan is unworkable. That, too, has happened.

Simulation can be done by a computer. Often it's more effective if workers or a team can move pieces around on a table top. They have more intimate knowledge of the complete process than can usually be built into a simulation model. In any case, if one is going to do a Kaizen Blitz, the impetus is to stop planning and try something. See if the major thrust of a improvement idea is going to work for real. Then follow up to keep it working.

There's much more to it. People need a sense of direction to avoid playing cowboy with a process while accomplishing nothing. But for many of us, staring at everything that must be done to improve process flow becomes a fixation—doubts and fears take over and nothing gets done. Properly used, Kaizen Blitz is the hammer of implementation.

The roles of various team members in a typical Kaizen Blitz are sketched in Chapter 1. To keep the attack going, a Kaizen Blitz needs an experienced facilitator. In this context experience is more than having read the book. Having worked through several prior intensive improvement episodes is a must. As much as anything else in life, Kaizen Blitz is a learn-by-doing experience.

No two Kaizen Blitz experiences are the same. There are many similarities in the time compression of all processes, but the specific personnel, the beginning state of the process, and the technical problems to overcome compose a unique set for each one. And implementation requires working with what really exists, using what is available, right now.

■ THE BACKGROUND OF KAIZEN BLITZ

The term *Kaizen Blitz* is only half Japanese. *Kaizen,* a Japanese word, means continuous, small-step improvement. *Blitz,* a German word, means lightning or lightning strike. When the words are literally construed, Kaizen Blitz is an oxymoron—"continuous small-step improvement lightning."

However, Kaizen Blitz was coined in the United States. In American football, a blitz is a rush by defenders to sack the quarterback before he can do anything—literally, make a big hit. By implication, Kaizen Blitz is a fast attack to achieve a tactical objective. Japanese have long experience with the methodologies but not the context of the term Kaizen Blitz.

After World War II, Japanese industry lay in ruins. Quality was nonexistent. Industrial productivity was one-eighth of the U.S. level.

With nowhere to go but up, the Japanese began to soak up anything they could find on productivity and quality improvement. They turned first to U.S. industrial training. Training Within Industries was developed to train workers for rapid ramp up of defense production during World War II. It was introduced by the occupation forces into Japan about 1948 and grew rapidly thereafter. Much of the Training Within Industries material emphasizes basic problem solving and standard work.[3]

Then the Japanese turned to quality, listening to teachers such as W. Edwards Deming and Joseph Juran, a much better-known story. By the 1950s they were trying to figure out how to match U.S. productivity with no money—how to achieve cheaply the effects of a smooth, automated flow of production—but strictly by simple process improvement. The only way was to be creative with process basics.

Another happenstance was that, although General Douglas MacArthur outlawed labor unions in Japan, violent strikes continued. The only way out was cooperation within the plants. By the mid 1950s, Japanese managers were discovering how to develop trust with the workers. Quality Circles were born. The only way for

---

[3] Alan G. Robinson and Dean M. Schroeder, "Training, Continuous Improvement, and Human Relations: The U.S. TWI Programs and the Japanese Management Style," *California Management Review* 35 (Winter 1993): 35–57.

the Japanese to meet their objectives was for the workers themselves to improve the processes.

This was not easy; command and control managerial instincts did not go into remission without struggle. Quality Circles became a success only after managers learned to work with the people. Slowly these methods evolved into skilled process-improvement groups at the bottom of Japanese companies. At higher levels the traditional seniority-based hierarchy remains intact to this day. Sometime in this era kaizen was born. *Mangi* publications (comic-book style) for foremen popularized simple process-improvement methods.

The most process-innovative company at the time was Toyota, whose reputation is now well known in the West, but not always very accurately. At Toyota, from 1960 to 1966, Taiichi Ohno led the charge into just-in-time (JIT) production. The company's situation then was desperate. Mr. Ohno was an earthy man; he later colorfully referred to kaizen and JIT as "the last fart of the ferret." (A ferret exudes an unbearable stench when cornered.)

Ohno's groups learned the effectiveness of 5 S, U-line cells, pull systems, fail-safing, visibility systems, fast flow with pull systems of control, and much more, including *jidoka,* which is stopping the line for correction or improvement.

Kamigo Engine Plant No. 9, A Shrine to Kaizen

By 1966 the kaizen method for developing JIT production had resulted in Kamigo Engine Plant No. 9, a factory that chunked out 1,500 four-cylinder engines a day using 160 to 170 people (and no computers) in one-piece flow. Technically, the equipment is basic. Instrumentation consists of little more than lights, limit switches, and relays, but the concept for integrating the process was brilliant. Today, Kamigo No. 9 is still a world benchmark among engine plants and a shrine to kaizen—to working people making a process world class themselves.

During this period many Japanese companies dramatically improved process quality, although the productivity improvement of most remained far behind Toyota. Japanese productivity through kaizen did not explode until the oil crisis hit in 1973. Americans only griped about gas lines, but Japanese were utterly dependent on imported oil. Many Japanese companies found themselves up against the wall, as Toyota had been previously.

Toyota organized a program to first assist suppliers. Toyota teachers stormed from plant to plant, implementing JIT by methods similar to AME's Kaizen Blitz. Nonsuppliers lined up to visit Toyota plants to learn the methods. Competitors assimilated Toyota's practices in their own ways. By the late 1970s only a fraction of Japanese companies had progressed substantially with kaizen, but results were astounding. Japanese exports to the United States had become so threatening that Americans and Europeans began to tour Japanese industry to view what was going on.

■ TOKAI RIKA: CONVERTING TO JIT THROUGH KAIZEN

Tokai Rika was a typical example of a Toyota supplier conversion. The company makes many of the items that go in the instrument panel of a car. In 1974 Tokai Rika had already achieved substantial improvement in process capability—quality. Quality Circles functioned well. Many worker suggestions were readily implemented. But when Tokai Rika first attempted to convert an entire plant to cells and JIT production, the management underestimated the challenge. They declared failure.

To kick off the second try, top management assembled the entire workforce. They said very little. Instead, they cleaned machines and swept the floor before them to demonstrate that they, too, were going to get dirty in a second attempt.

What followed was a five-month *blitzkrieg* campaign, seven days a week with all employees, including executives, fully engaged. Each night they moved machines and tried a new set of ideas. By day they made production, observed the outcome, and figured out how to do it better. The next night they did it again. They not only changed production processes but revised all the support processes necessary to make the new system work. Charts throughout the plant bore evidence of their progress.

The intensity at Tokai Rika during this time appears to have been greater than during defense plants during World War II. Survival was at stake. One of the top managers, Susumu Okada, said that in five months he did his job by day, worked with the workers every night, and went home from the plant only three times. It was up to him and other top officers to demonstrate leadership and passion, but the workers had the best ideas.

This level of warlike fervor cannot persist long. It didn't at Tokai Rika either, although processes are still regularly subjected to what we have dubbed Kaizen Blitz. However, Tokai Rika's story demonstrates an important point: If a revolution in primary processes is necessary, top management must not take lightly the leadership necessary for the change in work culture that comes with it.

By the early 1980s explaining the "Japanese miracle" became popular not only in the United States but everywhere. But there was no miracle. By the late 1980s there were cases in which "Japanese manufacturing" had come to the United States, then Americans went back to Japan to teach it to the many Japanese companies that had missed their own revolution. Sperry-Univac sending a lean manufacturing emissary to Okidata was one such case.

Furthermore, the same kinds of improvement approaches have become known everywhere that industry has expanded. One can find plants with smooth process flows in Mexico, South America, Southeast Asia, and Europe. The notion that process expertise is concentrated where the industrial financing has been located is outdated. And today, variations of concentrated process improvement exist everywhere. An advanced version that is becoming popular in Germany is called *Produktklinik*.[4]

The concepts behind Kaizen Blitz are not new. They have a long history and are being used in different variations by many organizations worldwide. But for all the fun experienced in an intensive session, great implementation of a radical process change remains a major barrier to fast-flow, high-performance processes.

Kaizen Blitz is a tactic to implement JIT, lean production, time-to-market, quick response—time compression of operations under whatever name. This type of fast-flow work system has been emerging for several decades now, and it has many facets. It isn't done just by an information systems change, although information technology is an enabler if it is used to execute different process concepts instead of merely optimizing the old ones to death. Obsolete software itself chokes process flows. As has been said about boat racing, you can't turn a rowboat into a racing yacht merely by installing sensors and computers.

■ A ROSE BY ANY OTHER NAME

Some will insist that Kaizen Blitz is really just reengineering by a different name. Some might differentiate by using the term *reengineering* for business processes and *kaizen* for manufacturing ones.

---

[4] Horst Wildemann, "Produktklinik: Getting It All Together in Germany," *Target* [publication of the Association for Manufacturing Excellence] 13 (November–December 1997): 22–29.

Then there are company specific implementation program names, like PICOS at General Motors, or BP (Best Practice) at Honda. However, a growing number of companies, such as Dana Corporation and Applied Materials, use the term *Kaizen Blitz* internally.

Whatever they are called, these methodologies have many similarities in their principles, lists, and forms. Some variations in nomenclature and approach are inevitable between organizations. All of them must modify names for acceptance in the internal culture, but that's exactly the rub.

Everything has to be called something or people can't communicate. As long as people can communicate clearly, names are of secondary importance. Results count.

Ask almost anyone what's wrong with quality improvement or process simplification, and they respond that in principle nothing is wrong with them. It's a specific implementation effort that is an abomination.

A worker at an unnamed plant put his finger on the real problem of nomenclature with the following observation: "The management says we have JIT production now. You can't tell it by looking." Adopt a process name with pizzazz, declare victory, and give up. Move on to the next improvement campaign. Or conversely, state that "JIT production doesn't work" and try something else. There are plenty of "isms" to pick from.

Unfortunately, implementation is easily sabotaged by its promoters, wittingly or unwittingly. Kaizen Blitz is not immune to the implementation woes of approaches going by different names. By reading this book or any other one, you can gather ideas, tools, and background—and perhaps a little confidence. But you are learning *about* radical process improvement. Real learning is by *doing*. Learning about something doesn't guarantee accomplishment.

Upper-level management has the most important responsibilities for implementation of the Kaizen Blitz, although their hands-on participation is minimal. This responsibility covers four points:

1. *A consistent vision.* Answer the questions; "What are Kaizen Blitzes supposed to be implementing, and why?"
2. *Sustain human development.* Create an environment for human development, including incentives for it.
3. *Provide the resources.* Provide the budget (relatively modest) and human time (more generous), and assure technical support of the processes.
4. *Set priorities.* Everything can't be done at once.

Taken together, these four points are a test of leadership. Of the four, sustaining human development is the toughest challenge.

■ VISION: WHAT IS PROCESS IMPROVEMENT?

The objective of a single Kaizen Blitz is to make dramatic improvement in a limited process that a team can get its hands around. The objective of an ongoing series of Kaizen Blitz episodes is to improve *all* processes—"kaizen everything" and sustain the gain. But to what end?

The objective is to take the waste out of processes and keep it out. Knowing whether that is being done effectively is so involved that Chapters 5 and 6 are devoted to it. In brief, processes have improved if the following occur:

➤ Their duration time decreases.

➤ Space required decreases.

➤ Fewer resources are used (resources are people, machines, material, energy, and information).

➤ Outcomes improve (outcomes include quality, customer satisfaction, and cash flow).

In a manufacturing facility, an objective larger than a single Kaizen Blitz might be the implementation of JIT production. In turn, the main objectives of JIT production are the development of processes to flow and to eliminate waste, so these objectives are compatible with Kaizen Blitz.

Use of the phrase "just-in-time" is unfortunate, because it creates the surface impression is that the objective of JIT production is only to cut inventory, make shipments in small quantities, or to deploy a "pull system" of material control. Those are means, not ends, and only a few of the means at that. Not being coupled with aggressive process improvement, such as Kaizen Blitz, has been one of the weaknesses of JIT in practice, not only in the West but in Japan where it began. A full discussion of JIT production is a book in itself, and those are abundant.[5]

---

[5] See, for example, Robert W. Hall, *Attaining Manufacturing Excellence* (Burr Ridge Ill: McGraw-Hill/Irwin, 1987). This book is still a good overview of the subject; numerous other books on the subject exist.

Implementation weaknesses hobble the spread of process concepts such as agile manufacturing, quick response, lean manufacturing, and others. People want an "implementation road map." However, road maps can be only crudely sketched, not drawn in detail. Every set of processes to be attacked has uncharted territory. People can only learn what happened in now-charted territory and go off on their own adventure. Upon entering new territory, the explorers have to find their own way. If they learn well, they can apply similar ideas in different settings.

■ HOW TO MAKE PROCESS FLOW IMPROVEMENT

To improve the flow of a process—any process—four principles, shown in Figure 2.1, are employed. They are so commonsensical that people often use them without giving them much thought. However, sometimes people "rediscover" one of them and tout it as if it was the only key to business success.

➤ Step 1—Compress a Sequence of Process Steps

Compressing a sequence of process steps is basic to almost any Kaizen Blitz. The time duration is shortened by identifying waste and cutting it out. The notion of waste, or non-value-added, is so important that an overview is given in Table 2.1; the list is repeated twice in slightly different forms in Tables 6.2 and 6.3.

➤ Step 2—Put Process Steps in Parallel

Putting process steps in parallel is done everyday. People are quite capable of doing several things at once. Watch what people do while driving, or what the average teenager does while doing homework. On a larger scale, a major advance in reducing the time to develop and launch a new product is often called *concurrent engineering*—doing as many project steps as possible in parallel. In production, Mazda's Hofu assembly plant deviated from the world automobile norm by creating a "spider" line, which shortens the time of assembly considerably by assembling modules on feeder lines, then joining them on a short final line. (Some observers think that Suzuki's Ohta plant is even more flexible.)

1. **Compress a sequence of process steps.**

   From this:

   ☐ ☐ ☐☐ ☐ ➝

   To this:

   ☐☐☐☐☐☐   (The open gaps are wasted time and activity.)

2. **Put process steps in parallel.**

   From this:

   ☐☐☐☐☐☐☐☐☐☐☐☐☐☐☐ ➝

   To this:

   ☐☐☐
   ☐☐☐ ➝
   ☐☐☐

3. **Build on process "platforms." (One platform is standard work.)**

   a. Copy only.
   b. Copy and amend.
   c. Copy and improve.

4. **Expand the view of the process.**

   From separated workstations to a sequence of operations (as in a work cell).

   From a sequence of operations to a total flow in one location (as in a plant).

   From process flow at one location to those spanning multiple locations (as in a "supply chain").

   From single-purpose processes (such as production) to a full set of life-cycle processes (as with the dirt-to-dirt life cycle of a product).

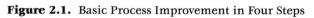

Figure 2.1. Basic Process Improvement in Four Steps

Table 2.1. The Classic Process Wastes and How to Eliminate Them

Waste of:	Action on Shop Floors	Action in Administration

Overproduction	Reduce lot sizes
	Reduce set up times
		Reduce work batch sizes
		Reduce mental set up time:
		    Shorter search routines
		    Easy access to information
		    Eliminate unnecessary data
		    Simplify processing

Waiting (Long lead times)	Synchronize work flow
	Use cells
	Balance workloads
	Cross-train
	Cues from visibility systems
		Combine work at one
		    workstation
		Colocate sequential work
		Cross-train to balance
		    workloads
		One-touch information access
		Cues from visibility system

Transport	Use cells
	Compact space
	Have fewer but closer
	    suppliers
	Minimize number of moves
	    for material
		Paperless or reduced-paper
		    processes
		One-stop workstations, etc.
		On-line to suppliers

Processing Itself	Redesign—eliminate parts
	Redesign—simplify design of
	    parts
	Review—are all process steps
	    necessary?
	Establish standard work
	Fail-safe to eliminate rework
		Simplify—eliminate
		    unnecessary work (e.g.,
		    must every order be credit
		    checked?)
		Establish system of standard
		    work
		Fail-safe processes to
		    eliminate rework

Inventory	Reduce lot sizes
	Reduce lead times
	Synchronize work flows (e.g.,
	    JIT pull systems)
	Minimize flow interruption
	Create capacity to handle
	    peak loads
		Reduce batch sizes for
		    processing
		Minimize checks and reviews
		Synchronize work flows
		    (system for immediate
		    prioritizing)
		Minimize flow interruption
		Create capacity to handle
		    peak loads

Table 2.1. (continued)

Waste of:	Action on Shop Floors	Action in Administration
Motion	Make every move count—whether by people or machines	Eliminate searching—one-stop access rather than running around
	Organize layout: 5 S	Organize layout: 5 S
	Visibility system	Visibility system
Defects	Logical quality standards	Logical quality standards
	Disciplined but flexible documentation	Disciplined but flexible documentation
	Standard work	Standard work
	Improve process capabilities	Fail-safe processes
	Fail-safe processes	
Information*	Decreases process waste	Decreases process waste
	Improves process outcome	Improves process outcome
	Easily comprehended	Easily comprehended
	Visibility systems	Visibility systems
	Ease of database access	Ease of database access
	Record accuracy	Record accuracy

* Three questions about either computerized or noncomputerized information methodologies are helpful:
  1. Does it simplify primary value-adding process flows?
  2. Does it complicate primary value-adding flows?
  3. If it complicates, does it add value to the customer in itself?

The same concept is used over and over to reduce setup times—or to cut pit-stop times at a race track. Do as much as possible in parallel while the machine is running. Then do as much as possible in parallel when it is stopped.

➤ Step 3—Build on a Process Platform

Building on a process platform is more subtle, but pervasive, and the idea is sometimes expressed as "Don't reinvent the wheel." Copy good methods shamelessly, whether they are your own or someone else's, then work to improve them. This is the basic idea behind process benchmarking and reverse engineering of products. It also provides much of the basis for Kaizen Blitz events repeated on a process that has already had a daring revision tried and standardized. Building on a process platform is the development of standard work, the follow-up phase of a Kaizen Blitz, and is also the idea behind repeated application of problem solving using a Deming Circle approach: Plan-Do-Check-Act.

Truly dramatic innovation, such as inventing the Xerox machine, is rare. A breakthrough innovation forces a scrapping of old processes and may instigate a major change in the way we live. The automobile was a classic innovation at the beginning of the twentieth century, the computer was a classic one at mid-century.

Innovation is most prolific when a breakthrough technology and the processes to support it are new, as is true now in the biotechnology industry and has been true in computer industry since its birth over 50 years ago. A twentieth-century pattern in the history of technology is to see prolific innovation early in the life of a major breakthrough as different organizations search for solutions.

After a time, these settle down into a more mature phase. Marketing, production, distribution, and service settle into routines that, unfortunately, can be regarded a way of life. As a breakthrough ages, adaptive innovation again picks up in frenetic efforts to diversify market niches or customize the product. At this stage the producer with a superior process has an advantage. Superior processes are the combination of a host of little ideas. A few ideas may be truly novel, but most are a new twist on old concepts.

That's the usual kind of innovation associated with the Kaizen Blitz, but don't underestimate it. Accumulating good process innovations is not easy to do, and it can make a company's total offering distinctive. As can be seen by the speed with which the personal computer passed from an innovation to a commodity, transition from uniqueness to commodity status can now take a very short time. No one can bank long on their technical superiority. Customers are starting to expect breakthrough innovation to be provided from superior processes starting with the prototype.

The automotive industry is a current example of product and process improvement and variation built around platforms. Unit body designs prevail, and the sheet metal underbody of a car is a subassembly literally called the platform. A well-designed platform with good vibration dampening characteristics is hard to develop. Once one is designed, it is much easier to design multiple vehicles for different markets from that platform than to design every new model from a clean sheet of paper (or a blank screen).

The same is true of production processes. Toyota, for instance, is famous for not designing a new plant from scratch. Instead, a layout and equipment that has been proven elsewhere is replicated. They then train people and modify the old process to fit the new setting. With enough kaizen, the new process may eventually become superior to the one from which it was originally cloned.

Intel is even more rigorous than Toyota in building on an established process platform. The Intel practice is called Copy Exactly! When Intel builds a second semiconductor plant to fabricate a chip already in production, the equipment, conditions, settings, measurements, operators' activities, and controller codes are copied exactly—no deviations.

With this discipline, as soon as the cloned plant is loaded and chips begin to appear, Intel is able to reach the same yield and output from it as from the original. There is no long debugging process. From that time onward, process improvement is done by a disciplined process with all the same plants in lockstep.

When a fabrication plant is built or modified for a new chip design, no more of the process than is necessary differs one whit from the processes in an established one. This production strategy is supported by a policy of modular product design, so that each new, faster chip is also a disciplined, modular change from the last generation. By this strategy Intel beat competitors to market with new generations of "X86" chips for about 10 years running. (Customers now expect next-generation chips to instantly carry Wal-Mart prices, so Intel's cash flow strategy is weakening, but the Copy Exactly! policy retains merit.[6])

Of course, there comes a time when a major process change cannot be put off. That is now happening for Intel and the rest of the semiconductor industry with the pending changeover from 200-mm to 300-mm wafers.

➤ Step 4—Expand the View of the Process

Expanding the view of the process is usually an unspoken objective of a Kaizen Blitz. If the purpose of a blitz is to remove opera-

---

[6] David Kirkpatrick, "Intel's Got a Bigger Problem Than the FTC," *Fortune,* July 6, 1998, pp. 30–31.

tions from separated departments and join them in sequence in a cell, the physical side of this objective is obvious. However, equally important is the long-term objective of getting people out of their cubicles and workstations and giving them a chance to experience how their work fits into a larger scheme of things. Likewise, an objective—and improvement tool—for most Kaizen Blitz events in plants is to improve the operators' process visibility. Redesign work so that people can see anything important happening at a glance. The reverse side of this is for the computer-bound to experience first-hand what a physical process is all about.

The perspective broadening also goes beyond a company's formal boundaries. Customer and supplier personnel may be invited to participate in a Kaizen Blitz. Many companies have sent teams of people to assist suppliers with process improvement. Xerox was already famous for it by the mid 1980s. Honda of America Manufacturing has a 13-week program of hands-on supplier development called BP. The Toyota Supplier Support Center has the mission of coaching Toyota's North American suppliers and other companies. In all cases the people involved began to get more of a sense of process flows across companies—or through a supply chain, as is often said now.

Attempts to improve a customer's operations have been a part of sales, engineering, and product development for decades. At least one company, Hil-Rom Division of Hillenbrand Industries, bases its market on improvement of hospital patient room operations. If a hospital had personnel who were ready, they might even do a Kaizen Blitz with them. Hil-Rom strongly promotes kaizen events internally.

How far can the human perspective be expanded? A long way, but not all at once. Learning takes time. A major step in making the Kaizen Blitz gains permanent occurs when the process support people self-discover that they should proactively keep value-added processes flowing. For example, maintenance should prepare to do more than just fix things when called. Once that is understood, maintenance may reorganize to better support both ongoing operations and process improvement. In almost all cases, cross-training people in support work as well as direct process work increases versatility in keeping processes moving.

Human self-discovery and learning rates usually determine the limits of process change at each stage. For example, creating a cell of complex machining equipment in which operators are cross-trained can tax them beyond their learning limit, at least in the short run. It's not a good bet as a first-time blitz project.

■ STANDARD WORK

Although standard work connotes the rote motions of a production operator, it is used everywhere. Elsewhere, it is likely to be called standard operating procedure (SOP), standard macro-programming commands, or other names. Standard work is how equipment creates quality output, within spec, time after time. Standard work is the reason that a welding robot is much superior to a human for repetitive welds. It doesn't tire and waver, so it tracks a bead along its programmed path every time—barring malfunction, of course.

On a grand scale; Intel's Copy Exactly! is standard work. On a workstation scale, a standard work sheet may be a procedure an operator develops by hand to summarize his or her activity, step-by-step, at that station. It may include operator instructions developed by staff to ensure quality or safety. It may pop up on a computer screen when a bar code is scanned. Standard work information tells people—or machines—what to do. But standard work isn't the documentation; it is actual accomplishment by an established method.

Some standard work is established by a computer protocol. For instance, most of us are familiar with how a standard transaction menu on a point-of-sale terminal guides a store clerk through recording a sale and taking payment. Sometimes the clerk is even prompted to say thank you or even attempt stimulating an impulse purchase.

However, people ignore much operational information available to them for the same reasons that football players don't review the playbook before running a play—there's no time. They go with whatever they know, however they actually do it. In some cases, operating instructions are consulted only after something goes wrong, and maybe not even then.

In practice, work has not been standardized if a "once-blitzed" process has to be completely flowcharted anew to be sure what is actually taking place. Likewise, work is not standardized if workers on the same job, but working different shifts, do not actually agree in practice with how the job should be done. The telltale sign is when one person adjusts the process differently from another, and not just for ergonomic reasons, like a new driver adjusting the seat and mirrors in a car.

Standardization of work is the last step of the Deming Circle: Plan-Do-Check-Act. The intensive portion of the Kaizen Blitz generally covers only the Plan-Do-Check phases of the Deming Circle. "Act" in the context of Kaizen Blitz is to assure that a process can actually continue to operate in the way that was demonstrated at the end of the blitz, or better. For example, several tweaks that are proposed during a Kaizen Blitz probably cannot be jack rigged in time for the demonstration. A process is not really improved when a new method is demonstrated. It's improved when the process is routinely functioning in the new way and robust enough to handle a few crises. Then it is standardized. "Act" is finished when all the follow-up support activity is done.

Both the value and the difficulty of standard work are chronically underestimated. Toyota has long regarded the most difficult, time-consuming phase of developing the Toyota Production System to be the hands-on workers in any process learning to standardize their own work *themselves*. To actually do that, workers must *want* to do standard work. When that happens, the actual work process is likely to follow a standard much more closely, thus assuring that the same work is actually done the same way time after time.

Take a set of complex tasks in assembly, or perhaps in fabrication. No way can a person actually doing the work "follow a recipe" as they go. Documentation does not assure standard work, and standard work documentation is not always the neatest. Although the customers for documentation are not managers, technical experts, or quality auditors, many procedures are really written for them to read. If the people operating the process don't understand the documentation or follow it, its preparation is an exercise in bureaucratic futility.

The people actually doing the work tend to keep their own instructions very simple. To test whether the instructions are effective, check to see if another worker of the same skill level can follow them and perform the work the same way.

Some basic job skills must be mastered; some general work rules must become habitual. They may be written up somewhere, but tucked away. In daily work, a base layer of procedure for a specific workstation must be followed without checking. Anything needed for reference during a given cycle of work should be easily visible and understandable within that work cycle. Like actors, people can follow cues and prompts only if they have first learned their lines cold. Standard work assures that the same task is done the same way every time.

To develop standard work to this level, the people actually doing the work have to understand it, standardizing less by rote discipline than by designing it into their own work procedures themselves. Human work discipline is important, but it has limits. Work has to be standardized using equipment, prompts, and fail-safe methods so that it does not depend on superhuman discipline.

The value of standard work for improvement is illustrated in Figure 2.2. Once it has been achieved, standard work is a platform from which the next level of advance can be achieved. Without standard work and a way to evaluate whether a new method is better than the old, process improvement may not stick.

The use of standard work as staging for a new round of improvement has many implications in many contexts. For instance,

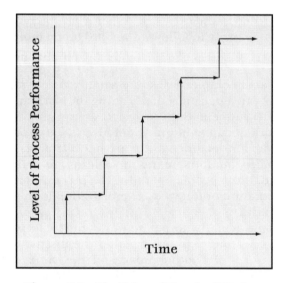

Figure 2.2. The Value of Standard Work

Adapted from: Robert W. Hall, *Continuous Improvement Concepts,* Research Report of the Association for Manufacturing Excellence, (Wheeling, Il.: Association for Manufacturing Excellence, 1987).

ISO 9000 examinations stress verification that the work is actually done as it is documented, sort of a first stage in development of standard work. Little weight is placed on process improvement. Unless organizations are prepared to build on standard work to improve and revise processes, the benefit is modest.

The role and importance of both standard work and process improvement is not as easy to understand, and it is easy to try to force people to do it "through the back door." For example, in the medical field, it has long been known that treatment of patients with the same diagnosis varies greatly from doctor to doctor, and from hospital to hospital. In the United States, the cost variance from this was one of the major inducements to move toward managed care—that is, an attempt to force standardization and improvement by cost pressures from people removed from the scene.

Today, the medical profession is becoming more interested in managing *clinical pathways,* an attempt to standardize postdiagnosis patient care by those who are more involved. Patients themselves vary even if the two-line diagnosis summaries of them are identical, so they are not processable like so many cans of beans. However, any attempt to standardize procedures, study outcomes, and revise them is likely to lead to real improvement in medical care, not mere cost containment. (A clinical pathway for a particular diagnosis is a great candidate for Kaizen Blitz by medical professionals.)

■ STAGES OF DEVELOPMENT

Stages of development are summarized considering all the elements of a process, and therefore all the elements of improvement, so all descriptions are greatly simplified. Learning about process development is nonlinear. Usually the process development itself is nonlinear. Once a process flow is simplified, it all seems elementary, but when we look at the muddle before simplification, nothing is understood in a quick flash of insight. Real insight comes from actually simplifying the muddles.

Below is one way to describe stages of process development. The six stages represent systematic human development the Toyota way. Toyota's approach to development does not have to be replicated, but the list is something to come back to and chew on as people learn more about the Kaizen Blitz and process improvement on their own.

STAGES IN DISCRETE MANUFACTURING PROCESS DEVELOPMENT

1. Start-up, or traditional, manufacturing
2. Organize a flow of work
3. Standardize work or standardize methods: Assure process quality
4. "Pull system" methods: Self-correcting control introduced to processes
5. Small lot sizes: Improved efficiency
6. Lot size = 1: High flexibility

Note: These six steps are based on one of the logical explanations of process development that Toyota has used. It is not transferrable to other kinds of operations as either a slogan or as a strategy of improvement. It is a historical guide to think deeply about, because it does encapsulate many issues faced when trying to turn a "molasses process" into a "fire hose."

■ HUMAN DEVELOPMENT

The human side of process improvement is generally the most challenging. A short way to describe the progress of the people, "the blitzers," is by stages of human growth: infancy, childhood, teenage, adult, and old age (when both people and processes start to "lose it").

Another simple, people-oriented illustration of building up process improvement capability is shown in Figure 2.3. Stages of process development are cumulative. Everything builds on the base below it, and human development is the base layer for everything.

Without experience with kaizen or continuous improvement, Figure 2.3 may be a bit inscrutable. Its moral, however, is easily understood from the Christian parable that a wise man builds his house upon a rock rather than on sand. To keep adding to achievement, keep strengthening the base of human development, and don't neglect any base while building on top of it.

The base level is development of work skill, technical skills, and especially the ability to work in problem-solving teams. Once this is in place, people are ready to deal with technical issues often associated with quality. If they cannot tune processes "to do it right" and standardize their work, they are limited in how much they can reduce lead times and simplify. Once they can overcome

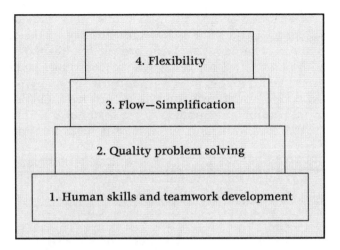

Figure 2.3. Human Development Process.
The lesson of the diagram is that "you can't pile very high
unless you have the base for it."

base problems in quality and efficiency, they are ready to create
more flexibility. That is, they can do multiple jobs and handle
many variations in requirements while still maintaining quality
and efficiency. Obviously, many technical issues with both hardware and software enter in, but this is the basic pattern for human
capability development.

The first two layers of Figure 2.3 are the critical ones. First
comes the basic teamwork and process skills. Next is the ability to
make process changes without a mess, so you don't screw something up trying to make it better.

There's more to level 2 in Figure 2.3 than formal quality training. Both quality technology and practical grounding in something like the Deming Circle approach to problem solving are big
plusses. Besides that, a Kaizen Blitz team needs the ability to revise
a process themselves, or at least be able to do so with the help of
readily available support personnel. If the process is dictated by
software that others have written, the team needs the ability to
amend it. If processes at different sites are supposed to be identical
or nearly so, people have not usually had much experience with
substantive process improvement. They execute processes that others develop.

If a process uses tools and equipment that others have designed and installed, a Kaizen Blitz team is also limited in the scope of change that can be undertaken. If the process is a "turnkey project" developed by a supplier, the Kaizen Blitz team must come up to speed with it before being able to modify it. In many cases the turnkey supplier would be happy to be involved. But if the involvement of equipment suppliers raises issues of trust and confidentiality, that, too, is as much a human issue as an intellectual capital issue.

Process development with Kaizen Blitz is a do-it-yourself approach. If grass-roots folk have not been trained to go much beyond turning the crank on their process, they are limited in how much they can improve a process until they work themselves up to the skill levels needed.

Toyota, the grandfather of what we call the Kaizen Blitz, has long had a policy of relying on "peopleware" rather than software. One reason is to avoid having processes locked in by software. Another is to promote small-group process improvement—substantive improvement—not just changing the locations of the waste cans. Manufacturing engineers, who might be called expert tinkerers, support improvement groups and work close to product floors or other process areas. Foremen are expected to spend little time with routine personnel matters, but much time as the assigned kaizen support person for their group.

Figure 2.3 is a variation on diagrams constructed by Japanese companies to explain the successes and failures of their buildup of continuous improvement. There and elsewhere, successful leaders understand that their achievements are built on a human base. It is no accident that many events sponsored by AME have been planned to concentrate on subjects other than human development, but in every meeting that issue always comes up.

Close involvement is not the only way to improve processes, but when this approach is doggedly pursued, it is very effective. Figures 2.2 and 2.3 are useful to keep in mind when planning a process improvement strategy to be implemented with Kaizen Blitz. You can create your own variations for different purposes.

■ LIMITS TO THE BENEFITS OF IMPROVEMENT

Is there a limit to the benefits of improvement? Yes and no. No, there is no process that cannot be improved. Yes, one can run into diminishing returns, after which a process needs breakthrough in-novation, a new start on a new platform, if possible. Then im-provement processes can start over.

This phenomenon can be illustrated by classic learning curves, shown in Figure 2.4. Most learning curves show unit cost or labor hours. The curves in Figure 2.4 are labeled with duration times, or

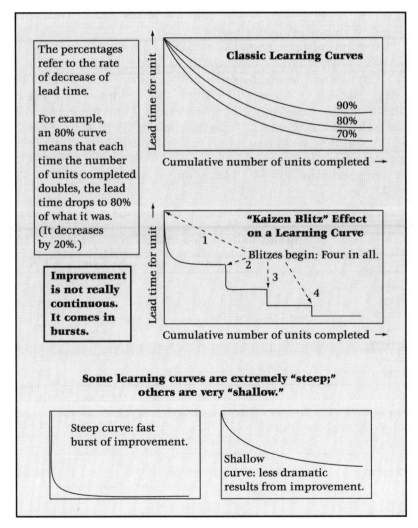

Figure 2.4. Learning Curves for Process Duration (Lead Time)

process lead times, which is a common performance indicator for the Kaizen Blitz. The learning curve phenomenon holds for any indicator on which improvement takes place.

The basic flaw in the classic learning-curve equation is that it is continuous. Actual improvement has historically been discontinuous. Changes in process measurement were most marked when significant changes were made in the process—a different process layout, for example. A Kaizen Blitz is a deliberate effort to make a large number of process improvements all at once and see a big shift in process performance quickly.

Sometimes improvement is extremely rapid. For example, in the AME Kaizen Blitz event held at Farmington, Connecticut, a blitz team zeroed in on the order-entry process at Dell Manufacturing (not Dell Computer, although that company is great in kaizen, too). *In three days* the team identified how to decrease the lead time from order entry to production by 75 percent. That's a big drop. It took about six months of follow-up to standardize results and actually achieve it in practice, with plenty of potential for more lead-time reduction left. Some details are shown in Figure 2.5.

	Initial Process	Development Track		Express Track	
		New No.	% Gain	New No.	% Gain
Operations	43	25	42	16	63
Players	8	5	36	3	63
Hand-offs	20	8	60	2	90
Decisions	10	3	70	3	70
Delays	6	4	33	4	33
Files	4	2	50	2	50
Opportunities	11	1	91	0	100

Dell's products can be configured from existing engineering, which is the express track for order entry shown above, or it may require customer engineering, which is the developmental track. The objective was to knock the waste out of both tracks.

Figure 2.5. AME Kaizen Blitz Changes in the Order Entry Process at Dell Manufacturing for a 75% Reduction in Lead Time.

From John St. Onge, "Return of the Kaizen Blitzers[SM]," *Target* [publication of the Association for Manufacturing Excellence] 11 (September–October 1995): 40.

Not all processes will be so dramatically improved through a Kaizen Blitz. Administrative processes are often good candidates for big reductions in lead time, especially the first time around. Much depends on whether anyone has paid improvement attention to the process before.

Unstudied setups are also good candidates for at least 50 percent time compression the first time around, even on complex equipment, just by cutting out the wasted time and movement. That allows lot sizes, inventories, and lead times to also be cut. However, cutting one setup time has little effect if an entire process cannot change over quickly because setup is only a part of a bigger process.

With an experienced expert around, process improvement can be done very quickly. One of the late Shigeo Shingo's favorite ploys was to suggest a few setup changes on a small press to a work crew who would make them quickly, then demonstrate results at the end of the day. The first-cut formula was routine to Shingo: standardize die heights, install stops so that the incoming die would properly position with one push, and simplify the clamps and connects.

In 1985 Shingo pulled off that trick with a bit of "show biz" in Helsinki, Finland. He asked to visit any nearby plant with a small press early in the morning before going on stage all day. Setup time was 45 minutes, they said. In about 15 minutes, Shingo made a sketch and handed it to technicians, asking them to make the alterations and practice a few times. At 4:30 P.M., just before airplane departure time, Shingo swept in, followed by a gaggle of reporters and a television crew. On national television, the workers demonstrated a die change in 1 minute, 28 seconds and then broke a bottle of champagne over the press. The cost of the modifications: about $16.00 (U.S.).

That's what can be done if a process has not been studied before. In percentage terms, further reductions of a press setup time from 1:28 may be dramatic, but not in the amount of time and resources saved. That's the message of the learning curves.

The initial bites into process improvement should be whoppers. Thereafter, the apple keeps getting smaller as one gets closer and closer to the value-adding core.

There is no good excuse for living with waste. It's like being overweight. Companies can live with it as long as they don't have to engage in top-level competition. If they do, extra weight is a hindrance at minimum, and it may be fatal.

■ REGRESSION

Figure 2.6 shows a learning curve with "toe up." Not many such curves have been captured. People "sorta know" it's happening, but attention is directed elsewhere, so no one pays enough attention to measure the regression.

Like gaining weight, regression in process performance is easy for most of us. All we have to do is relax and stop training. Training, for work processes, means a regimen of process improvement in which something like the Kaizen Blitz becomes a lifelong habit.

Performance regression, like weight gain, is a process filled with excuses. There are few real studies of regression, but there is much speculation about regression's causes.

One area of concern is complexity. For example, the serve time at McDonald's is not as fast as it was 25 years ago when the menu was more limited. But McDonald's doesn't operate to set serve speed records; it operates to please the customer. And customers in the 1990s want more choices. The problem is how to remove the waste from processes that give the customer what they want.

Much the same has happened to Toyota, and the company continues to be a leader in process improvement. To take just one performance indicator, the worldwide inventory turns of Toyota Motor Manufacturing Company dropped from 64 in 1981 to 12.5 in 1997. During that time the company expanded from remarkably compact operations mostly on the Japanese isles to operations in every

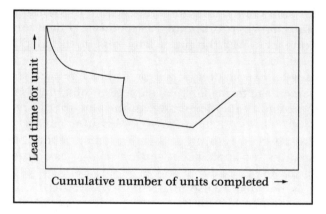

Figure 2.6. "Toe Up" of a Learning Curve

part of the globe. None of the overseas operations yet match the performance of those in the home country, and those, too, have been affected by product complexity.

In the long run, some form of kaizen needs to be ongoing if an organization is to avoid strangling in the increasing complexity of its own operations. Without an offsetting approach to simplify the waste, who knows how badly Toyota might have regressed.

Another potential problem is believing in magic answers. That's an addiction to a particular technique or to one or two pet measurements for guidance. It leads to vacillation and faddishness. Getting in mind a simple approach for telling whether processes are efficient and effective is not as simple as it seems. That's the subject of Chapters 5 and 6. The alternative is cycling through a series of conflicting improvement objectives, perhaps under different managers, and going in circles.

■ THE CASE FOR KAIZEN BLITZ

Kaizen Blitz is an approach for rapid improvement of a limited process area. Development of a production cell is a common blitz objective, but all kinds of processes can be improved, including those for customers and suppliers. At least a part of the improvement team should consist of workers in the process being improved. The stimulus is to use innovative thinking to eliminate non-value-added work and to immediately implement the changes to a demonstration stage within a week or less. Making the follow-up changes so that the demonstrated improvement sticks generally takes a little longer.

One of the major benefits is ownership of the improvement by the process work team and those that support them. People less readily accept improvement that is thrust on them, no matter how ingenious it may be. This seems especially true if the changes are simple ones—elimination of waste that is obvious and perhaps embarrassing. Another major benefit is the development of skills. To make most improvements, people must expand their on-the-job skills, and they should develop skill in problem solving and future process improvement as well.

Few companies are close to realizing the limits of process improvement. Low-tech process improvement will not yield returns that are as big after an initial round or two of Kaizen Blitz, but that makes it no less important. An organization that intends to play in major-league competition cannot afford to get out of physical condition.

Chapter

Improvement Strategy
Implementing the Big Picture

Kaizen Blitz is about execution. It can be appied somewhat randomly or to implement a clever strategy. Strategy is itself a complex subject. It must consider much more than operations—market shifts, technology, competitive threats, acquisitions, alliances, political changes, legal environment, globalization, and on and on. Considerations can come from any direction.

The purpose of strategy is to set a direction that will produce future business results. In business, "results" mean taking in more money than is spent, but a well-done business strategy considers much more than the assumptions behind a few periods of pro forma financial projection.

For many organizations, such as law offices and investment offices, the operations aspect of strategy would seem a relatively insignificant determinant of long-term success. Few law offices will take up process improvement using the Kaizen Blitz. Companies such as Southwest Airlines, for example, for which operations are the key to strategy should be much more excited.

■ EXAMPLES OF OPERATING STRATEGIES

Southwest Airlines

Southwest Airlines is a classic case of a company with a distinctive operations strategy. As a low-fare airline, it uses one type of aircraft, the Boeing 737, each identically outfitted, which simplifies maintenance, crew training, and turnaround time on the ground. Turnaround time is, well, pivotal to the strategy.

Southwest makes light use of computer systems and keeps transactions simple: no seating assignments, for instance, and virtually fixed ticket prices. (Major airlines have 30 or more ticket prices for each city-pair served depending on lead time before flying, times of flights, and so on.) Southwest's frequent-flyer plan credits customers for each flight segment—not total miles—so no database tracks frequent-flyer miles. Computer systems for flight operations are equally fundamental.

There are many other aspects of Southwest's lean operating strategy. The airline is famous for humorous flight crews who keep passengers at ease by making light of the spartan service. Southwest has won several awards for best airline service; notably and publicly, management gives full credit to the employees for the awards.

On short-haul jet routes, Southwest keeps loaded airplanes in the air a large fraction of the time, but the strategy also limits the route options. Coast-to-coast flights would negate much of the competitive advantage of simplicity and short turnaround time. Southwest's cabins would have to be reequipped for meals, and perhaps entertainment. The complexity of operations would rise.

Southwest has made trade-offs to tailor operations for the market it serves. If the carrier outgrows the short-haul, no-frills market niche, expanding its lean operating strategy will be a great challenge, but don't count it out. The equivalent of a Kaizen Blitz team just might concoct a lean version of long-flight operations and try it out. To make a new long-flight process into a real customer offering, Southwest's current training and culture would have to adapt to the demonstrated process—and afterward improve on it. (Southwest Airlines made a trial run of its first coast-to-coast flight in November 1998.)

Mazda

Having "world class" processes, however, is not by itself a sufficient strategy for success. Mazda is an example of a company that developed itself to become very strong in both engineering and manufacturing. Its production processes rival anyone's. Its products are high quality. At least two distinctive car models, the RX-7 and the Miata, have practically sold themselves in niche markets. But like American Motors before it, Mazda has not been able to escape periodic financial crises. The company cannot sell enough cars.

Wiremold

For most manufacturing companies, operating excellence is not the only key to success, but it is vital to making any strategy work. A good example is the Wiremold Company, one of the most publicized of all U.S. companies profiting from the Kaizen Blitz.

According to Art Byrne, president and chief executive officer of Wiremold: "One ingredient essential to our success has been the way we look at kaizen. At Wiremold, we believe it's a fundamental part of our business strategy. After all, our business delivery systems are what the customer sees. If we fall behind in quality or in lead times, we disappoint our customer and we won't succeed no matter how good our strategy. On the other hand, if our systems can outperform the competition, then we can outrun them."[1]

■ SLICING A STRATEGY DOWN TO THE IMPROVEMENT LEVEL

A core Kaizen Blitz event is an execution tactic and is itself only one local episode carrying out an improvement strategy. The overall improvement strategy needs to be tied to a broader view of where the organization is going. In the broad sense improvement kaizen is like a training program for athletes. Kaizen conditioning gives an organization a bigger range of options and the ability to execute them, just as athletic champions in top physical condition can make moves that others find impossible.

Operations strategy is usually embedded in business strategy. A typical operating strategy considers operating locations, distribution channels and logistics, key supplier partnerships, centralization versus decentralization of operations, and so on. Process improvement strategy is a subpart of operations strategy, but it may drastically affect everything else. Normally, ambiguities in a strategic plan become more solidified when it is converted into a budget.

Part of an improvement strategy includes initiatives to shift an organization and culture to be compatible with the "grand vision."

---

[1] Art Byrne, "How Wiremold Reinvented Itself with Kaizen," *Target* [publication of the Association for Manufacturing Excellence] 11 (January–February 1995): 8–14.

Process improvement planning is easier than planning somewhat unpredictable human changes, but one depends on the other. Changes in work culture must overcome the ghosts of strategies and cultures past. When the ghosts are big and ugly, leaders must personally demonstrate the behavior desired within the organization and take actions that dispel them.

For most companies, strategic planning isn't really a clean sheet. It starts from the history, existing commitments, and anticipated changes in conditions. What comes out is the big-picture plan to transition from where you are to where you want to be. This can be detailed further into subplans, including those for process improvement.

"From Strategy to Process Improvement," outlined on the following pages, sketches the framework of a strategic planning approach that drills down into the operations and process development side of strategy. Marketing, finance, technology, mergers, or other big-picture elements are crucial to strategy, and their actionable implications can be likewise detailed, but the link between business strategy and process improvement is the focus here. Bridging the gap between grand direction and improvement initiatives isn't always done well in strategic planning.

The first four steps of this six-step strategic planning process are similar to those used in certain divisions of Texas Instruments. The last two steps resemble the planning process of companies that use policy deployment to develop improvement initiatives. Together, the six steps should assure that, as much as possible, improvement initiatives are connected to the needs of a broader business strategy.

Because most companies already have a strategic planning process, the six-step process is not meant to replace the current one. Rather, "From Strategy to Process Improvement" is a reference planning system for discussing some of the common issues senior executives should consider when committing an organization to rapid process transformation.

■ SOMETHING TO BLITZ FOR

Getting your processes in great shape is becoming a prerequisite just to hang around in a tough competitive industry. An improvement regimen based on the Kaizen Blitz is work, it's self-disciplinary, and

FROM STRATEGY TO PROCESS IMPROVEMENT

Note that operations include *all* processes—customer service, logistics, design, and so on—not just production.

1. **Assess the current situation** (leadership team)
   a) *Do a business "SWOT" analysis:* Write out Strengths, Weaknesses, Opportunities, and Threats.
   b) *Operations review*
      (1) Compare processes with external benchmarks where available.
      (2) Compare the level of performance of all processes with the desired level, or with "world class." (Various checklists and tools are available to help with this.)
2. **Long-term projection** (a leadership team exercise, perhaps with research)
   Where is the industry (not the company) going? Where will it be in 10 years—or as far as can be projected to the "limits of the headlights"?
   a) *Avoidance.* No crystal ball is totally clear, so one objective is to avoid obvious dead ends. For example, avoid the following:
      Becoming "an excellent buggy whip manufacturer"
      Making a major improvement effort in manufacturing only to see that you should not do your own manufacturing (What processes will be outsourced?)
      Competing on commodity cost if the obvious trend will be to high-service, highly differentiated market niches
   b) *Dominance.* A more ambitious objective is to become or remain an industry leader using a "blow-out" strategy—changing the rules of the game with a radically different product line, different technology, or level of process performance that competitors cannot match quickly. An effective blow-out strategy probably has a mix of all three approaches, or another one that is both innovative and highly promising.

(continued)

FROM STRATEGY TO PROCESS IMPROVEMENT

(continued)

3. **Near-term vision, changes, and goals** (leadership team)

In the next operating planning periods (six months to three years, depending on how fast conditions transform), what changes do you visualize for the operating organization and its processes, consistent with the long-term projection?.

At this stage, pay close heed to the basics of operating or manufacturing strategy: outsourcing, new markets or customers to be served (or dropped), partnerships and alliances, capacity, locations, technology changes, work skills required, and the like.

Human development is just as important, perhaps much more so if radical transformation is to take place using Kaizen Blitz or the equivalent. It is very heavy on participation, and the human setting for that is hard to maintain — easily upset by sudden top-level shifts and haunted by specters from past practice.

To achieve this, what goals need to be reached? Be specific. Quantify any goals you can. Saying that we will "deliver the highest customer satisfaction of anyone in the industry" isn't quantifiable if no industry-wide rating system for this exists. Hitting a goal figure on a customer satisfaction rating or index is better.

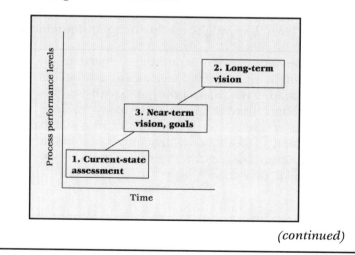

(continued)

FROM STRATEGY TO PROCESS IMPROVEMENT

(continued)

4. **Refine and prioritize goals** (leadership team)

Boil down the goals to the big ones that count. Call them "critical success factors" or anything else you wish, but they must affirm what the operating organization should accomplish and by when. About six major goals is the maximum that an organization can focus on during one operating period, so prioritize and boil the plan down to size.

Establish performance measurements to know if these goals are being reached. (Not all measures are numerical. For instance, securing a distribution partner in India is not a scaled measurement, but success is easy to verify.)

For an operating unit dependent on grassroots participation in improvement, at least one goal will likely concern the development of people. Here's a sample list of six such one-year critical success factors:

1. Improve the customer satisfaction index from 3.1 to 3.6 (on a 4.0 scale).
2. Introduce new product X to customers A, B, and C, and train them. Target for sales of X to A, B, and C is $30 million.
3. Reduce product costs by 20 percent per pound.
4. Reduce standard customer lead time to one week from four.
5. Ship 90 percent of all customer orders direct from production.
6. All associates will have participated in "culture withdrawal" sessions.

These are top-level goals for a company that has already accomplished some degree of process improvement and that has a sound quality-improvement process. Many more changes may be desirable, but this is a plateful for a year's improvement effort. It's not hard to see how all parts of the organization can derive stretch goals from this guidance. Implementation of changes to meet these goals may instigate a number of Kaizen Blitz events, but the ability to engage in rapid improvement is implied. It is not a goal in itself.

(continued)

FROM STRATEGY TO PROCESS IMPROVEMENT

(continued)

Note that all near-term critical success factors have goals, so the organization can track whether they are being met. Goal 6 refers to facilitated meetings in which associates develop their own thoughts on policy and behavior that must change if the organization is to move from its current state to the near-term one envisioned. The critical success factors, or goals, mask a mass of detail, some of which is known to senior management, and much of which may not be known to them.

5. **Develop and prioritize major new projects or initiatives.**

Projects and Initiatives

	Kaizen Blitz	Trade show preparation	Switch to Velcro material	Improve service school	Work environment meeting	New Solvent recycler	ISO 9002 certification	Customer hot line	Supplier visits	Team-leader training	Goals in 18 months
Customer satisfaction	2	3	2	2		2	3	3	2	1	Index of 3.6
New product line, X		3	3	2				2	1	2	$30 million in A, B, and C
Product cost reduction	3		3		2	2	1		2	2	Cut by 20% per lb.
Fast customer lead times	3			2	2			2	2	2	One week
Ship from production	3							1	2	1	90% of all lbs. shipped
Remove behavioral legacies	2				3					2	Associate satisfaction 80%
Sum of priority weights*	13	6	8	6	7	4	4	8	9	10	
Management's priority	1	2	4	7	8	9	10	6	5	3	
Accepted for budgeting**	✓	✓	✓	✓	✓	✓		✓	✓	✓	

*The figures 1, 2, or 3 are simple important weights assigned.
**Both dollar budgets and associates' time budgets should be considered.

(continued)

FROM STRATEGY TO PROCESS IMPROVEMENT

(continued)

Developing all three phases of a Kaizen Blitz is only one initiative. Another example is development of a new product, X, and the processes for it; another, a major thrust requiring development and training. Prioritize according to the contribution to the six critical success factors.

This is a huge amount of process change for most organizations. If the dollar budget is affordable, the time budget for associates has to be checked, but it may not be a big problem. A little waste killed frees time to kill more waste.

A more serious question is whether associates have learned enough to make rapid improvement. If they lack experience in quality and kaizen, they may be slow to take charge of process change and so not advance as quickly as was hoped.

6. **Roll out, including policy deployment**

The plan includes both staff-directed projects and decentralized kaizen plans. Examples of staff-directed projects are the planning system revision and the new product, X. Decentralized, grassroots improvement can be stimulated by a Kaizen Blitz. Senior management should commission each blitz so it does not interfere with a staff project, but with that in mind, give the Kaizen Blitz teams running room to diagnose problems and find solutions.

Where decentralized improvement has taken root, teams take cues from the senior leaders' statements of goals and proceed to develop work plans based on them. Many of these plans will need management blessing and budget. These improvement proposals bouncing back and forth is called *catchball,* or policy deployment.

Most of the time Kaizen Blitz proposals don't change strategic direction but rather they enhance it with detail. Catchball also allows everyone to become comfortable with the strategic direction so that they are not executing orders blindly. Policy deployment has been tried with associates green to improvement processes. It works better after people have kaizen experience. If an organization is not ready for catchball, the strategy with early Kaizen Blitzes is to make limited gains while developing the staff and associates.

After all this is done, you are ready to approve time and money budget requests for support of kaizen, including the Kaizen Blitz preparation and follow-up activities.

it's often fun. Although it does not assure market victory, enterprises that hope to be winners without something like it had best have a trump card that beats operational excellence. The fitness standards to survive are being raised.[2]

Most companies that acquire a serious interest in Kaizen Blitz already have an improvement history, a plan, and ongoing activity in support of it. If the organization's strategy, culture, and improvement direction fully support the deployment of Kaizen Blitz episodes, a brief strategic review will quickly lead to tactical preparation: how to prepare an organization before a blitz and how to follow up afterward to preserve the demonstrated gain.

If senior managers have zero experience with Kaizen Blitz, it may be a good idea to have a trial event or two with little expectation of retaining the gain. Just observe the demonstration and have people think about what must be done for the organization to actually operate in a very different fashion. The long-term cultural change to sustain the gain is the real revolution. Planning for this will be easier if the planners have first-hand experience with the potential for improvement *in their own environment*.

■ THE THREE-QUESTION READINESS TEST

To instigate a revolution with Kaizen Blitz, senior managers need to test whether an organization is ready to support the changes. One such test is to ask three questions:

1. Will a series of Kaizen Blitz events implement something consistent with the long-term direction of the company?

2. If it will, has that something been defined—is there a vision of future operations? Without one, Kaizen Blitz episodes will stir excitement but fizzle out before they can establish a lasting effect.

3. If strategic direction and an improvement campaign are clear, is the organization culturally ready? An acid test is to honestly evaluate whether prior improvement initiatives

---

[2] See Robin Cooper, *When Lean Enterprises Collide* (Boston, Mass.: Harvard Business School Press, 1995). Cooper addresses the need to do more than just go for world class operations, tough as that may be.

have stagnated. If they have, why? A legacy of failed attempts to revolutionize operations is not a good indicator that some new initiative called Kaizen Blitz will succeed. Perhaps a more basic set of problems needs to be addressed.

Ideally, prior to a Kaizen Blitz members of the blitz team and those working the process to be attacked should be able to answer the above questions. Answers need not be elaborate. Eighteen years ago, workers at Kawasaki Motorcycle could easily quote the strategic vision: "To build the best motorcycles in the world." Most could also describe Kawasaki's improvement initiatives of the time—quality and JIT manufacturing. The organization's culture had been developed to support grassroots-level improvement projects. (Operationally, the company was acclaimed, but marketing went flat for well-designed products—a caution about relying on operating improvement alone.)

Beginning with the strategic review, senior management leadership is critical. Success depends on a blitz's neither being smothered in overcontrol nor a directionless exercise in populist anarchy. Point the way, give them their head, keep them out of the ditches.

Once a major improvement initiative is underway, Kaizen Blitz events can demonstrate new process achievements—capture a beachhead so to speak. But as with island warfare, a blitz is only a successful landing. To finish capturing the island, and to hold it and change the work culture of its inhabitants, a long period of occupation and follow-up is essential. For a successful campaign, many islands need to be captured and held. Senior management has to have an overall improvement strategy—something bigger than a small island to go for.

The annals of war emphasize the derring-do of raids and the grit of stalwart defenses. Battles may be high-drama turning points, but whether a battle is a real turning point is only determined by the subsequent history of stressful change in the occupied territory. Did the work culture really change? Without a successful outcome, the entire war was just another waste of lives. A plan to win a war allows people to learn from defeats in some of the scattered battles.

■ BREAKING THE OLD PATTERNS

For a strategic business unit, traditional business strategy is fundamental: products, markets, and offerings; operations and asset deployment; management and personnel; and a plan to tie all this together so that it makes a profit. Unfortunately, for many companies continuing business as usual, strategic planning is little more than a fast review of the business situation prior to making a financial projection.

If an organization is to transform itself with Kaizen Blitz, that is far from enough. Senior management should estimate how much breaking the old patterns will change the performance of the processes. Visualize what that can do competitively and how to take advantage of it. Then pay considerable attention to how the associates must change to make the transformed process work: their work skills and responsibilities, their perspective of their work, the support required, motivation, mutual trust, organization, and so on. Transformation of the work culture is where the big alligators lie in wait.

For many people, breaking established patterns of thinking about operational design compromises is the first step toward radical change. What is the potential? The traditional notion is that a process designed for a particular type of efficiency can't break out of its pattern. It is summarized by the diagonal line in Figure 3.1. However, the bold arc that swoops away from the diagonal represents the effect on unit cost by making processes flow better, and there are many additional advantages.

Broadly speaking, the assumptions of the diagonal in Figure 3.1 are commonsensical. One does not build a one-of-a-kind satellite in an oil refinery. Every manufacturing process has its limits. However, they can be stretched, and a great deal of the stretching is done by modifying processes for better flow. Cost reduction is the benefit that flows most directly to the bottom line, but indirectly it may not be the most important one.

In the long run increasing the flexibility and capacity of a process will have more benefit than immediate cost reduction. Take the Southwest Airlines example. Their competitive milieu is short-flight, where rapid turnaround and fast maintenance translates to more flights per day per aircraft and more passengers (but not passenger miles) per employee than any other airline. The added capacity is the real source of profit, not a lower cost to do the same thing. To fly passengers cheaply, Southwest doesn't really do the same things as other airlines.

■ IMPLEMENTING THE BUZZWORDS

Breaking out of the product-process diagonal in manufacturing is the strategic intent of many of the buzzword movements of the

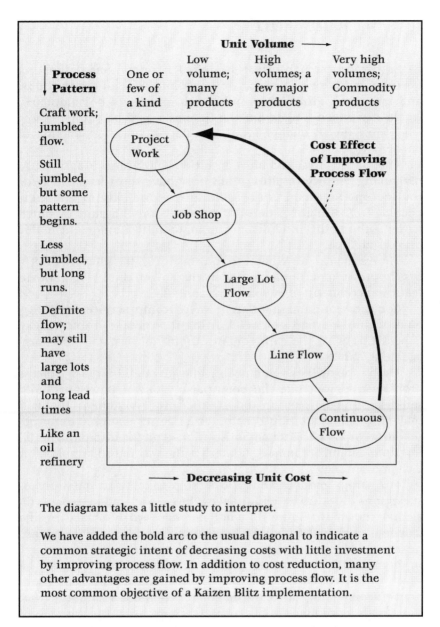

The diagram takes a little study to interpret.

We have added the bold arc to the usual diagonal to indicate a common strategic intent of decreasing costs with little investment by improving process flow. In addition to cost reduction, many other advantages are gained by improving process flow. It is the most common objective of a Kaizen Blitz implementation.

Figure 3.1. Bending the Classic Product-Process Matrix

This basic diagram has appeared in many contexts. It has been embellished and modified for service operations. The original concept appeared in two articles in the *Harvard Business Review:* "Link Manufacturing Process and Product Life Cycles" (January–February 1979): 133–140, and "The Dynamics of Process-Product Life Cycles" (March–April 1979): 127–136. Both articles are by Robert H. Hayes and Steven C. Wheelwright.

past two decades, such as just-in-time (JIT) operations, competing on time, building a learning organization, six-sigma operations, and mass customization. A full list, if one could be completed, would run much longer, but the themes would be similar: short lead times, higher quality, lower cost, flat organization, and lots of participation.

One of the latest and most ambitious buzzwords is agile manufacturing. Agility implies to not only have short lead times for routine operations but to be able to react quickly to the unexpected. Unfortunately, none of these visions amount to much without the ability and discipline to actually implement major process change.

Here's the carrot: Whatever your business, the purpose of process improvement, implemented by the Kaizen Blitz, is to perform feats that competitors in your class can't do.

You can beat them in different ways: prompt service, flexibility, quality, and—perhaps—price. Turning that potential into reality depends on what the *entire* organization, not just staff and management, can do.

Here's the drill: develop people to overcome their own process problems, demonstrate the potential by Kaizen Blitz, and build self-discipline to follow up and fix other process elements that will make the demonstration become an ongoing reality. Careful observation of Kaizen Blitz demonstrations and the discipline to follow up to establish them as standard is the way to fully implement a change strategy.

For senior management a first step may be to question assumptions they think are implied by the classic product-process diagonal shown in Figure 3.1 (but not necessarily shared by the diagonal's original authors). One assumption is that processes are nearly fixed by their original design and by the capital investment in them. Or that once a new process is shaken down, it cannot be much improved. Or that the only way to reduce costs is by economy of scale—going down the diagonal. A dubious assumption that starts with more merit is that process improvement is limited unless products are redesigned for it, which is true, but it concludes that redesign is prohibitive.

Many other assumptions are summed up by the often heard comment, "But we've always done it this way." Translation: We're going to coast on what we've got for as long as we can.

The point of improvement using Kaizen Blitz is at first to make a radical improvement. Create a jolt, wipe out a process as is, go back to where everything is simple again, and create a better process flow. Subsequent blitz events may only improve on the first, but no basic process concept may be unchallenged forever. With a truly radical thought in mind, tear up a process refined by many blitzes, go back to the most simple base, and start over again.

If senior managers think "on the diagonal," the first move is to start thinking off the diagonal and into a new operating range. To create a jolt, some seemingly outrageous goals must be set. But most of them should be within the reach of an imaginative Kaizen Blitz if the team also learns to think off the diagonal.

■ ANTICIPATING THE ISSUES

The obligations of senior management are implied by the strategic planning process, "From Strategy to Process Improvement," shown on pages 61–65. The specifics of any given case cannot be fully anticipated, but some kinds of issues have been relatively common. By going through a planning process somewhat like that given above, fewer issues in a specific case should come up by surprise.

To lead a process of rapid improvement, senior management has to be on top of the following: (1) where we are, and who we serve, (2) where we are going, and what customers we will serve, and (3) how do we develop the human will and skill to get there. Of these three, human development is usually the big crunch. The strategic planning should provide answers to these questions. Added to the challenges of running the business, it's a full workload for senior management, which must start to think of itself as "senior leadership."

➤ Where Are We?

Start with step 1 of "From Strategy to Process Improvement"—Assess the current situation. Senior executives of fast-changing companies have been around and continue to get around. They have seen operations other than their own—and some impressive ones, such as Wiremold, Critikon, or perhaps even a Tokai Rika. Much of the learning is first-hand self-discovery. Books and benchmark figures only start to make one ill at ease.

Dissatisfaction comes from self-discovering that where we are is not where we ought to be and that it is a long way from where we should be going. Dissatisfaction spawns improvement action. But if senior executives learn by self-discovery, so do the people who are going to execute the changes. They need to get out and about, too. Action is much more aggressive when large numbers of people realize that substantive change is needed, so their leaders are not taking them into an ambush.

(The Association for Manufacturing Excellence [AME] was originally founded as a vehicle to promote people going to see a live operation having a few lessons others could absorb. That's a first step. Kaizen Blitz events are held today just to promote participation in making rapid process improvement.)

➤ Rapid Assessment

Various assessment tools are available to help companies organize their own evaluation of where they are. The Association for Manufacturing Excellence has one called ASSESSMENT for EXCELLENCE.© Other organizations also have various checklists and rating systems. And of course, a critical part of self-assessment is knowing how the organization stands with primary and secondary customers.

Many issues should be anticipated by working through steps 2 and 3 including long-term projection and near-term vision, changes, and goals. Industry changes we need to take into account include outsourcing, technology, centralization-decentralization, use of software, avoiding false promises, and so on. All these are better handled if they are anticipated before deciding how to direct a Kaizen Blitz campaign. But of course, you might just dive right into the swamp and get lucky.

➤ Where Are We Going?

Some changes create a market where none seemed to exist before. Apple Computer was once in that position. Nike turned athletic shoes into a fashion business. Starbucks led the rise of coffee kiosks.

There are few concerns facing producers that can actually completely destroy their market, but nearly all producers face significant challenges. For example, first-and second-tier automotive suppliers are being asked to shoulder a significant load in automotive development—a big change from 10 years ago when most were make-to-print manufacturers.

Tune into the major shifts now occurring in operations. Supply chains are being tightened, software is embedded in everything, and considerable service is being bundled to accompany product. For example, personal computer manufacturers such as Dell and Compaq are recognizing that their hardware and factory-loaded software have become "commodity modules." They should use them as platforms to get into the software and Internet access business.[3] Hewlett-Packard, Motorola, IBM, and other companies design products to a distributed process. For fast response, customization is deferred until the last possible step—within distribution, perhaps at a truck terminal, or even at the customer's site.

Hewlett-Packard calls this strategy *postponement*. This strategy shifts the core competency processes for the various players. Such shifts need to be evaluated before stirring up a Kaizen Blitz on processes that will move elsewhere.[4]

➤ What Operations Will We Retain?

Likewise, some outsourcing (and insourcing) is unavoidable for technical reasons. For example, when printed circuit board (PCB) technology accelerated into multiple layers, high-part densities, and surface-mount technology, a company with a low volume of PCBs could not afford to maintain either the equipment or the technical pace no matter how much they attacked the process flow. Staying at the same defect rate level per board took concentrated effort from the most astute players of this game. In-house PCB departments faded as contract PCB houses grew. Such trends are harder to spot by foresight rather than hindsight, but one must try.

Although outsourcing is an operational cutback to the outsourcing company, it is an increased challenge both to the contractors and customers. A company that specializes in contract manufacturing had best become very good at their core competency, plus very good at making their operations flow into those of

---

[3] David Kirkpatrick, "Old PC Dogs Try New Tricks," *Fortune,* July 6, 1998, pp. 186–187.

[4] Hau L. Lee, Edward Feitzinger, and Corey Billington, "Getting Ahead of Your Competition through Design for Mass Customization," *Target* [publication of the Association for Manufacturing Excellence] 13 (April–May 1997): 8–17.

their customers. For smooth flow, both sets of operations need to fit with one another.

Localization of globally marketed products makes a fair amount of outsourcing inevitable, and it is not limited to parts for products. Brightpoint, for example, is a "value-added" global distributor that simply takes over the distribution and customer service of manufacturers of cellular telephones. Distribution and customer service for various manufacturers are handled using packaging and menu screens customized for each client so that end customers don't know they are really dealing with a contractor, not the manufacturer. Clients find that it's a huge advantage not to have to create localized distribution in far-flung parts of the globe.

In a company such as a Brightpoint, distribution and customer-service processes cover the world in geographic scope. An improvement campaign must take into account that processes must have a few elements tailored to each client, and that systems remain compatible worldwide.

■ IMPROVEMENT OF INTEGRATED VERSUS MODULAR PROCESSES

In the not always so good old days, B.C. (before computers), process integration depended on humans. It wasn't tied together with software and telecommunications connects. Most processes weren't well integrated either.

Even Henry Ford's famed Rouge Works had near-fatal process flaws. It wasn't very flexible (for years the only color was black) and the cost estimates were rough, to say the least, in an era when accounts payable were estimated by comparing the total weight of all invoices with the weight of sample stacks that had been totaled.[5] However, Henry Ford did not rely on cost figures to keep costs down. He turned technicians loose in the plants to constantly devise better methods and machines. In the B.C. era that's also how companies such as General Motors, which targeted improvement possibilities with far better cost systems than Ford, also improved manufacturing processes.

---

[5] Robert Lacey, *Ford: The Men and the Machine* (New York: Ballantine Books 1987), 451.

During this era production material flowed through processes, but the processes themselves were modular. For instance, methods and machines for making camshafts could be modified without affecting anything else as long as the resulting shafts met fit, form, and function. That's still true if one considers only the physics and geometry of processes. It's not true if information systems connecting them are not modular, or if processes become exceedingly complex.

■ CENTRALIZATION-DECENTRALIZATION AND COMPLEXITY

Where operations are centralized and uniform, process improvement quickly runs into systemwide conformance policy issues—the McDonald's problem. Most customers expect that whatever is presented at one McDonald's outlet will be virtually identical to that from any other. A Big Mac is a Big Mac is a Big Mac—anywhere—and although there are differences in the size and layout of outlets, customers also expect the service to be quite similar.

That policy severely limits local experimentation with either menu or core operations to appeal to local taste, the outcome of which may be a big hit or fall flat, but which in either case does not conform to the cosmopolitan McDonald's image. Changing the recipe, presentation, or methods for a Big Mac is a big deal—a centrally directed, coordinated change to appeal to a mainstream market segment. McDonald's imposes standardization through standard training, standard ingredients, standard equipment, uniform point-of-sale software, and so on.

In manufacturing, centralization-decentralization issues are perennial, both in processes and in organization. They affect both overall improvement strategy and its implementation, part of which may be by Kaizen Blitz. Some issues are as basic as assuring that the same parts from two different processes are interchangeable. Others are more subtle, but still fundamental, such as how to assure that the organizational culture between different locations (or countries) is compatible.

For example, Copy Exactly!, Intel's key to rapid deployment of both new product and new capacity, also dictates that local Kaizen Blitz teams are not going to be turned loose in production. If all production processes in different locations within Intel are to be identical in minute detail, then all production improvements must be centrally orchestrated in detail, an impossible feat without broadband digital communication. On the other hand, Intel's corporate order entry system, if it is modular in design, might be a good candidate for Kaizen Blitz.

In Intel's case, Copy Exactly! applies to chip development and production. The process has become so complex that there is limited time to experiment with core processes. At lesser levels of process complexity, experimentation to achieve better results makes progress, but when the science behind a recipe is not always fully understood, "same or better results" becomes lost in a tangle of process variables. Copy Exactly! clones the process more like replicating a DNA code, and changing such a process is like checking out genetic mutations. A few mutations are beneficial; most aren't.

In organizations with less need for integration—DuPont, for instance—centralization consists only of sharing of best practices. Within DuPont, best practice councils promote process improvement and sharing of excellent practice "the DuPont way" between divisions. DuPont's production processes in different locations may be similar, but with a wide product line, they cannot be identical. The diversity and modularity of DuPont's business increases the chances of a local Kaizen Blitz being successful.

By comparison, a small company does not have the financial backing or training resources of a large one. However, it is also much less likely to have big issues in centralization, so local teams can be much more the masters of their own process fate.

■ SOFTWARE MONUMENTS

Today, software permeates processes so that it is often a major consideration when commissioning a Kaizen Blitz. Centralization-decentralization dilemmas are particularly acute with systems software packages if the package is large and tightly linked at multiple points. By contrast, modular software systems communicate between modules through input-output. They don't use common variable lists or common subroutines so that reprogramming one module also reprograms several others.

Changing a large, tightly interconnected software package is time-consuming work not to be undertaken lightly. A limited programming staff must ignore most change requests and spend much time swatting software bugs. A huge, nonmodular integrated package is a software monument tough for an island-hopping improvement campaign to cope with.

Enterprise resource planning (ERP) software embodies these issues. A major selling point of such a package usually is that it will permit most business systems of multilocation companies to be integrated very easily: common formats for summary statistics and accounting data, all on the same system, and as current as the latest data captured. Large ERP packages have many options. Picking options is like finding a system to fit a set of processes located somewhere on the product-process graph of Figure 3.1. Once committed, the danger is that processes are locked in to the assumptions in the software. Afterward, process improvement attempts to work around this software monument.

■ CONTROL BY SOFTWARE

The role of software needs critical review if your company does not want "the tail to wag the dog." Software is often used for process guidance and control. It enables never-before-possible feats. But software can also encumber a process with delays and tollgates. At a tollgate everything stops for a check or transaction.

As a simple example, scanning a bar code of material literally on the move captures data on the fly with little delay to the value-adding process flow. But a major tollgate stop for a scan is such a ridiculous monument to control systems that you would think anyone would see it. Not so if the existing culture worships control.

Such a problem actually occurred in a cell-building conversion. A process that had been done by job shop methods had "required" nine stops to monitor material transfers between departments. The process could be converted to two cells connected by a small buffer. No database for inventory was needed because it was all visible to anyone in the area. Input-output counts for the total process were all that was needed.

The first reaction of remote staffers was that the process would collapse because it was out of control. Furthermore, no data from the new process could be compared with the data from the old one. Team members had to personally go look at the new process to realize that the old control system was no longer necessary—if it ever had been—and then, because they were not involved in the process changeover, their self-esteem prevented ready acceptance of the scene before their own eyes.

When processes simplify, control systems also simplify. As a process advances into rigorous standard work with fail-safe methods, control systems shift to prevention rather than mess management. Because computer systems allow us to capture more data, it can easily lead to the delusion that, if a mess is manageable, it isn't really a mess.

A Kaizen Blitz demonstration will show how to eliminate process waste—mess management. But the job is not done until the mess managers and the systems that support them have been displaced into something that adds more value.

■ KAIZEN BLITZ VERSUS IMPROVEMENT BY SOFTWARE PACKAGES

Changing the nature of any process to a flow changes the need for supporting software. Likewise, forced use of an information package also dictates that the process conform to it.

A popular way to improve processes is by purchasing a software package that mandates changes in order for it to work. Software package–driven process change is not the same as turning people loose to blitz a process and take it as far as it can go. A charge to a Kaizen Blitz team asks them to examine a specific process as it is and improve every aspect of it that they can deal with. That's fundamentally different from shopping for a software package with features that offer an improvement in the process, no matter how aggressively the shopper seeks process improvement.

Look down the left-hand-side of the product-process graph in Figure 3.1. A process with jumbled flow takes a great deal of communication to manage—lots of checking and calculating and verifying—and lots of continual matching of resources to needs.

For instance, when a contractor "stick builds" a house, the house sits; it doesn't flow. Crews and material must come to the site. Because contracting crews work on several houses at once, each house normally sits with nothing happening until the next critical crew can arrive. In some stages of house building several crews can work on different jobs simultaneously, but this process has to be coordinated on the fly. In addition, much judgment and adjustment by on-site crews replaces detailed process planning. Outcomes may exhibit considerable variance.

But house building has been done in ways that improve the process. When choreographed in detail, a house can be built within a few hours with crews waiting nearby to jump in when it's their turn. If standard house modules are built on a balanced line, much of this waste is eliminated. The elapsed time is short, and the pre-planning is simplified. If a house is built from precut, standard-size components, the total time of stick building on-site is also short. Crews are mostly engaged in assembly, not measure-cut-fit field fabrication. Each method of work flow has a different information system requirement.

The process assumptions embedded in a software package may or may not be a major advance over prior practice, but both the development and support of a complex package costs less if one is purchased. The risk is that the level of subsequent improvement may be limited by an inflexible software package. The difficulties of modifying complex software are nicely illustrated by the end-of-century "year 2000" bug—buried code that will crash if it can't interpret dates beyond the year 1999.

Anyone who has implemented a new Materials Requirements Planning (MRP) package realizes that if the software itself is not "buggy," the major problem is revising processes to fit the software. If committees obtain a package that can manage waste because they are more comfortable with it, they forego big opportunities for process simplification. They may even want a system that adds transaction complexity.

■ SOFTWARE ENABLES MORE COMPLEX OPERATIONS

Indeed, one reason for software is to be able to handle more complex tasks. For instance, consumer banking software allows tellers to handle more types of transactions and more complex ones than 25 years ago. More can be done for the customer within an acceptable customer-service time.

Unless an error was made, a teller's cash count should also instantly balance out at the end of the shift. The software also allows branches to stay open longer. Twenty-five years ago, "bankers' hours" allowed tellers the downtime to balance their drawers by the green eyeshade method. Now the push is on to shift basic teller work to the customer (and a software package) through on-line banking.

In these circumstances a Kaizen Blitz of teller operations by branch personnel makes little sense. Few improvements will be dramatic without dealing with system wide software. A cross-functional, strategically guided kaizen team that includes tellers and systems personnel makes sense, but any blitz demonstration will be for a systemwide solution.

Regardless of the type of process change assumed by a software package, people will resist it if they are not convinced that the new processes are the way to go. Even in smooth conversions, training and process change constitute the bulk of the effort and expense.

At Toyota and almost anywhere else in the 1960s, process improvement meant dealing with physics, geometry, and simple visibility systems for human communication. In the 1990s almost all operations have software issues that must be considered in developing an improvement strategy. Software monuments cannot be completely avoided, but they can be made more pliable if packages are not densely integrated and thus are easy to modify.

Survey data indicate that many manufacturing managers are aware of the problem, but perhaps not as much as they should be.[6] A couple of planning cautions help to alleviate the impediments of software. First is that old adage, "simplify, integrate, then automate"—that is, improve the process *before* creating a new software-based system for it. A Kaizen Blitz demonstration, or the equivalent, comes first so that process performance is not held hostage by software. If much better process performance can be demonstrated, but software is not compatible with it, then software change is a follow-up action.

Second, to develop software that can be modified with minimum effort is easier said than done. It should be modifiable, upgradable, and scalable—which means modular, relatively simple, and well documented. Features no longer needed can be turned off. Features that need to be changed can be changed.

When manufacturing plants went through rapid change early in the twentieth century, the key actors closely supporting the

---

[6] *Industry Week 1997 Census of Manufacturers* (Cleveland, Ohio: Penton, 1997). Table 1.15 lists some investment criteria that manufacturing companies use for information technology. Cost was only one criterion. Functionality, supportability, and ease of use were rated higher than cost. Upgradeability, time-to-implement, and scalability were rated lower.

shop floor were manufacturing engineers, equipment mechanics, tool and die makers, and so on. (It was no accident that Henry Ford and many other early industrial pioneers were mechanics.) The major process advances were by people who could create a process themselves, just as winning race-car teams have always been capable of developing advantages themselves.

Today, close-support systems developers and programmers have joined the cast of key actors in process improvement. Where processes and software are modular, they should be part of Kaizen Blitz teams. Where they are not modular, and where good reasons for centralized uniformity of processes exist, a bigger, more coordinated version of the Kaizen Blitz concept is necessary.

■ AVOIDING FALSE PROMISES

➤ Outsourcing

Trying to foresee obvious issues helps to avoid making false promises to Kaizen Blitz teams. With an all-out improvement campaign, all associates are involved in modifying existing processes. Their motivation is boosted if the results pay off for them. If outsourcing is necessary, let them in on it up front. For example, a company in Germany, where costs are high, determined that costs had to be reduced by revising the entire process for cellular flow production. However, before starting conversion, they estimated that, even with fast-flow production, German costs would still be too high. Workers in the Czech Republic could run cellular production as well as the Germans. The whole process was blitzed and transferred to the Czech Republic in 18 months. German workers were transferred to other work because the company was growing. It is better to have such a scenario mapped out sooner rather than later.

Avoiding false promises is a major reason to peer hard into the crystal ball in steps 2, 3, and 4 of "From Strategy to Process Improvement." If drastic process improvement will unavoidably reduce employment, get it out of the way fast. Several years ago Cincinnati Millicron Electronics Systems Division converted production to JIT. There was no Kaizen Blitz methodology then. Staff and management detailed the process changes, which took six months, then directed the execution. In one weekend excess workers were laid off because there were far too many, with no foreseeable business growth to occupy them. The plant reopened on Monday morning.[7]

Without a strong growth plan or a highly expansionary business, people will be displaced by startling productivity improvement. Enthusiasm for Kaizen Blitz wanes quickly if workers suspect that their reward is cessation of a paycheck, and especially if they think management doesn't care.

➤ Omark

In the early 1980s Omark (now Oregon Cutting Chain Division of Blount Industries) more than doubled labor productivity in just a few years. The company then had more than half the global market share of chain-saw blades, and still does, so no growth in market share could offset the productivity improvement. Oregon Cutting Chain's senior management made several valiant attempts to broaden the product line and take on other kinds of work. None met with outstanding success. In the end a plant had to be closed and the total workforce reduced. Because the downsizing was done through attrition as much as possible, there wasn't much rancor.

As long as the leadership obviously tries and is not capricious, most people accept setbacks if they understand the situation. A little bit of pain sharing also helps. Executives getting big bonuses for throwing loyal troopers to the wolves is not a morale booster. Senior managers should shun policies that wreck their leadership status.

One of Dr. Deming's 14 points was to "drive out fear." That's a tall challenge. No one gives a formal lifetime employment guarantee, not even Japanese companies famous for it. Their "guarantee" is an informal understanding that, in a pinch, personnel will not be eagerly sacrificed to the bottom line. Everybody, including top management, hurts together—equality of sacrifice.

However, in the United States talking about equality of sacrifice is not much of a morale booster. Much to be preferred is a growth strategy to soak up excess personnel. Sometimes the unemploy-

---

[7] Cash Powell, "Cincinnati Milacron-Electronic Systems Division," *Target* [publication of the Association for Manufacturing Excellence] 3 (Summer 1987): 28–32.

ment can be exported to competitors, but that's hard to count on. They may be improving too. Senior managers who anticipate dramatic productivity improvements need to develop an aggressive growth strategy.

■ INVOLVING ASSOCIATES IN THE BUSINESS

Sometimes production workers can be peripherally involved in marketing. For example, Jeff Anderson, general manager of Williams Technologies, frequently invited prospective customers to tour his rapidly improving plant and talk to workers. If they said "Wow!" the probability of landing their business went up. Direct contact with prospective customers was great experience for the workers, too.

Avoiding false promises is not always possible because customers are fickle and plans don't always work out. A much bigger issue than Kaizen Blitz is developing all associates to have a degree of understanding of the condition of the business. Adopt some version of open-book management. Treat associates as adults and expect adult behavior from the time of hiring until outplacement if that becomes necessary. In most cases an organization can't give anyone much assurance of a long-term career. It's much more realistic to promise that, if you acquire great experience here, you won't have trouble finding work elsewhere. Develop people to be employable rather than dependent.[8]

■ ARTICULATING AN IMPROVEMENT STRATEGY FOR EVERYONE

To articulate an improvement strategy, an imaginative buzzword name may help generate enthusiasm if leaders have to talk it up a great deal. It can be called anything from "Fast-Flow Operations" to

---

[8] A pioneer in treating employees as adults was the late Scott Myers, whose last book was a classic: *Every Employee a Manager* (San Diego: University Associates, 1991). Myers made a career of bringing managers and workers together. He began formulating his concept of nonpaternalistic management in the 1960s.

"Drive Away the Buzzards," but if the commitment is not real, a name won't help for long.

Giving a separate name to the larger-scope business strategy may be useful too. One of the most colorful business strategies of all time was that of Komatsu in the 1960s and 1970s: "Maru C," which means "surround Caterpillar." It referred to grabbing niche markets in the heavy equipment business where Caterpillar wasn't and to all the activity necessary to support that approach.

If a company is in dire straits, awareness of impending disaster can be turned into a great motivator if senior management has a plan and associates can contribute to it. When chasing benchmarks in a catch-up campaign, understanding what to do is usually easier too.

However, if people are "fat and happy," it's a huge challenge to motivate them "to go where no one has gone before." That's a strategy to dominate an industry or market niche—to do what others cannot do. People need a sense of adventure plus long-term rewards (such as stock or stock options) to take an offensive plunge.

■ LEADERSHIP FOR RAPID CHANGE

Senior leadership for rapid change needs to be considered up front. Besides other "walk-on-water" qualifications, the most valuable characteristic of senior managers leading transformation by Kaizen Blitz is the ability to induce people to change themselves—to create a new work culture. Culture change must overcome the legacies of the past.

Legacies are old software systems and old processes, but most of all old habits and behaviors—"instincts" about how to get things done. Old software and old processes can change when there is a will, but creating the will is a leadership challenge. Behavioral legacies die hard.

Some managers are remarkably prescient about the forces of status quo surrounding them. For example, one general manager, aged 61 and coasting to retirement, was subjected to a plant tour and exposition on fast-flow processes and the implications by an expert in it. Within a few hours he understood the concepts quite well. He also understood the legacy of his organization: "Me lead all that? With the people I've got? I won't live that long!"

Some of the legacy issues can be blown through with colorful leadership (which the coasting manager didn't want to exercise). Great leaders change the culture by "walking the talk" and telling the right stories. They extol examples that demonstrate how people are to behave and work the new way. They discourage the recounting of injustices past. They intervene in the oral history of the organization—lunch-room talk—by creating something new to talk about. A Kaizen Blitz episode is something to talk about. The difficulty is stirring up support for it, holding the gains, and moving on.[9]

Good leaders make dependable promises but they may have expectations that seem unpredictable and outrageous at first. Thus, all keep things stirred, but with differing styles. Art Byrne at Wiremold writes poetry back and forth to his troops. Burgess Oliver at Nortel has a vast repertoire of folksy, colorful stories and expressions to inspire his Nashville-based organization. Dick Nordquist at Guidant-Temecula has, well, irrepressible Californian enthusiasm and energy. All of them spend more time with people than on any other aspect of the business. In dry sociology speak, these guys are change agents.

However, the risk is that an initiative based on a leader's "personality cult" will not survive the departure of the leader (or leaders). This risk is real anywhere, but it is pervasive in large companies that regularly rotate managers between locations. Large organizations have a long tradition of partially involved local personnel following a survival strategy. Play along, hunder down, and wait out the limited tenure of the current zealot-in-charge. The next one will try something different.

In a large organization with managerial transience, nothing approaches cultural stability until it survives several generations of management. Likewise, any practices that have survived several management generations will not be dislodged easily. Finding or creating good leaders is the first step in an improvement strategy that is built on human development. Without top level leadership, facilitated Kaizen Blitz events are unlikely to go beyond demonstrations of potential.

---

[9] Sandra Egli and John Whiteside, "Changing Corporate Culture Overnight with Oral History and Legends," *Target* [publication of the Association for Manufacturing Excellence] 13 (January–February 1997): 14–17.

The leadership challenge intensifies after a Kaizen Blitz demonstration. That is when those who support the new process must work through the postblitz changes to convert the demonstration to established practice. That is also when the old work culture fades out and the new one emerges.

■ EXORCISING THE CULTURAL GHOSTS

Realistically, not every employee will become a fast-flow enthusiast. To make a durable change requires a critical mass of enthusiasts, a majority that will go along and few that are really opposed. With either a union or nonunion workforce, the deep-seated legacies of the past are the toughest to deal with, and the legacy drag is apt to come more from staff and supervision than hands-on workers. Supervisors and staff are the personnel who carry the baggage of the control-systems legacy with them. Also, overcoming the legacy drag usually leads to discharging a few recalcitrant personnel who cannot escape their old way of life. They don't get it.

But discharging of all the fearful and reluctant is not feasible. They carry with them a wealth of experience that is difficult and expensive to replicate. If colorful leadership can't turn attitudes fast, the sources of legacy problems must be found and corrected to turn people from dysfunction.

Some dysfunction is normal—just charming individualism. Every family and every working culture has a few dysfunctional quirks. Among the novelties displayed at tourist traps occasionally can be found a plea embroidered in sampler style: "God Bless Our Dysfunctional Family." However, corrosive dysfunction will undermine the process of change, and it hides as an unspoken attitude that, like a stealth aircraft, goes undetected by leadership radar.

When useful, hold ceremonies to bury old resentments. Sherry Ford developed the culture process shown in the box copy on page 88 while working in economic development with industries near Athens, Georgia. She likes to tell of the plant where it was discovered that workers had long harbored a four-letter-inducing dislike for managers whose presence in the plant was marked by wearing white hard hats, exclusive to them. Managers and workers held a ceremony out back, dug a hole, and literally buried the white hard hats, figuratively burying the hatchet with them.

Steps 4 and 5 (refining and priotizing goals and developing and prioritizing new projects or initiatives) in "From Strategy to Process Improvement" appear to be rational planning, but strategists must consider the irrationality of human relationships and legacies. Much human development is not technique training.

Several break-out moves can be made. One of the simplest is to change the assignments of a few people in leadership positions in the same organization (not site transfers). Most of us can figure out how to overcome someone else's legacies easier than we can figure out how to overcome our own. In one case, by designating a division controller to lead a manufacturing improvement campaign, staff personnel readily became involved, recognizing that they must support the changes.

But when legacy ghosts are truly ethereal, they will not be easily exorcised by selective dismissals, leadership changes, or cheerleading. They have to materialize before they can be banished. One way to scare legacy ghosts out of hiding is with facilitated meetings designed for the purpose; even the meetings are not effective however, if issues are not addressed after they are identified.

An outline of such a series of meetings is shown in the box titled, "Breakthrough Process to Assess and Change Plant Culture." Some ghosts, once identified, can be seen by anyone and quickly exorcised by a few redemptive actions, such as burying the managers' white hats, getting rid of assigned parking spaces, or painting a drab area.

Other ghosts haunt only a small set of people that have been affected, such as the comment, "Nobody trusts night people to get the stuff they need." Such specifics come from detailed comments that individuals silently write on cards. Once they are revealed, corrective follow-up may take cooperative action to fix. In the case of the night supplies, some years back the hoot-owl shift had a history of removing stock and leaving storeroom records in a shambles, so the stores were double locked. Working out a fix for this kind of problem is the beginning of the kind of follow-up that can make Kaizen Blitz demonstrations permanent achievements.

It never fails that an assessment process such as the one described have produces more cards with an affinity to "communication" than to any other category. Working out how to continue

BREAKTHROUGH PROCESS TO ASSESS AND CHANGE PLANT CULTURE

➤ Half-day sessions, interactive, maximum of 15 employees.

➤ Segregated by level (management, supervisors, operators, maintenance, indirect)

➤ Structured brainstorming, flip-chart responses to the question "What changes do you expect in the next three years for market, customer, competition, technology, product, cost of doing business, organization?"

➤ Structured brainstorming, three-by-five cards, response to the question "What kind of work culture will it take to handle these changes?"

➤ Silent affinity mapping of over 100 three-by-five cards, into up to seven affinity groups.

➤ Relations diagramming, "What is the relationship of influence among these seven affinities?"

➤ Compare the top affinities of each session (reveal a plant's legacy systems).

➤ Build turnaround strategy from these top affinities.

➤ Introduce "world-class" concepts only after legacy systems have been addressed.

➤ Train on a JIT basis, right people, right time, right topic.

➤ Follow up at least twice monthly for a year to sharpen skills and keep the turnaround strategies relevant.

Don't abandon the process if results don't show up immediately! This process digs out many legacy problems without a seeming eternity of focus groups and gripe sessions, but it is still very time consuming.

Courtesy of Sherry Ford, Change Partners, Athens, Georgia.

operating with radically different processes is a never-ending stream of trivia fixing by the people running the processes. Creating the atmosphere in which that can be done is a leadership responsibility not to be taken lightly. A thoroughly poisoned atmosphere does not clean up quickly either.[10]

■ PREPARING TO WRESTLE ALLIGATORS

When a process is improved, it's analogous to draining a swamp full of alligators. The first noticeable effect is an increase in the concentration of alligators. The alligators, deprived of home and food, are not happy about shrinkage of their territory, and they may not be fearful of humans. The moral: When planning to drain a swamp, be ready for the alligators.

A Kaizen Blitz drains part of the process swamp. During the final Kaizen Blitz demonstration, it looks much nicer; process performance is much improved. But the alligators have not yet become hungry. As soon as they appear, people not prepared to deal with alligators will quickly resort to the easiest fix: Refill the swamp.

Alligators are a protected species—not an endangered one. Nonetheless, one can liken the overall process change using Kaizen Blitz to alligator extermination. That is, improvement of process quality and flow requires an organization adept in problem solving. That takes time to learn. One of the toughest concepts to learn is that a fast-flow process has to be closely supported. Auto assembly is probably the best-known flow process in discrete manufacturing. When an auto assembly line is down, the alligator team immediately goes into action. But people accustomed to taking their time solving their problems have a different gut reaction: Make the alligators go away by refilling the swamp.

---

[10] Sherrie Ford, "Competition May be Global, But All Quality Is Local," *Target* [publication of the Association for Manufacturing Excellence] 12(November–December 1996): 33–37. A more extensive discussion of the methodology is in Sherrie Ford, and Susan Dougherty, "A Work Culture Renaissance through Effective Assessment," *Conducting Needs Assessment* (Alexandria, Va.: American Society for Training and Development Case Studies, 1995.)

Creating an artificial sense of urgency doesn't work very long. It has to become real, and alligators tend to twitch a lot before they die. People need to acquire confidence to become alligator exterminators. Will plus skill equals rapid progress.

■ DEVELOPING PROCESS SUPPORT

Where rapid problem solving is in progress, there isn't much time to dress up analyses for presentation. The wall boards and flip charts remain unbeautified. The place for clear explanation is at the action point, where a fix must be checked out and standardized.

The strategic implication of all this is that process improvement the Kaizen Blitz way is done by people. From a leadership standpoint, the secret, if there is one, is to develop the people to do the improvement—including most of the alligator kills. Then they take care of the processes and the customers as well.

The key areas to make improvement stick are in process support. Paradoxically, process support is not very effective until the people in those roles realize that they serve the real value-added processes. They must adapt to make to those processes run smoothly rather than making the processes adapt to their convenience or their compulsion to control.

Support staff will not realize this until they self-discover it. One of the best ways for them to self-discover is by including support people on Kaizen Blitz teams. In a factory with physical flows, that's maintenance, tool and die, programmers, manufacturing engineers, accountants, schedulers, sales, customer service, and one too often forgotten, human resources. Whatever they do to genuinely improve a process is helpful, but more important in the long run, they acquire experience to develop themselves.

In a plant that cannot seem to get support people motivated, a reasonable early strategy is to do a Kaizen Blitz on a support area itself. In a plant, for example, do a blitz in a maintenance shop, a tool-and-die room, or in programming development.

The emphasis on broad human development is necessary to induce awareness of the need to totally back fast-flow processes. Otherwise, performance tops out at the level that the organization, as is, can deal with. For example, Texas Instruments has employed team-based process improvement for years. For years a nagging issue in team problem solving was that they could not obtain meaningful cost data quickly from accounting when that happened to be an important consideration in a problem. The accounting databases were not set up to do it effectively—a big alligator that twitched a long time.

■ FIRMING THE PLAN

As with anything strategic, there's a lot to think about, and it comes from many directions. It's a good idea for a leadership team to set a time limit for coming up with a firm plan. Taking a long time won't produce a much better plan. No plan will be followed exactly but having one signifies that the leadership team has looked ahead, then agreed on goals and what must be done.

The firming process is step 5 in "From Strategy to Process Improvement." Doing an exercise similar to the matrix helps to tie an action plan into a neat bundle with some relationship to long-term direction. The format can be adapted to the needs of the individual case, which come partly from the business strategy and partly from the current status of people to engage in rapid improvement. The crucial step is boiling it down: deciding on a few overall critical success factors, how they will be measured, and the goals to achieve them. A good question to ask when doing this part is, "Six months from now, at the first management review of this program, how will we know if we are making the kind of progress we had hoped for?"

Some of the goals for critical success factors should seem outrageous, so that people have to learn quickly what they imply. Until people see how outrageous goals can be reached, they will think them insane. On the other hand, goals that require no more than tweaking of current processes do not create a revolution. For example, Motorola's Six Sigma quality goal was considered outrageous when it was first put forward by Bob Galvin. But "Motorolans" quickly understood that such goals could not be reached by continuing with business as usual.

When deciding the initiatives or projects to sponsor, you may find that the budget precludes doing as much as you would like. However, the limiting factor is almost always the improvement time available and the limitations of people to fight and kill alligators. A few specific projects must be directed toward human development. Some human development will be indirect through experience with the improvement effort itself, including Kaizen Blitz. Other development will teach people, both behaviorally and technically, how to fight alligators.

■ ROLLING OUT: START ALLIGATOR WRESTLING

As mentioned in step 6 of "From Strategy to Process Improvement," a workforce experienced in improvement processes will probably take to policy deployment. They understand process detail that simply can't be seen by senior managers.

However, early on some associates need to be stimulated to fight alligators. They don't want to. They are afraid. They don't know how. They see legacy ghosts. Others will have a big burst of enthusiasm until they find an alligator that seemingly refuses to die. Senior management has to be prepared to lead the alligator war. By this time it should be obvious that planning ahead may be an intellectual exercise, but winning the implementation itself, like any kind of war, depends on leadership.

Getting Ready
for Kaizen

If you are reading this book, then, presumably, the Kaizen Blitz concept already interests you. What you need to assess now are which specific business needs or goals need improvement. Perhaps you plan to concentrate on productivity improvement, inventory reduction, capacity expansion, cost reduction, leveraging capital investments, or processing time reductions. Or, perhaps you just plan to demonstrate the possibilities for rapid and radical change that exist within an organization. Articulating such goals will help to focus initial efforts and make the results more meaningful to the rest of the organization.

It is very difficult to master the kaizen process without a guide. No individual or organization will go very far without help from someone who has walked the ground before. Finding that resource, the appropriate guide or mentor, in a nearby company or through a competent consulting organization, is often the critical determinant of success. Here and elsewhere we repeatedly point to the need for experienced guidance as each new phase of learning is reached. And beyond the initial phases, even spectacularly successful practitioners point to the benefit and need for constructive criticism and feedback as the organization moves forward.

The appropriate source and level of mentoring will, of course, differ from one organization to another. What's important is to recognize the need and to begin to seek out the right mentor for your organization.

■ THE LEARNING PROCESS

Kaizen begins with learning—about lean manufacturing, the Toyota Production System, and kaizen and its applications. We can characterize this initial learning phase as an exploration.

Readings from this book and other reference materials can provide a good introduction, but successful kaizen practitioners almost invariably cite the need for experience-based learning and guidance by experienced practitioners as the primary path to success.

Senior management should take the lead role in the resource selection, education, and training processes, ideally by benchmarking with the management of other firms using kaizen. As with most change processes, the chance to share the experiences of those who've walked the path before, particularly if they are willing to share their failures as well as their successes, can be invaluable. Often they can also identify or introduce key resources they employed in beginning and promoting the process in their own organizations.

Next, seek opportunities for the management team to visit facilities where kaizen is being employed. If these visits can also include the chance to speak to a broad cross-section of the staff, they can rapidly advance the understanding of how the whole organization perceives, adapts to, and finally adopts kaizen as an effective improvement tool.

For a fortunate few, contacts with practicing companies may evolve into an invitation to serve as a team member on a real kaizen team. If possible, senior management should participate on an actual team in another company to gain first-hand knowledge of the process. This is perhaps the best way to begin to develop a real understanding of the true nature of the kaizen process.

Unfortunately, most practitioners will not have the opportunity to develop direct contacts who can arrange site visits or team participation opportunities. Although many business consulting firms offer educational services in this field, companies may wish to find other ways of advancing their understanding, or even of sampling the process, before making a real commitment.

Professional organizations such as AME offer a variety of educational resources and often serve as effective avenues for establishing contact with individuals in practicing companies who may be sources of guidance. The Kaizen Blitz events of AME, for example, offer opportunities for attendees to participate on real kaizen teams, in host companies willing to share their experiences. These unique events can be real eye-openers for the beginner and provide contacts for further learning opportunities.

■ KAIZEN AS A SELF-LEARNING PROCESS

The kaizen process itself is a self-learning process. Mastery of kaizen—that is, developing the ability to effectively practice kaizen to bring about real change and improvement as needed—requires experience, experience gained through repetition of the application of key principles as skills are developed.

Developing a skill—the ability to effectively apply knowledge to achieve a desired result—has three steps:

1. Education
2. Training
3. Experience

In terms of kaizen, we can look at the three steps in the following way.

➤ Education

Education creates an understanding of the underlying principles of lean manufacturing—as with the Toyota Production System, for example. Through education we explore how these principles apply to and can benefit the business. Education also explains the principles of the kaizen process itself: how projects are selected, teams chosen, goals set, and results achieved.

➤ Training

Through training one learns the specific techniques and tools that the kaizen team uses to do its work. Some are new tools, such as value- versus non-value-added analysis, takt time and cycle time calculations, standard work, time observation, and cell design. Others, such as brainstorming, flowcharting, and pareto analysis, that are already in the organization's repertoire are reviewed in the context of their application during a kaizen project.

➤ Experience

Experience is the kaizen process itself: applying the knowledge and new tools acquired in education and training along with other known improvement tools; mastering skills through practice, repetition, mistake, and correction.

➤ Applying the Three Steps

As with the practice of law or medicine, the necessary skills of the profession can only be developed through application. It is only through a well-thought-out process of education, training, experience, feedback, and correction that we can develop the skills to successfully practice kaizen.

These three steps are really the framework of all learning in the process. They do not apply only to the team members themselves. They have application at every level of the organization, from the first-line supervisor to the top manager responsible for the business. They have particular importance in developing in-house facilitators or kaizen experts who must be skilled at all levels of the process and have a clear understanding of the various roles, needs, pressures, responsibilities, and limits that apply to each of the participants in the process.

For these reasons it is important that basic education begin with the management team and that management participate at all levels both to develop a clear understanding of the process and to develop and hone the skills needed throughout the organization to master the kaizen process—to achieve lasting improvement through its application.

Once again, we see the need for mentoring, for an experienced guide to give the critical feedback needed to correct and improve.

■ THE FIRST PROJECTS

Choosing the first project sites and goals are important steps that should be carefully considered. Areas that can significantly change the business are ideal starting points. They should be evaluated for selection of projects that are more or less self-contained with

DESIRABLE CRITERIA FOR AN INITIAL KAIZEN BLITZ PROJECT

➤ Be clear and unambiguously measurable—for example, reduce setup time, improve output, and so on

➤ Enjoy management enthusiasm or support in the specific area

➤ Satisfy a perceived business need—break a production bottleneck, and so on

➤ A highly visible process or location

➤ Be an easy project, a confidence builder (think about where and for whom)

➤ Take advantage of availability of team and support resources

➤ Have a strong environment for follow-up—a management team that can be counted on to strongly support the kaizen team's changes into the future

➤ A simple, easy to understand process

➤ A stable, repeatable process

➤ A people-based project highlighting the workers contributions (don't make it look like a technical exercise)

➤ A self-contained process, one not subject to considerable influence and change from outside sources

WHAT TO AVOID IN A FIRST KAIZEN BLITZ PROJECT

➤ Out-of-control processes

➤ Unreliable equipment—prone to breakdown, and so on

➤ A machine or process that's not capable

➤ A process highly dependant or easily affected by another process or outside influence (e.g., one that may require major adjustment due to minor variations in raw materials)

➤ An unnecessary improvement area (e.g., setup reduction on equipment that seldom needs to be changed over)

➤ A machine or process soon to be obsolete or replaced

➤ Any process (a computerized system, for example) where an immediate improvement can be stymied by technical limitations (can't reprogram it in three days, etc.)

clearly identifiable boundaries. Don't try to overreach, particularly with an initial kaizen. Projects need to be cleanly completed in the time allowed without a carry-over list of unfinished items. As kaizen is a highly focused improvement technique, broad gains are best achieved by linking together several projects along a product flow until the desired result is achieved.

Pay attention to the physical layout of areas under consideration so that any "monuments" that should be dealt with prior to the kaizen are identified. A monument may be a centralized process (heat treatment furnaces, chemical processes, an enormous stamping press, etc.) that is difficult, impossible, or expensive to move or modify—something that appears beyond the reasonable capabilities of a kaizen team, particularly in an organization new to the process. It may be possible to work around or build a project around the monument, but be careful not to choose something that requires a lot of prior preparation and thereby gives the impression that this is typical of the kaizen process. It isn't.

Weighting of the various criteria varies widely from place to place. This is one of many areas in which the advice and guidance of an experienced hand shows its worth. Remember, the real objective is to make the first project a success, one that can be recognized by the whole organization.

Along with desirable criteria, there are of course, things to look out for, to guard against.

■ DEFINING THE SCOPE OF THE PROJECT

The project scope and objectives can vary widely, but early kaizen efforts generally will focus on the following:

Productivity improvements. Those that increase output or reduce resources required to do the job.

Changeover time or setup reductions. Reducing the time equipment is down or out of production while changing from one product configuration or operation to another.

One-piece flow. Focusing on building cells or eliminating interruptions in operations to cut inventories and process times.

(Pull-system projects—providing signals for action based on consumption or demand—are common kaizen team projects. As first projects, however, they may lack the impact of the types noted above. Often the improvement, although it is real, is not obvious to the casual observer, and administrative process changes, reporting for example, frequently require more management intervention than is desirable in an early demonstration. For these reasons, it's often best to begin pull-system projects in a second round of projects.)

Goals for improvement in these areas are set high to challenge the team to get out of the box and try radically different approaches to the problem. Setup time reduction goals will typically be set at 90 percent, and those for productivity improvement at 20 to 30 percent. One-piece-flow projects commonly call for 50 percent or greater reductions in inventories, process times, and walking and part-travel distances.

Although all of these goals require a real stretch on the part of the team, less challenging goals are in reality sometimes harder to meet as the need for radical new thinking may be less apparent. If the goal seems reasonable and achievable by the team at the outset, many may be unwilling to stray very far from the existing process or too timid about trying alternatives. A 90 percent setup reduction goal, for example, forces the team to completely rethink the process; a solution probably can't be seen simply by refining existing methods.

In choosing the site and specific event, you'll need to spend time developing the baseline data from which results can be measured. The final details of this fall to the chosen team leader under the guidance of the kaizen facilitator.

Think all of these things through in the context of support resources available. For example, building a cell from functionally located equipment might not be a good first project if heavy plant maintenance support can't be provided by a small staff. Take this one on later using outside support resources once the organization is more accustomed to the process and has gained confidence.

Another reason to reject a project like this early on is to avoid creating the impression that kaizen is a high-cost, resource-intensive process. Bringing in a crew of professional riggers to do the "heavy lifting" is fine in a mature lean organization, but it leaves the wrong impression in the minds of first-timers.

Is there a project area where a likely team leader is already involved? (But don't be surprised if, in retrospect, the "ideal" team leader turns out to be a dud or a bad fit. The needed combination of personality, people skills, leadership ability, and drive to succeed are often hard to define outside the context of real kaizen team experience.)

Unfortunately, the first teams are often entirely composed of novices. That's why prior experience on a team and advice and guidance from experienced practitioners are so important. Kaizen must always be a *team* process.

The results that last come from the ideas of the team, the people who do the work, and must be owned by the team to be sustained. Perhaps the most common failure in organizations trying to adopt kaizen is in doing too much preplanning, or in populating the team with individuals who "start with the answer." Above all, avoid the brilliant engineer who has the whole solution preprogrammed in his head before the team starts.

A kaizen team isn't just an implementation team; its job is to develop solutions, that is, to develop and test its *own ideas,* and *then* to implement them.

■ CHOOSING THE TEAM

Team composition will vary from project to project depending, of course, on the specific nature of the areas addressed and the team's objectives. All teams, however, must have as a core the people who do the work: the individuals who operate the machines, change them over, move the materials, and so forth.

Any good kaizen team does a lot experimentation—running parts, changing over machines, and so on. The team needs several people who can do that capably and safely—the people who usually do the work. In addition, these are the folks who'll be expected to maintain the new practices and techniques the team develops. Their ownership of the changes is critical to the fulfillment of this expectation.

A successful kaizen project often creates a radically different process that, by its nature, moves many people out of their comfort zone. Sustaining such change can be difficult even when the changes were self-directed. Imagine how much more difficult this can be if the changes appear to be imposed from outside the workplace environment.

Choosing the right operators, machine setters, and so on from among those available in a department is important. In a setup reduction project, look for one or two of the most skilled setup people—individuals who have a reputation for getting the job done well. (This isn't stacking the deck with people who can outperform the average associate or an attempt to achieve results that can't be repeated. It's merely a practical recognition of the strengths of potential team members.) Look also for innovators, open-minded people who might like to see things change.

Don't go too far in trying to set up an all-star team, however; most people can learn to contribute effectively on a kaizen team. Including the occasional "doubting Thomas" on a team can be a real plus because converting the attitude of a well-known naysayer can pay real dividends in enhancing kaizen's reputation and desirability in your organization.

Support the core of the team with the variety of skills they may need to get the job done. These will vary, of course, but look for people who have some expertise in product, process, or machinery: an engineer, a tooling technician, a production control specialist, an inspector.

Also include some outsiders, people outside the process, from sales, accounting, administration, or even outside the company. They can look at things from different points of view, with fresh eyes. They often see things that those familiar with the process won't and can ask the "dumb" questions that often lead to the most remarkable improvements.

Finally, consider someone who may have a particular expertise in some of the basic improvement tools your organization routinely employs, such as brainstorming or flowcharting, skills that can be put to work with good result by the team.

➤ Volunteerism

The attributes and skills to be considered in choosing the team members should not be applied at random. Particularly for early teams, volunteerism is almost essential. A kaizen team is asked to make extraordinary efforts to bring about radical change. Working hours can be long, and tasks performed and skills employed are often outside of the normal assignments of team members. Their work can be seen as changing the way they and others work in the future. Many associates will be uncomfortable with some or even all of these aspects of the kaizen process. Because the objective of the team is success, for itself and the whole organization, it is prudent to limit team membership to volunteers. Eventually, after long experience, some organizations mandate participation by all employees, but this is definitely not the way to start.

Kaizen is about teaching people how to change the culture of their own workplace, to carry out process improvements for themselves. As such, it is bound to generate strong feelings among many associates who will, at least at first, be uncomfortable with its concepts and its impact on their routines. Voluntary participation is the sensible way to begin, to build trust and win support for the process.

■ THE TEAM LEADER

The team leader is sometimes the supervisor, the immediate supervisor or someone a step or two up, of the project area. Recognize, however, that the title *leader* does not mean *supervisor*. The team leader isn't expected to be in charge in the sense of directing specific solutions, but to lead the team in developing solutions that draw on all of their skills. The team leader's job is to make sure that the team meets its goals, not to have all the answers or, worse yet, to have a preconceived set of solutions.

For these reasons, the first few teams in a company may look outside of supervision for the team leader. This can help create a less-intimidating environment for many of the team members, at least until the open, no-rank style of a well-run kaizen team can be broadly recognized. In cases like this, it's good practice to make the area supervisor a team member. He or she, after all, will be called on to follow up and support the results of the team's work.

The choice of a team leader involves more than just his or her position in the organization. Ordinarily, after a number of kaizen projects have been conducted, a pool of former team members who have first-hand experience with kaizen becomes the source of future team leaders. On the first teams, of course, this isn't an option. As with team members, at least at the outset team leaders should be volunteers.

Look for people who are biased toward change or who at least demonstrate an open-minded attitude toward change. In addition, look for people who can perform well under pressure.

Strongly directive leaders are not a first choice, but a certain tough mindedness, an ability to stay the course under pressure is desirable. Kaizen is a time-bound, goal-oriented process, and the goals are often challenging indeed. As a consequence, the pressures on a team leader can sometimes be severe—getting the team leader through the tough spots is a primary challenge for the facilitator.

■ EDUCATION AND TRAINING

The ranking manager, his or her staff, and other key personnel need to provide the necessary support, the foundation, for the success of the team. They need a shared commitment. That can't come without understanding, so begin with education for these key individuals.

You may start with a broad overview delivered by an executive from a practicing company nearby or by a consulting resource. After that, arrange for a formal class that begins with lean manufacturing education (the Toyota Production System) and concludes with all of the elements of kaizen training. Make sure that this is the same curriculum to be delivered to the real team.

At this stage, it is critically important that everyone have a common understanding of the overall philosophies, principles, objectives, and techniques involved. None are so complex that they can't be simply and clearly communicated and well understood by all levels of the organization. In fact, the ability to create this common understanding or common language across the organization should be a key test of the effectiveness of the education and training program. If your people, at all levels, can't get past the jargon, look for another educational resource before you go forward.

It is particularly important that key supporting resources, the maintenance staff, for example, understand the context of the exercise they'll be asked to support. (It's hard enough to deal with people who won't take no for an answer when you *know* why they're so persistent.)

■ EDUCATION AND TRAINING
FOR THE TEAM: LEARNING TO SEE

The team's education and training class should follow the same path and ideally be exactly the same package as that delivered to management, including an introduction to the Toyota Production System, the principles of takt time, one-piece-flow and pull systems, and the basic concepts and tools employed by the kaizen team to put these principles into practice. It may be helpful, in building trust, to have one or more members of the management team participate in the class, but only as participants; classes, like kaizen teams, should have no rank and should encourage open and frank feedback and discussion *among equals*.

Ordinarily, education and training can be accomplished in a three-to-four-hour class. Depending on the duration of the project itself, this can be included as the first half-day of a three- or four-day project or conducted a week or more in advance for a week-long, five-day project.

The real focus of education and training is to familiarize the team with the concepts of continuous improvement they'll use in their project and to create the "blameless" environment within which they'll be asked to root out and eliminate waste, non-value-adding activities, of all kinds.

For the first several projects an organization carries out, it is desirable to hold the training class a few days in advance, even if projects are of short duration, to allow time for adjustments and preparatory work by the team leader under the guidance of the kaizen facilitator.

Classes are generally conducted by an experienced facilitator who will guide the kaizen team, its leader, and the management team through the process. Emphasis is not solely on teaching specific skills or techniques—confidence building and developing a sense of the team as a cohesive unit are equally important. Some of the teaching techniques themselves are tailored to these ends.

A good example of a confidence-building teaching technique can be found in a common approach to time-observation training. The objective of time-observation training is to develop the skills needed to observe an operation, break it down into several steps or elements, and then repetitively time each step in sequence and record the time required to perform each one. The data gathered can then be used in a variety of ways to help the team eliminate wasted effort, ease the difficulty of operations, simplify tasks, and so on. It is a basic tool for cell building, productivity improvement, and setup reduction projects.

In the classroom the basic use of the stopwatch is taught by playing a videotape of an operation and having the class time its various elements. Participants can then compare results with each other as well as with the instructor's answer sheet. Frequently, a shop-floor associate will outshine a technical professional in this exercise, helping to build respect as well as confidence.

Another tactic is to ask the team members in the class to observe the video, usually of an operation none of them are familiar with, and offer improvement suggestions. The result is often astounding, particularly to the class members themselves, with many small improvements apparent even to the novice observer. Techniques such as these are important to building the team's confidence so that it can meet goals that at first may seem impossible. As an organization becomes adept at improvement through kaizen, home-grown examples can become part of the confidence-building routine in the classroom, reinforced by the testimony of fellow workers who have served as team members.

It is important, particularly for the first few teams in a facility, to make sure that all of the team members have attended a full training session. The focused, results-oriented approach the teams employ is usually radically different from any that team members will have experienced themselves. It is, therefore, crucial that they begin with a good understanding of the process. Even with excellent training and facilitation, it will still be difficult for many to come to grips with what they can and are expected to do.

■ BASIC MEASURES

Following the class work, the facilitator works with the team leader to develop necessary baseline information for use by the team in its initial analysis and to make arrangements for materials the team may need to do its work. Using some simple techniques and forms that are described more fully in Chapters 6 and 7, the team leader gathers the basic information needed for the team to present its project at the kick-off meeting held at its inception and from which progress toward its goals is measured.

Often this basic data-gathering step validates the true status of the process so that specific improvement targets can be established for the team. Finding the answers to seemingly simple questions— What is the cycle time? or What is the setup time?—can turn out to be dauntingly difficult. The answer to this problem is to stick to simple, basic techniques.

A good example of the type of problem we're referring to is in determining a starting point for a setup reduction project. An initial investigation often yields several different versions or interpretations of what the current actual setup time is. Some of these stem from simple differences in definition. A company may ask workers to report the time spent actually changing tooling from one job to another, while time spent waiting for prints or for raw materials to show up may be reported in another category.

In a kaizen project a typical strict definition would be "last good part to first good part," that is, all of the time elapsed from the completion of the last part on one job until the first good part is being produced on the new job. Most organizations cannot begin to give a consistent or valid answer to that question.

For a team leader gathering data for his or her team, a few simple approaches usually suffice. First, the team leader questions the people who do the work, asking them how long it usually takes, not on a good day or a bad day, but on an average day. Then, perhaps, the team leader might ask an associate to time a setup, not break it down in a formal sense, just keep track of when the process started and when it finished. This sort of approach is often good enough to start. In the case of setup time, the answer will more often than not turn out to be a great deal longer than what common wisdom might suggest. The objective is to try to establish a *realistic* starting point and then to bring about a dramatic improvement.

Another example is the determination of cycle times, the actual time it takes for certain operations to be performed or for a part to be produced. Once again, examination of shop-floor records or labor- or production-reporting forms, may be misleading. Sometimes a simple approach such as observing the interval or spacing between products coming off of a production line or completing a process give the most direct and truest answer. Again, the objective is to approximate what is really happening in the current process in a simple direct fashion so that targets can be set and performance improvements easily gauged.

Two common baseline measurements are the distances traveled by people and materials. These are not parameters normally measured by typical cost-accounting-based shop-floor measurement systems. The preferred technique here is, not surprisingly, to actually walk the paths taken by people and materials, pacing off the distances to establish a baseline. In the case of a setup reduction project, one might follow along as a setup person went from place to place during an ordinary changeover, both at the equipment being addressed and on the many common excursions to tool cribs, inspection stations, print files, and the like. Unless a great deal of attention has already been paid to easing the operators burden, the results will usually be a surprise and sometimes a shock. Walking distances during setups often total thousands of feet, even in small facilities. Precision of measurement isn't the objective, just the establishment of a baseline that everyone feels is realistic. The Kaizen Blitz can then be tasked to take a large bite out of the base.

Material travel distances can be measured in a similar fashion, taking along a few people familiar with the flow of the work and a set of routings or any other process instructions that may exist and just walking the path, pacing off distances. As with walking distances, the results will often amaze even the long-time employee. We're just not used to thinking about and measuring material or people movements in this way.

These basic measurement steps, as imprecise as they may seem, are fundamental to a successful kaizen program. They help reveal the reality of operations and reinforce teachings on the opportunities for eliminating waste in most environments. Furthermore, these simple, easily learned and understood techniques complement the self-learning, self-improvement philosophies that underlie, and are in great measure the real objectives of, the kaizen process.

■ LOGISTICS

Aside from the project-related support (maintenance resources, hardware, etc.), virtually all kaizen teams need some level of logistic support from outside the team to do their work effectively. The team is, after all, working under special circumstances to do something radically new or different in a short time. Hours worked are often long and unpredictable, many are away from their regular workplace, and everyone needs to keep focused on the tasks at hand.

Over time every organization develops its own set of work patterns and consequent needs for kaizen teams. Working hours vary, group preferences and regional customs vary, and so on. Here are several areas that should be considered as a start—

➤ Meeting Area

Most teams need a breakout or meeting area equipped with a blackboard, flip chart, and other similar materials. They'll need a place to gather from time to time and work out ideas. Nothing fancy is required here; movable dividers on the factory floor often suffice.

➤ Meals/Coffee Breaks

Depending on working hours and the specific environment, provide the team with appropriate meals (breakfast, lunch, dinner, coffee, and soft drinks). Sometimes it's fast food in the workplace, sometimes a more formal serving in a cafeteria. Do what makes sense in your company—the aim is to keep the team on task by taking care of these items for them.

➤ Tool Kits and Cleaning Supplies

Almost every factory kaizen team finds it needs a basic set of standard hand- and small power tools, cleaning supplies, and gloves or protective garments to do its work. Consider making up some simple tool kits and clean-up kits for the teams in advance; this spares them much begging and borrowing as they get started. Most teams quickly become adept at acquiring help and needed materials, but this gets them off to a good start. Look for advice on contents during your benchmarking visits or from your guide.

➤ Celebrations

A celebration is perhaps after the fact, but it is still important. Provide some real recognition for the team: a team dinner one evening at the end of the project; a plantwide gathering to celebrate their accomplishments. Remember, you expect the team to do a first-class job for the company; make sure they and everyone else recognizes the value of their contribution. This also provides an ideal forum for promoting the kaizen process to the whole organization.

Many organizations find that it is useful to appoint an individual to organize and serve as a focal point for the kaizen teams on all logistics issues.

Some of these issues may seem petty when viewed in the context of the overall lean manufacturing or kaizen initiative, but as they relate directly to the people who bring rapid change through kaizen, they deserve real attention.

Benchmarking, education, selecting projects and teams, training, setting baselines and goals, and logistics preparations are all prerequisites for beginning the real Kaizen Blitz process. Success depends on commitment, a commitment to the teams and more important, a commitment to the process of learning through experience that kaizen teaches. Regardless of the success of initial projects, real success for the organization can only come from an ongoing, steady, step-by-step process that relentlessly applies the kaizen improvement process to eliminate waste and enhance value-adding activities throughout the enterprise.

Chapter

Timeprints and Takt Times

Since the arrival of just-in-time (JIT) manufacturing from Japan about 20 years ago, Western manufacturers have become more accustomed to time-based performance measurement. In the intervening years, practices from lean manufacturing to information technology have likewise promoted what is sometimes sloppily referred to as "the need for speed."

Our biggest problem figuring out how to improve is probably the human factor, part of which is mutually understanding and accepting time as both a descriptor of a process and a guide to its improvement. For example, using the term *speed* to describe time-based measurement connotes a faster work pace or higher output rate. Neither objective necessarily leads to real improvement. A much better overall indicator of improvement is reduction of process duration indicators, such as material flow times.

■ A FAST RUN THROUGH THE HISTORY OF TIME

One way to view history is by tracing how people learned to sharpen their use of time to coordinate activities. Rhythmic coordination by dancing or marching has been understood for millennia, but our sense of time has rapidly changed in recent times. "Native" people with a vague sense of time do not easily adapt to the modern world.

Most ancient societies' sense of time was so limited that they blurred the distinction between the past and the future, which profoundly influenced their reasoning. Because cause comes before effect, they had difficulty comprehending the relationship between the two.

For example, like most ancient languages, Middle Egyptian did not clearly distinguish between past, present, and future tense. Although Egyptian astronomers developed a calendar that foretold the annual floods of the Nile, their language did not clearly convey the concept of a forecast to the average Egyptian. Those who forecast an imminent flood or solar eclipse were likely regarded as having the power to cause the event themselves, a power the astronomers wisely attributed to gods or to the pharaoh.

Considerable evidence indicates that in all ancient agricultural civilizations—including Egypt, Babylon, China, and the Mayan Empire—astronomer-priests invented and reinvented calendars to guide planting and harvest and to set religious observations. That is, their discoveries set the patterns of life. Some calendars were quite accurate by present standards. Perhaps the most accurate was that of the Mayan Empire, which collapsed about 600 years before the Spanish arrived.

For centuries, separately kept calendars did not agree. Medieval Europeans going to a different city sometimes found themselves in a different year! Without a clear concept of time, a practice now as precise as interest-rate calculations were crude. Besides, time was usually considered to belong to everyone, so time charges for money were considered immoral.[1]

Before mechanical clocks, the measurement of time in intervals of an hour or less was approximated using water clocks, sundials, and burning candles. No times were recorded for the ancient Olympic races because timing a dash was not feasible. However, both the Greeks and Romans used *clepsydras* (hourglasses) to limit the time of lawyers' speeches. And before mechanical clocks, day

---

[1] G.J. Whitrow, *Time in History* (Oxford, England: Oxford University Press, 1988). The first few chapters summarize the connection between concepts of time, measurement of time (including calendars), and the basic assumptions of ancient cultures. Usury, the direct charging of interest on a loan, was officially banned by the Catholic Church until 1832, but not enforced. It is still banned by the laws of Islam.

and night were often separately divided into six hours each, so the length of these depended on one's location and time of year.[2]

The first all-mechanical clocks are thought to have been invented in Italy in the fourteenth century (along with double-entry bookkeeping). Although they lacked minute hands, mechanical clocks began to create a new sense of time in daily life. Soon bells from municipal clocks signaled the beginning and end of the workday for Italian textile workers, thus beginning centuries of argument over how long a workday should last and how much should be done.[3]

After that, new needs for clocks became technology drivers. For example, in 1714 the English commissioned a prize to develop a marine chronometer accurate enough to enable the calculation of longitude at sea. Indeed, the volume and accuracy of timepieces produced roughly corresponds to the advance of manufacturing capability.

Watches were first mass-produced in the 1850s, and the habit of looking at a watch began. Rail schedules were one reason to look at them. Before the railroads, each town could keep its own time, and some did. As rail traffic increased, the observance of time zones became necessary. By the 1890s the need to synchronize rail service drove time technology; the spec for a railroad watch of that era was 17 jewels and accuracy within 30 seconds per week.

At the beginning of the twentieth century, synchronizing U.S. power grids to the 60-Hertz frequency was still a challenge. By century's end, many of us assume that 60-Hertz electricity is a birthright. We don't reach the limits of time-keeping science unless we manage something like satellites or Internet operations.

---

[2] A simple *clepsydra* ("water thief" in Greek) is a water-filled equivalent to a sand hourglass. Ancient civilizations from Greece to China also built much larger, more elaborate water clocks.

[3] Juliet B. Schor, *The Overworked American* (New York: Basic Books Division of HarperCollins, 1992) Schor's Figure 3.8 indicates that in England and the United States, nonagricultural working hours peaked in the nineteenth century. The work hours of industrial workers in Dickinsian England were longer than anywhere else before or since. Converting from the seasonality of agriculture to the industrial clock has also been a social jolt everywhere in the world. The pace and constancy of work expected during industrial working hours varied considerably, but it was quite different from rural work patterns.

Computers and computing networks are clocks. Everyone who uses telephone systems or computing networks leaves "timeprints" in many databases, but we are not always conscious of them.

Foggy time characteristics indicate that a process does not have a definitive time pattern, meaning that the process itself lacks a pattern. The clarification of a process is accompanied by clarifying or creating its time characteristics. To do that, we need to develop sharper time consciousness in the process performance measurements that we use.

■ SCIENTIFIC MANAGEMENT

Other than a track coach, the man most symbolized by a stopwatch is probably Fredrick Winslow Taylor, who surfaced in manufacturing soon after stopwatches were produced in quantity. An excellent amateur athlete, Taylor sometimes used watches to improve his performance. As an engineer, one of Taylor's favorite tools to improve work processes was a stopwatch.

Taylor focused on how a person, machine, or the two together could accomplish more in less time. From his analysis he set time standards—procedures first detailed second by second and later in hundredths of a minute.[4] He argued that each worker who beat the expected number of daily repetitions of such a standard should be rewarded with individual bonus pay. At the time it was thought that few workers could relate pay to the performance of processes much beyond their immediate reach.

Taylor called his system Scientific Management. Its purpose was generally to maximize the output per day of individual workstations. During the twentieth century Scientific Management influenced all managerial thinking in government as well as business, and it dominated industrial management. Today the set of practices that evolved is often called Taylorism.

■ TIME AND TAYLORISM

Taylor's assumptions are still with us because they were built into Taylorism. Two limitations in Taylor's early work were crucial. First,

---

[4] By 1915 the Gilbreths and others used motion pictures to analyze in fractions of a second, frame by frame.

Taylor, an expert analyst, studied work as independent processes, station by station. Second, his usual objective was to maximize output per hour or per day. (He began the formal standardization of work but could never leap much beyond an issue that began in the fourteenth century.)[5]

These two limitations led to a third one that today gets a lot of press—Taylorism does not engage the worker. Except for skilled work that cannot be partitioned, Taylorism breaks down work to repetitive cycles requiring minimal skill. Such tasks are not intrinsically exciting. Even where considerable skill and judgment must be used, just complying with standards set by analysts is demeaning. The reaction of medical doctors to the standards set by HMOs and insurance companies is a recent example of reactions to the system.

Early Taylorists did design assembly lines and techniques for balancing them, but their mind-set generally limited the objective to achieving a desired line speed (often at a maximum capacity) while minimizing the idle time of resources used (primarily labor) at each station. Until the last few decades, hardware manufacturers rarely conceived of processes in which product flows all the way from raw material to customer. A concept such as Henry Ford's Rouge Works was an exception to general practice.

■ WORKING OUT OF THE TAYLORIST BOX

To "get out of the Taylorist box," we must (1) expand the scope of a process mentally as far as possible and still deal with it in a practical manner, (2) think of work flowing through a process, thus establishing a time pattern, and (3) devise time indicators (along with others) for process performance. All this implies broad participation in process improvement rather than process design by "industrial astronomers" who work for management "pharaohs."

---

[5] Robert Kanigel, *The One Best Way: Frederick Winslow Taylor and the Enigma of Efficiency* (New York: Viking Division of Penguin Books, 1997). Kanigel uncovers many flaws in Taylor's assumptions and attitudes in the light of today's scientific standards and sociology. (Taylor was an out-and-out engineer and the very first management consultant. In his time he was neither scientist nor sociologist and referred to workers in groups as "gangs," which was customary usage at the turn of the century. It was enough for him to develop the basis for standardization of work.)

One other concept is fundamental: The process should minimize waste by doing *only* what the customer needs, and one of the major ways to do that is by maintaining as constant an interval between job completions as possible. Under Taylorism the conflicts between independent processes working at different rates was usually solved by buffering them with inventory.

The essence of time-based operations is to serve customers' requirements as they need them. If customer demand has a time pattern, the timing of supply processes can be organized to match demand. The ideal is shipping material to an assembly line that consumes it at evenly spaced intervals. If customer demand patterns are chaotic, look for a time pattern that can best serve them anyway. Like the swirl of a galaxy, a process time pattern is usually waiting to be discovered by people who seek it.

■ A PROCESS CAN BE A CLOCK

Time itself is defined by a reference system in which something moves, whether it is the solar system or an oscillating atom. Likewise, the motions or shifts within man-made work processes create their own time patterns according to the relationship of various activities to each other, in sequence, duration, and repetition.

To make a man-made process highly repetitive requires careful attention to the timing of its elements. If a process's activity cycles can be refined and interconnected, it can begin to "run like clockwork" itself.

Most people are accustomed to work done by accounting cycles or school semesters that are tied to the calendar. However, a manufacturing process can also have intrinsic cycles, depending on the methods and resources in use. Such a time pattern is occasionally called a shop cycle. It may be as simple as an industrial machinery manufacturer "turning out, on average, a machine every 7.2 days."

An outside observer may regard such a shop as self-organizing into a regular, repeating pattern. Workers time their various contributions by a planned overall cycle, or by one that simply emerges as the process self-organizes. One objective of a Kaizen Blitz is to establish guiding time cycles whenever possible. Another is to be able to alter the time cycles when desirable. That is, workers should learn to engineer and reengineer the process to fit a new time pattern when needed. To do so, workers must learn not only how to run a process like clockwork but how to reset the process clock, or even how to rebuild it.

■ TIMEPRINTS: DESCRIBING A PROCESS WITH TIME

Every method of performance measurement, including costing, attempts to understand something about a process that is not seen just by looking. However, without having a basic understanding of the process itself, all performance indicators are misleading, so it's worth thinking through what an indicator represents.

Timeprint measures describe a process exclusively with time: how long it lasts (duration), how frequently something comes out (interval), or how long it takes to make a change (like a setup time, for example). (See Figure 5.1.)

Timeprint measures are direct characteristics of a process, not a ratio of something else with respect to time—such as speed (distance/time) or output rate (units/time). Even a value-added ratio, to be discussed in Chapter 6, is not a timeprint measure. The value-added ratio is omitted from Figure 5.1 because, although it is a time ratio, segments of time must be classified as either value-added or not.

Timeprints of similar processes can be compared globally without adjusting for currency translation, cost allocations, and so on. For example, comparisons of manufacturing process duration and order-to-shipment duration can be made with data from *Industry Weeks'* annual America's Ten Best Plants competition.[6]

■ UNDERSTANDING WHAT IS BEING MEASURED: FLOW CHARTS

Most processes can be described by the four basic elements, long known as the four Ms: man (all persons), machines, material, and methods (which includes measurement and information). The sequences of these elements can be described by flow charts, and de-

---

[6] *America's Ten Best,* an annual statistical profile published by *Industry Week.* The latest annual report is available from *Industry Week* Customer Service, Penton Publishing, Cleveland, Ohio (800-326-4146).

Definition of Timeprint: The characterizing pattern of a process using only time.

Timeprint Characteristics of an Actual Process
Duration (flow-through time of key process elements)
Cycle (time between output unit completions)
Process Cycle (takt time) Range
Change Time (time to change a process for different output
    volumes and mixes)
Customer-Response Lead Times
Information Feedback Times

Timeprint Characteristics of Process Planning
Planning Horizon
Replanning Cycle
Firm Point
Granularity (length of time increments used for planning)
Takt Time Planning Lead Time

Four-M Elements of a Process
Man (all persons)
Machines
Material
Method (includes measurement and information)

By strict interpretation, even a value-added ratio, the fraction of total process time that value is added, does not qualify as a timeprint by a strict interpretation. The numerator of this ratio requires classifying activity as value-adding or non-value-adding, which is one additional assessment factor beyond just taking a time measurement.

Figure 5.1. Timeprints

tailed flow charts constructed by knowledgeable people are part of the improvement process.

Seeing a process the same way is not elementary. In most factories it is not possible to grasp the general flow of either processes or material at a glance. If all the production floor cannot be seen in one sweep of the eyes, workers' ideas of how a process flows outside their own area will be limited. Offices are worse if no obvious material flow marks the processes.

High visibility of process flows aids communication, a part of which is a common understanding of process measurements. As people start to be responsible for outcomes of larger processes than those which they directly control, they must engage in teamwork. Visibility of processes is essential to cut teamwork communication times. Although they are difficult to measure, information feedback times are conceptually important timeprints, and high visibility eliminates a great deal of both communication time and effort.

Identify the key value-adding elements of the process that should flow, usually material in manufacturing. Making those elements flow becomes the focus of the improvement and of the time measurement. Flows of other elements are also to be greatly shortened or even eliminated.

Practically speaking, value added is a strict interpretation of something a customer is willing to pay for. Not everything that adds value is material. For example, Motorola's process to assemble and test Iridium satellites must not only create hardware; it must also create accurate "as-built" physical configuration data, plus software configuration data, which is vital to the management of each satellite during its lifetime.

Some aspects of defining a process using time are intuitively obvious. Others may take some getting used to. And any time description is ambiguous unless people have a similar mental picture (or overall flow diagram) of the process. Several time characteristics of processes are listed in Figure 5.1. Fortunately, some relatively basic flow diagrams and timeprint estimates are sufficient to provide objectives and ideas for a first-time Kaizen Blitz.

■ DEFINING TIMEPRINT CHARACTERISTICS

➤ Duration

Duration is the start-to-finish time of work going through a process. The longest process duration time normally attracts interest, but there is great opportunity in shortening all flows—or compressing the timeprint, illustrated in Figure 5.2. The compressed process should be capable of the same interval between completions.

The diagrams are greatly simplified. Complex ones may help determine exactly what is occurring, but the objective is to simplify. Therefore an objective is to decrease the diagram complexity as well as shrink its time coverage (its timeprint). Note that the configuration of the compressed process is not the same as the unimproved one.

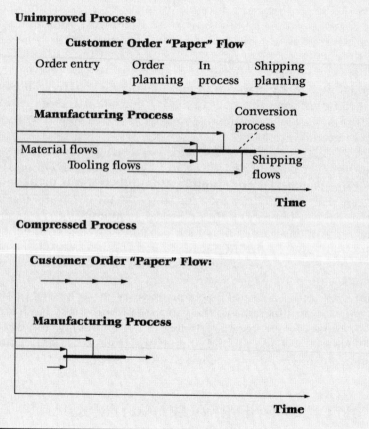

Figure 5.2. Simplified Timeprint Diagrams

Sometimes flows merge, like parts flowing into assembly. Both the main flow path of assembly and the material flow times are part of the timeprint. Assembly duration is the time for a primary platform to go from start to finish. The flow-through time, or duration, of the inventory added may take a longer or shorter time, and each part may have a different duration. In addition, the flow duration times of software, documentation, or just information may also be significant.

Think of a bare printed circuit board starting through assembly until it finishes, component-laden and fully tested. The bareboard flow time is the duration of the PC board assembly and test process. The time-on-hand of inventory is an indirect estimate of materials flow-time duration.

If a process flow diagram is imposed on a time line, as shown in Figure 5.2, the duration part of the timeprint becomes the time equivalent of the flow diagram. A Gantt chart does the same thing for a project. If one compares duration to a process layout, the timeprint becomes a crude form of space-time relationship. If some kind of timeprint cannot be conceptualized for a process, it is really muddled. The more precise the process, the more precise its timeprint.

As the scope of processes increase, defining the flows becomes messier. Suppose a manufacturing process is defined to include the entire supply chain. The longest duration time has often been called the cumulative lead time and may include active process duration times, transit times, and inventory time (just sitting).

Unfortunately, the terminology used in time measurement has long been both nonstandard and hard to standardize. Until the 1980s the term *cycle time* in most industries implied a repeating cycle, or process interval, like a machine cycle time. In the auto industry and a few others, cycle time also meant process duration time, or lead time, which is what cycle time means in general usage today. The meaning of a term can usually be inferred from its context and knowledge of the process.[7]

---

[7] The common use of the term *cycle time* to mean duration began with Ed Heard's presentations to Motorola in the early 1980s when that company was beginning what we now call lean manufacturing. Cycle time stirred more interest in improvement than lead time, a subject then considered to be a concern only for materials planners.

➤ Process Interval Time

Process interval time is the time between unit completions, or job completions. It has been called cycle time (in its original sense), pulse time (by Motorola), drumbeat, and other terms. Interval time is the actual time between units—an outcome. Takt time is a planned time between units. Interval times in this sense are the inverse of rates. Think of a 1-minute mile instead of 60 miles per hour.

➤ Interval Time Range

Interval time range becomes more important as a flow process is refined and so is a more appropriate objective for later kaizen of a flow process. Process range is the ability to reorganize processes to produce different mixes and volumes, using different interval times, or pulse rates. People are far from ready for this when first organizing a process flow, but as process flows start to become a familiar work pattern, achieving this objective makes processes flexible or agile.

➤ Change Times

Change times are of two basic different types. The most fundamental one is setup time. The shorter the setup times, the smaller the batch sizes, and the quicker to adjust to a change in unit mix. If setup times can approach zero, a process may be able to run a mix of units in one-piece flow. Attention generally should be paid to setup times starting with the first Kaizen Blitz.

The second type of change is reorganizing the process to run a different volume and different mix of units with a different interval time between—that is, based on a different takt time. In production that's an exercise in repositioning and substituting tools, materials, and even equipment. In a factory this could be called layout change time. Small, labor-intensive custom-packaging operations are an example of a type of business that for decades has changed layouts for different jobs several times daily. Other manufacturers with heavy equipment or those with a long history of stable production more likely regard a layout change as a major engineering project.

➤ Customer Lead Time

Customer lead time may apply to almost any service offered, but in manufacturing it's likely to be order-to-customer-receipt time—the lead time that the customer actually sees for a product. Several nonmanufacturing processes consume part of order-to-receipt time duration, and if the deliverable expected by the customer is not hardware, all processes are service processes. Kaizen applies to them also.

➤ Information Feedback Time

Information feedback time is the time to obtain and act on needed information. The importance of such measures seems obvious in a decentralized organization. However, if people are coming off a Taylorist bureaucratic mind-set, "information" covers a universe of phenomena. *Information* is a neutral term, but an information process can either promote value-added flow or plug it up.

Customer information is very important. Ideally, everyone would like to minimize the time needed to respond to complaints or other information from customers—and to external needs of other kinds as well.

Perhaps the need for rapid feedback is easiest to see when it is applied to conformance quality issues. If stops to fix quality problems are combined with the reduction of process duration times, then quality will improve and rework will decrease. Feedback time is shortened and action takes place.

The best way to overcome conformance quality problems is to set up fail-safe methods so that errors are difficult to make. Instead, they are anticipated by process deviations and corrected before they happen. And fail-safe methodology, or *poka-yoke,* is a subject in itself.[8]

---

[8] Shigeo Shingo, *Zero Quality Control: Source Inspection and the Poka-Yoke System* (Portland, Ore.: Productivity Press, 1985). Although fail-safe methods have long been used in reliability engineering, Shingo popularized inexpensive fail-safing as part of process improvement by workers in the Western world under the Japanese name *poka-yoke.* He contended that intelligent use of *poka-yoke* eliminated the need and expense of much quality-control monitoring and information because problems were stopped before they occurred.

Jim Swartz, a former GM executive turned lean manufacturing consultant, has a convenient way to explain information time reduction from a quality viewpoint. "Time to detect" is the lag time after an error occurs before it is noticed. "Time to correct" is the time after detect until correction is made. And "time to prevent" is the duration time until the process is revised so that errors are permanently corrected—that is, a fail-safe solution is applied—a key element in developing standard work.

Much is now made of creating learning organizations. Whether they are formally measured or not, decreasing information feedback times is a form of learning. As Swartz puts it: "Time to detect + time to correct + time to prevent = Time to learn." And there may not be much need for actually gathering data on feedback times. Any lag times that one can eliminate don't need to be measured.

➤ Compression of Process Timeprints

Compression of process timeprints should benefit the customer. Compression refers to duration times or lead times. One can devise various response-time indicators that suggest whether customers are getting what they need within a short elapsed time. Of course one can ship almost instantly from inventory that has been sitting for years, but the idea is to create what the customers want so quickly that they will never know the difference.

➤ Process Planning

Process planning also has time characteristics: planning horizon (how far out the plan or forecast reaches), the replanning cycle (how often to replan), and the firm point, which is the point at which action is committed and cannot be changed easily. If the timeprint of a process compresses, the time pattern of its planning process may also need to change. It is common to discover that the time characteristics and reporting requirements of an old planning system do not fit a revised process.

■ WHAT IS A TAKT TIME?

Takt-time planning may seem strange at first. Once the process is understood, however, calculating takt times does not take very long. Determining the time period that the takt time should cover and having confidence in a forecast that covers that period are challenges, but ones very familiar to planners.

For any planned schedule period, divide the time available in which to do work by the number of units to be completed. That's the planned time interval between unit completions—takt time in its simplest form.[9]

Figure 5.3 shows two basic takt time calculations. In practice, allowances must be made for planned process downtime. The number of units needed must include everything that is required of the process—samples, tests, spares, and so on, plus the regular requirements of customers. However, these planning adjustments are necessary whether calculating a takt time or not. Figure 5.4 is a more complex illustration adapted from an old Toyota calculation for pick-up truck beds.

A simple calculation such as that shown in Figure 5.3 will probably do to start. Because the idea is that the actual interval between completions should match takt time as closely as possible, be generous allowing for downtime at first, and put the effort into developing the process station-by-station to match the takt time without having waste. A calculation more like Figure 5.4 is more appropriate once steady flow in a cell is actually established in practice.

Even the masters of running to a takt time, for example, Toyota in top form, allow three to five percent of the time in each shift as downtime for people to adjust, study the process for improvement, or just recover from screwups. Any mishap should be fixed on the spot before it is passed on. Otherwise, its effect multiplies as rework, or worse, as a customer complaint. Toyota calls this practice of downtime *jidoka*. Too little *jidoka* is as bad as too much. If people don't take *jidoka* time, they aren't paying enough attention to the process, and things will slide.

The use of takt times usually accompanies a change of mindset in how to design processes. For example, suppose a press can be developed to form sheet metal 10 times faster. One should question

---

[9] The term *takt time*, sometimes spelled *tact time*, came to the United States from Japan, but the term *takt* is not Japanese. English speakers often assume that it is German. Actually *takt* is Swedish for "cycle" or "cycle time." Regardless of the language, it useful to distinguish between a planned time interval and an actual interval that results from execution of the plan.

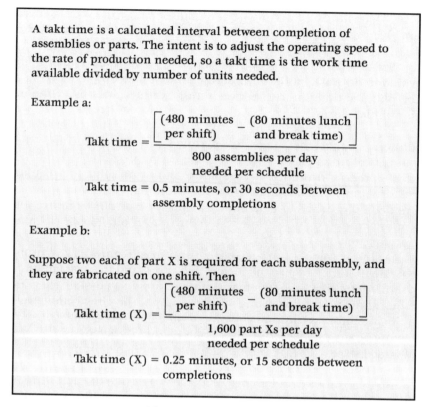

A takt time is a calculated interval between completion of assemblies or parts. The intent is to adjust the operating speed to the rate of production needed, so a takt time is the work time available divided by number of units needed.

Example a:

$$\text{Takt time} = \frac{\left[\begin{array}{c}(480 \text{ minutes} \\ \text{per shift})\end{array} - \begin{array}{c}(80 \text{ minutes lunch} \\ \text{and break time})\end{array}\right]}{\begin{array}{c}800 \text{ assemblies per day} \\ \text{needed per schedule}\end{array}}$$

Takt time = 0.5 minutes, or 30 seconds between assembly completions

Example b:

Suppose two each of part X is required for each subassembly, and they are fabricated on one shift. Then

$$\text{Takt time (X)} = \frac{\left[\begin{array}{c}(480 \text{ minutes} \\ \text{per shift})\end{array} - \begin{array}{c}(80 \text{ minutes lunch} \\ \text{and break time})\end{array}\right]}{\begin{array}{c}1{,}600 \text{ part Xs per day} \\ \text{needed per schedule}\end{array}}$$

Takt time (X) = 0.25 minutes, or 15 seconds between completions

Figure 5.3. Takt Times

whether it is worth doing. The interval time for the forming portion of its total function might be much faster than the times for moving material in and out, and it could be a huge plug in the process flow if the setup times were long. Slower presses often plug process flows, as can be inferred from studying Figure 5.4. The ideal press would form the part needed next to where it is needed at the time it is needed. That has occasionally been done with slow "minipresses," but the physics, footprints, and costs of metal-forming processes generally preclude such ideal solutions. However, these issues become more obvious when the time pattern of a process is considered as a whole.

➤ How Do People Use a Takt Time?

Using a takt time, operators can determine how to do the necessary work within that time interval while eliminating the wasted effort.

The forecast is for 11,227 truck beds in May, which has 21 work days. Assembly is on two shifts, 350 line minutes per shift allowing for lunch, breaks, and *jidoka* time. *Jidoka* is an allowance for downtime to make corrections or to improve the process—about 10 minutes per shift, and it is expected to be taken. Otherwise people are not paying attention to the process.

Subassembly takt time = [(350 minutes/shift) × (2 shifts)
× (21 days)] ÷ [11,227 truck beds]

Subassembly takt time = 1.31 minutes, or about 77 seconds
between completions.

What about parts?

Most parts are formed on a press line, and only one part of each type is used per truck bed. Take a right-side fender skirt, for example:

Right fender skirts required: 11,227 for assembly
+ 239 for spares (some customers
have wrecks)
+ 7 for engineering tests
_____
Total   11,473

The same press line runs 10 parts and also operates on two shifts. All 10 parts have about the same volume required, and each part will run once each day. Ten minutes are allowed for each setup. The press line also has the same operating times as assembly, so:

Press takt time for right fender skirt:

Minutes available per month = [(350 minutes per shift)
− (50 minutes setup)] × 2 shifts × 21 days ÷ [10 parts]
= 1,260 minutes for each part.

Takt Time = [1,260 minutes ÷ 11,473 fender skirts]
= 0.11 minutes, or 6.6 seconds.

(continued)

Figure 5.4. Takt Times for Truck Beds

If only one part of each type goes into each assembly, and the assembly takt time is 77 seconds, all 10 parts can theoretically be pressed during one assembly takt time allowing for the 10 setups. Because 6.6 seconds is a rather slow working-cycle time for a press, more can be done. Other parts can be added to the press, but that exacerbates the imbalance between the press and assembly takt times, a common issue. Ideally, each of the 10 parts could be formed just as needed next to assembly. That's infeasible with present forming technology because of press size, speed, and expense, even after great effort to better balance actual output timing with assembly consumption.

Figure 5.4. (continued)

They develop their standard work based on a takt time interval, or a multiple thereof, which is very different from the Taylorist notion of maximizing usable output. Those who focus on maximizing output think about increasing process rates. Those who think about eliminating waste need to have a takt time work window that ties together all the parts of the process flow. Takt times are derived from schedules that tie the linked processes together.

■ NONMANUFACTURING TAKT TIMES

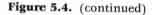

Takt times are not confined to manufacturing processes. They bring a new perspective to all process thinking. For example, in running a golf course, a classic management problem is how to set the time interval between scheduled tee times, which is a takt time. If tee times are spaced too closely (too short a takt time), more fast groups will stall behind slow ones. A course loaded with parties waiting rather than playing is loaded with frustrated customers. Here is a good first estimate of a takt time: Divide the time it takes a moderately slow group to play 18 holes by 18.

A complex example is the synchronization of traffic lights. On a through street traffic flows better if a wave passes through multiple lights before having to stop. At busy intersections, stoplight cycles (takt times) are frequently lengthened to allow traffic to clear. Complex traffic problems require simulation, but in the simpler cases everyone is familiar with the effects—and with the observation that racing ahead of sync speed to the next red light avails little.

To really move a volume of traffic, "lock" all vehicles together with an automatic control system so that the whole roadway moves at the same speed, like a conveyor belt, a proposal with numerous technical and social issues to overcome. In both of these examples the control of timing imposes more and more order on an otherwise chaotic process. In general, the search for a suitable takt time is an effort by "process astronomers" to create a pattern where none existed before.

■ DEVELOPING YOUR FIRST TAKT TIME

Takt time is meaningless unless some key elements of work can march along in some semblance of unison. The objective of a first-time Kaizen Blitz may be to develop a cell or a department to do exactly that. So where do you begin? Neither work standards, station-by-station, nor shipment forecasts are likely to have been created with takt times in mind.

Start by defining the family of parts or assemblies that a cell or department seems capable of producing. Then estimate the number of units in this family that is to be shipped for a month or a week. Because forecasts are shaky, even that number is often somewhat uncertain, but one must start somewhere with something.

Then estimate how many work minutes will be available to produce these items. If a cell is just being developed, allow plenty of downtime for people to make setup changes and sort things out. Then divide the time available by the number of units needed to get a rough estimate of takt time, as in Figure 5.3. It is normal to be queasy when estimating that first takt time, so start with an approximation and refine as you learn.

When a cell is new, sustaining any kind of flow is enough challenge. Any reasonable takt time will do when people are starting to learn how to design their own work to fit within a takt time window. Learning how to develop and adhere to standard work procedures is a fundamental practice that takes time. Until this is mastered and the hiccups that interrupt flow subside, it is hard to see the physical correspondence with actual work cycles and the takt time. With progress, both the process and the takt time become clear, and more refined calculations can be made, as shown in Figure 5.4.

What about large variations in product mix and volume from one scheduling period to another? Search for any stable pattern, first in total volume, then in mix. If volume requirements seem stable for a month, calculate the takt time for a month. Work on setup times so that the cell can respond to different mixes within that volume. The objective is to be able to handle requirement variances while maintaining a flow.

Some companies do experience considerable within-period volume variance. If this is within plus or minus 20 percent, you might start by holding a takt time and compensating by the usual methods—varying the work hours and perhaps (horrors) a little finished goods buffer stock. In the longer term, the ideal is to be able to convert to different takt times as needed.

■ HOW FAR CAN THE IDEA OF A TAKT TIME BE EXTENDED?

From Fredrick Taylor's time onward, if not before, it has been taken as axiomatic that revising processes to run repetitively removes much of the waste. Most work has potential patterns for standardization if one looks for them.

For example, product development processes are not highly repetitive. Nonetheless, companies that adopt standard New Product Development processes with decision-point "gates" have compressed their timeprints by establishing repeating steps as much as possible. New Product Development processes have been reengineered or "kaizened" somewhat like those that are highly repetitive. These processes are seldom repetitive enough to calculate takt times, but companies do manage product development capacity by roughly estimating the time interval between new product launches and the duration of each project.

On the other hand, some kinds of customer engineering are so routine that they can be done by expert-system configurator software. Then custom orders can march through customer engineering almost as the product marches through production. However, the time pattern is harder to see unless something visible, such as icons on a computer screen, artificially symbolizes the flow process.

Whether they are in production or not, some processes can be made to run like a clock. Others retain great variance in the value-added process times themselves. But by definition, any process that is repeated over and over will develop a time pattern. With attention, that time pattern can be captured and improved.

■ TIMEPRINT PERFORMANCE MEASUREMENTS

Direct process-time measurements, stated only in time units and here dubbed timeprint measures, have the advantage of a direct relationship to what has been done. One would think that they can all be captured using only direct observation and a watch. However, unless timing can be done almost automatically, a direct time measurement is only done once in a while as a check, or when studying a process for improvement. And not every possible element that could be timed actually is. Some well-selected indicators provide a timeprint of what is happening, and excessive time spent in measurement is itself a waste.

Table 5.1 lists some common types of timeprint measures, along with a brief definition of each. Takt time is not included because it is a planning time interval, not a performance measure. Consistently defined and regularly used, a few measures provide "stakes in the ground" that tell whether timeprints are compressing. Most measures are estimates, so great precision is seldom worthwhile. It's the persistent shrinking trend that indicates progress.

Takt times match the processes' timing to demand as closely as possible, so it is set according to "the customer's watch." The objective as not to compress it as much as possible, unless capacity is maxed out. Rather, it is to eliminate the waste from processes organized to deliver at the pace needed. The goal is for the actual interval between completions to closely track takt time.

A common way to check how well the takt time is being held is with a comparative process clock. The number of units actually completed is compared with those that should have been completed by the takt time clock. In manufacturing this is usually done only in assembly. Fabrication and subassembly processes simply track consumption in assembly using a pull system of material control. If a fixed amount of inventory is kept between points of use and points of supply, the time difference between the two is kept relatively constant without it having to be constantly measured.

Table 5.1. Common Timeprint Performance Indicators

Measure	Time Relationship
Interval time	Actual time between completions of similar units of work (often called cycle time). Done with a watch or with a computer.
Linearity	Cumulative actual completion time intervals versus planned takt time intervals (a graph such as shown in Figures 5.5 and 5.6).
Process duration time	Time for work to flow through the sequence of all steps of the process (also often called cycle time). Done with watches, computers (capturing the time between two different bar-code scans, for instance), or approximations.
Setup time	The time lapse between the end of processing one type of item and starting to process the next. Usually done with watches or videos. The smaller the setup time, the smaller the lot sizes or work-batch sizes can be.
Information time reduction	The time lapse between needing information and receiving it, or sensing that changes are needed or that errors were made, and the time of taking action. Often inferred from other process-flow duration times.
Customer lead time	Elapsed time from knowing the customer has a need until the need is fulfilled. Usually the sum of several subprocess steps.

All measures are directly time related—timeprint indicators.

Therefore, in many repetitive manufacturing processes assembly is the control clock. All processes that flow into assembly attempt to synchronize with it. The takt time for assembly is the control time, and the pull system is the control mechanism. But if operations are to actually run like clockwork, the actual intervals between completions in assembly should closely parallel the takt time "reference clock."

Some assembly lines literally have such a clock. A takt time count is kept by tripping the "should be complete" counter at every takt time interval. The actual completion count is kept by tripping a counter at the end of assembly. Then the two counts are normally shown side by side in an exhibit that everyone can see. For a large process such as an auto assembly line, several read-out exhibits may be maintained.

This process clock shows instant status to the assembly teams and everyone that supports them. Sometimes other information such as prompting or information signals is also shown. For example, lights may signal the locations in the process at which there is low stock, a stockout, or other problems. Note, however, that there is little point showing information if people do not act on it.

Linearity is a graphical comparison of accumulated completions with the accumulated takt time; that is, it plots how closely actual completions follow planned completions. A basic linearity plot, charted on hourly intervals, is shown in Figure 5.6. Note that bobbles began in the second hour of the shift, and after the team got behind, it could never catch up. At shift end they stayed and finished their planned completions. This kind of performance is not unusual when getting used to the system.

Figure 5.5 is based on a takt time of three minutes (7.5 hours—allowing 30 minutes for lunch—or 450 minutes, divided by the 150 units expected to be finished). Because little allowance was made for stops when calculating the takt time, the assembly crew is quite likely to get behind on the plot and stay that way.

Figure 5.6 is a linearity graph plotted every half hour. Standard work intervals are planned to a takt time of 2.7 minutes for the same 150 units expected to be completed. A greater allowance for breaks and downtime reflects more experience with the system. The takt time calculation is based on 405 available work minutes (allowing a 30-minute lunch, two 15-minute breaks, and 15 minutes of *jidoka* time).

Posting linearity so everyone can see it hourly is a good first step in measurement as soon as a work team can maintain a flow. The measurement gives them something to aim for in further refining the process, and it doesn't take special rigging or equipment. With several Kaizen Blitz episodes, and practice developing and holding standard work, the linearity may begin to approach the tracking shown in Figure 5.6.

The data for the actual interval time at each of a series of workstations is best kept by people near the stations. Experienced people know that, if work is tightly linked, a major imbalance in actual interval times will result in an obvious bottleneck or in obvious idle time that can be attacked as waste. These visual indicators are generally easier to interpret than a slew of numbers, thus minimizing the information feedback time.

The graph shows unit completions projected using the takt time versus actual unit completions for an eight-hour shift. Data is summarized by hour. In the third hour, a bobble put the team a little behind and they spent the rest of the shift catching up, finally working a few minutes overtime to complete exactly the number required. The takt time is three minutes between units; the actual cycle time between units is slightly longer. The expected completions line using takt time allows a half hour of downtime at midshift; otherwise it would be a straight line.

Human-controlled performance never tracks the linear takt time projection exactly; only automated processes actually work like a clock, and then only if no interruptions disturb them. This graph replicates how most such indicators look after a round or two of flow improvement.

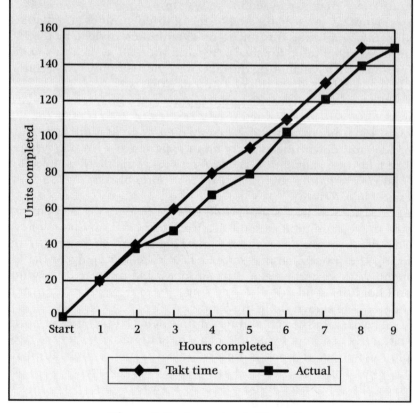

Figure 5.5. Approximate Linearity

Compared with Figure 5.5, the takt time in the chart below has been
shortened to 2.8 minutes. The number of working hours has
decreased from 7.5 to 7.0, alllowing for two 15-minute breaks. The
breaks are not just to rest. The first one comes at the end of the first
hour so that people can make adjustments to any problems that
seem to be occurring during this shift. As one can tell, actual cycle
times throughout the shift differ so little from those preplanned
with the takt time that it is almost imperceptible on the chart, and
it's not worth calculating the difference. The precise linearity of
this chart suggests more maturity with standard work and
management of a flow process.

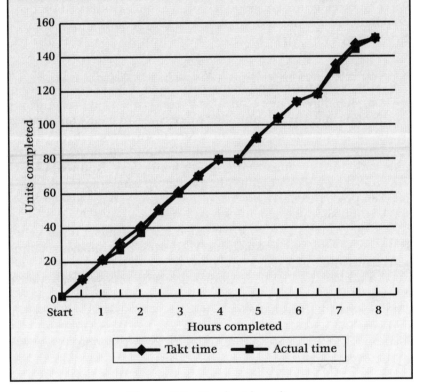

Figure 5.6. Precise Linearity

■ PROCESS DURATION INDICATORS

Duration times are the indicators to compress—without adding resources to do it. Adding resources is a trade-off, which is sometimes necessary, but it is not a true improvement.

Duration times are the elapsed times for material (or information or something else) to flow through a process. Sometimes it is called a throughput time, and very often "cycle time." Because a process duration repeats itself with the next unit through the process, the notion of it being cyclic makes sense, but it helps to adopt terminology that allows everyone to easily distinguish what is meant.

If a branch of a process consists of a series of operations, inventory is really in process much of the time, a situation that corresponds to "cars on line" in auto assembly, and that can often be timed directly by bar code ID's at the beginning and the end, direct timing etc.

If a subprocess consists of inventory passing through a conversion step, a duration is often approximated: Divide the amount of stock on hand by its rate of use. Or if a takt time is in use, multiply by the takt time. For example, 300 pieces on hand and consumed at a rate of 30 per hour yields 10 hours of inventory. If the corresponding takt time is 2 minutes, multiplying 300 pieces by 2 minutes yields 600 minutes worth, or 10 hours. Such approximations are quick and widely used. With more effort one can always time a marked piece through the process, but it isn't often necessary.

If a job shop has such jumbled processes that a flow diagram seems meaningless, an approximate duration time still has value. In this case one may be stuck just recording the time between job start dates and finish dates, and they will exhibit considerable variance, a subject that has been studied ad nauseum in production literature. A favorite solution is to revise the priority rules on the shop floor, which has benefit, but it's limited. Achieving more fundamental process changes through kaizen has more promise.

➤ One-Piece Flows

If one arrives at one-piece flow, process duration may be as simple as the takt time multiplied by the number of stations—a relatively constant number. The more refined the process, the less variance in interval times, and total duration times are the sum of the intervals.

Some processes cannot approach the timeprint precision of one-piece flow, at least not without substantial redesign of products or revision of technology. Others must serve chaotic customer demand patterns. Some seem intractable. But any action that can bring a simplified pattern to a rat's-nest process is likely to be marked by a compressed time duration, even if it is crudely measured.

Finally, try to define processes so that the duration time estimates of its various subparts are in sequence and therefore additive. For example, customer-order lead time might consist of the sum of order-entry, production, and order-shipping duration times. Some processes are in parallel, such as subassemblies and software that flow into a final unit. If the duration times of sequential processes are additive, the duration time of the whole is a simple addition.

■ SETUP TIMES

If a setup process has never been studied for improvement, the initial corrective action is to minimize process downtime for setup. In production, last-good-part to first-good-part is the duration of the downtime, usually taken with a watch or captured by video. Any wristwatch with a second hand or a read-out will generally do. Standardize the preparation and put away steps so a maximum number of steps can be done with the process (or machine) running, not stopped.

However, the full setup process includes all the preparation and put away with the process running, and that needs to be timed too. The interval between setups can be no shorter than the full time necessary to put away after one setup and to prepare for the next. And it is the interval between setups that determines how small lot sizes can be.

With great compression of setup time, it is possible to have one-piece flow with each item in the sequence being different. Usually one thinks of such rapid timing as being done with software, like a welding robot being instructed which program to trace for the next item. However, with ingenuity it can even be done by totally mechanical means. The author once observed a small press for door keys that loaded die sets from side-to-side while key blanks fed from front-to-back. The press could meet takt time exchanging dies with every stroke—a different key every time!

To achieve the flexibility of mixed-model, one-piece flow, the duration of the entire setup *pertinent to the machine* has to fit within the takt time allowed for the process at that station. To advance beyond this to agility (in the sense that each different item has some unique engineering), the takt time for engineering prep must match that for the production process. That is, the interval between engineering completions must be no longer than takt time. However, the duration of each engineering process may be longer—perhaps much longer—which starts to become a matter of resource use, not just timing.

■ INFORMATION FEEDBACK TIMES

With computers and computing networks, instant information has become a glamour subject. But unless computer feedback results in auto-activation, mere transmission and receipt of signals does not fulfill the purpose of the communication. Detection-to-action time completes the operational circuit.

The value of information feedback on quality issues is relatively easy to see. In a production operation the time required to feed back the information that a defect has occurred to its probable source is the same as the time lag between those two points in the process, assuming that a method for detection and near-instant feedback is in place. Without such a method, no one knows how long it will take.

The same logic applies to setup times, engineering flaws (and changes), customer problems, changes in customer perceptions, and so on. With or without using computer systems, process improvement should reduce delays in information time.

■ REDUCING MENTAL SETUP TIME: THE WILLIAMS STORY

Information time indicators are partly imbedded in setup times and process-change times. An example of this is Williams Technologies greatly shortening information lag times when designing a shop-floor information system.

Williams has about 500 employees; it remanufactures drive-train equipment, mostly transmissions in hundreds of variations.

To remanufacture a transmission to its current upgraded specification, the company must quickly implement a constant stream of engineering changes.

To get to one-piece flow, Williams Technologies workers first tackled most of the problems of physical flow, organizing cells and cutting physical setup times. Then they attacked "mental setup time." Understanding what to do at each workstation for the next transmission required numerous operating manuals. Keeping them up-to-date was a problem, finding the right manual took time, and trying to simply remember what to do led to misbuilds. Without a better system, Williams Technologies was stuck building batches of the same model transmission.

In 1993 they found a solution in a home-built system called Pro-Net. Digital cameras take pictures of the correct parts and document the engineering specs for each transmission. Now, when a transmission starts through the operation, its identifying bar code is initially referenced to that model's database. When the bar code is scanned at each station, the correct digital images pop up on a PC screen (486 models, not fancy or expensive).

Out with the manuals. On with one-piece flow. The system reduced the mental setup time so much that it was incorporated into the takt time of each station. Williams can also enter the simpler engineering changes into the system within an hour or so and be ready for execution in the plant.

This change also uncluttered the shop floor so much that a major changeover now involves only repositioning of tools and material in one takt time interval. Workers just skip a job along a line as the changeover rolls through. Process-duration time is one shift, so a transmission coming in (a *core* in remanufacturing parlance) can be returned the same day, literally better than new. (Remanufactured transmissions have a stronger warranty than when the same case was new because of upgrades and correction of original design issues. That, too, is a story of reducing information lags about transmission failures to engineering design departments.)

The Williams story illustrates an important aspect of information systems models—"instant" decentralized access to databases with the correct information. Once that objective has been defined, many indirect indicators can suggest whether it is taking place. Examples are system uptime, system response time, customer response time, and idea acceptance and implementation times.

Some kinds of information rate times are best reduced by non-computerized methods. The existence of 5 S (discussed in Chapter

7), visibility systems, kanbans, posted schedules, and the like are testimony to the existence of such systems. People seldom measure the reduced lag time effects of such practices; they just use them.

■ EXECUTIVE INFORMATION SYSTEMS

Problem-detection–to–correction time entails another set of issues. For example, in customer service, it is becoming more common to monitor how long customers are kept on hold waiting for customer service and also whether their queries are thought to be answered by the same call or much later. Phone systems or e-mail systems can be set up to collect time data, and service departments can record duration–until–closure of cases.

Monitoring duration times and intervals for routine information transfer can be done, but the best outcome of process development is to simplify it until a welter of information is made unnecessary, or at least manageable. One of the ways that is done is by promoting process visibility. For example, a basic kanban pull system is a version of a visibility process in which people can see what to do next without having to calculate anything or refer to a computerized formula. If everyone can see imbalances, trouble points, the "process clock," the duration-of-key-process flows, and other process indicators, many questions don't have to be asked.

Rob Lawton has developed an exercise on visibility in executive work. He notes that many executives spend more time receiving and answering questions than doing anything else. Many questions are for others; some are for themselves. This information process is often inefficient.[10]

Lawton suggests that executives start keeping a log of the percentage of times that they must respond to questions with "I don't know," "I'll get back," or "Ask someone else." All these responses he classifies as IDK (I don't know). But why isn't an answer known, or for that matter, why was a question asked? Recording duration times between questions and answers may yield clues, but it isn't as productive as investigating why such communications episodes were necessary. For any question that could have been avoided, the duration time should have been nil—a non–data point.

---

[10] Robin L. Lawton, *Creating a Customer-Centered Culture* (Milwaukee, Wisc.: ASQ Press, 1993). The discussion of IDK starts on page 9.

To start converting the data collected in this review to a Pareto chart on causes of IDK, one must focus on why questions were asked and why information wasn't known. That leads directly to regarding all inquirers as customers and checking what their needs really are. The principle of visibility applies to processes besides production, and some of those processes are those of real external customers. That can be a start with a Kaizen Blitz on information systems and communication methods, something with impact well beyond just improving internal operations.

■ CUSTOMER LEAD TIMES

Order entry is a favorite process selected for an early Kaizen Blitz, but order entry is only one subprocess that *might* contribute to total customer lead time—duration between learning of a customer need and fulfilling that need. Manufacturing companies sometimes assume that customer lead time is the duration between receipt of a product order and shipping that order, but a shipping time only indicates when the product left the dock, not that the customer's need is fulfilled. There's much more than that to customer satisfaction.

Most manufacturing companies, however, measure customer lead time as the duration between order receipt and order shipment. The commercial transactions that penetrate the barriers between customer and supplier leave the easiest timeprints to record. By tracking the logistics, some companies also know when the product was checked into the customer's premises. But whether the product arrived when the customer wanted it, or whether the customer is satisfied with it, can only be known by working with the customer.

The point of this is to set up the indicators of customer lead time to span as much of the gap between customer and supplier as possible. Typical lead time data is too producer oriented. For example, "on-time shipping" is often defined as shipping to the producer's original promise time, disregarding when the customer really wanted it, because that seems fair to the production folk. However, compressing process timeprints advances the ability to serve customers when *they* want. Performance measurement should no longer resort to old dodges in the interest of fairness.

Kaizen Blitz projects that address customer lead times or customer-response times are the ones most likely to make strategic breakthroughs. They focus on processes that directly intersect those of the customer. A beneficial change allows a customer to kaizen their own processes. For example, on-line ordering a la the website *Amazon.com* changes how customers buy books. They cannot browse the books themselves, but if they know what they want, it takes less time than going to a bookstore. Although it is affecting how books are distributed and marketed, on-line ordering is not accomplished just because customers can get on-line. Every sub-process of order fulfillment has to be substantially revised from the traditions of the industry.

Of course, *Amazon.com* and other digital businesses are entreprenuerial ventures beyond the scope of most limited-process Kaizen Blitz initiatives. But neither does one want to pursue a strategy of improving the flow of processes that can be completely superseded by a different approach to the customer. This situation can be partly avoided by maintaining at least one timeprint indicator for customer-response lead time. And if it is at all possible, make the timeprint cover the full sequence of processes necessary to serve customers. That sequence may include processes that belong to customers, suppliers, and intermediaries.

■ TIMEPRINTS ARE NOT ENOUGH

Despite the advantages of relative objectivity and close relationship to a process itself, timeprint-performance measures are not the only ones that are important. Costs, value-added ratios, quality fallout, customer satisfaction, and the like are all valuable, and everyone knows the importance of cash intake exceeding cash outflow. However, a little reflection on how time factors into each measurement generally convinces people that compressing timeprint measures by eliminating waste is not going to harm performance as indicated by any other measures.

Many performance measurements indirectly relate to time—various forms of rate ratios. For example, unit-direct-labor costs and unit-machine costs represent expenditure for the time used to make one unit, although the allocation of overhead and indirect costs often muddles the connection. The overall system of performance measurement, not just time measurement, is important for Kaizen. That is the subject of the next chapter.

Chapter 6

How to Tell If There Is Improvement: Adding Value, Subtracting Waste

A Kaizen Blitz is successful if the performance indicators for a revised process show improvement—and if the improvement is sustained. However, a single Kaizen Blitz treats a process that is limited in scope, so a larger issue is whether an overall program of improvement is working. To evaluate whether overall operations are improving, performance indicators should span a complete set of processes that serve customers, a total business, or perhaps a total supply chain. The objective is to eliminate waste, not just push it somewhere else, and most of us can only pay attention to a limited number of performance indicators.

Performance measurement can be as simple or complex as desired. The issues run deep, and this chapter can cover only a few of them. Our pragmatic advice is to use simple performance indicators, and just start. Then think carefully about what they imply and learn as you go.

■ HOW TO KNOW IF YOU ARE IMPROVING

Table 6.1 summarizes four categories of process performance measurement, with some subcategories. Many kinds of measurement methods and performance indicators fall into each category. The first step is to develop something workable from each category and

Table 6.1. Process Performance Measurement Categories

1. Time (timeprint)
2. Space (footprint)
3. Resource Use:
   Resource usage ratios
   Costs (stack-ups of "dollarized" ratios)
4. Results:
   Process Quality (error rates, deviations, yields, etc.)
   Primary customer satisfaction
   Secondary customer satisfaction (safety, environment, etc.)
   Financial cash flow

subcategory and infer what you can. No one can capture or interpret an overabundance of indicators.

Measurement itself is a process, and an indicator is an outcome of it. The term *indicator* itself suggests that no piece of data is "ultimate truth."

Genuine process improvement is suggested if performance indicators in at least one category improve with no offsetting decline in indicators in any other category. Otherwise, we are engaging in trade-offs. Trade-offs may better align a process to serve customers, but they aren't really process improvements for organizations tough minded about eliminating waste.

Table 6.1 is also limited to *process* measurement. Process performance indicators do not provoke larger strategic questions, such as whether technological advance will make a process obsolete, whether a line of business should be pursued, or whether the process should attempt to serve particular kinds of customers.

The process-limited categories in Table 6.1 do not include, for instance, at least three categories of performance that are often critical when a customer company evaluates a supplier to be a long-term partner. One is technical capability, including software crucial to keeping up in a fast-changing environment. Another is financial staying power. A third is the morale and capability of the associates. But all three of these capabilities are exercised with processes whose performance may be measured with process indicators.

Technology may or may not improve a process according to the indicators. For example, electronics and added features continue to complicate automotive designs, as anyone can see by looking under the hoods of comparable models today versus 1970 or so. As a result, processes to build, service, and dispose of cars became more complex. Timeprints expanded. Costs went up. To offset this, the automotive industry has made a great effort to employ "design for X" methodologies and process simplification to keep processes tractable. Many other industries have had similar experiences. Where complexity is burgeoning like kudzu, a victory for Kaizen Blitz is to prevent process indicators from getting worse.

Keeping it simple isn't always easy, but simple process performance indicators help a great deal. Interpreting process indicators requires one to be process oriented, but with practice, that's not a difficult mental set to acquire.

■ FULL-SPECTRUM MEASUREMENT

Each category of measurement in Table 6.1 represents a view of a process using a sensory system sensitive to a different "spectrum of light." A picture taken using radar, ultrasound, infrared, or ultraviolet light is not the same as direct sight in the spectrum directly visible to humans. The scope and resolution of the picture also makes a big difference. A picture from a nonvisual spectrum picks up information we do not see directly. It also misses information we *do* see directly.

"Truth" does not exist in only one spectrum, but it is easy to assume so if that is the light we are accustomed to using. For example, we frequently translate performance data into a cost model because we believe that will better tell us how an activity will affect cash flow or the bottom line.

Stereotypical finance-oriented folk interpret everything in dollars. They need practice in "process logic" to see the relationships of other measures to the bottom line. For example, reducing timeprints, space, resources used, and errors should lead to lower costs. Cutting process duration cuts the time from cash outflow to cash inflow. Cutting space decreases capital costs and also operating costs if the extra space was used for wasteful activities. Cutting resource use cuts cost—almost by definition. And reducing errors reduces cost, as has been described using "cost of quality" (better described as "cost of non-quality").

Translation is usually done with ratios, but by process logic, relationships are not always linear or immediate. In this chapter we will refer to all four categories of measurement in Table 6.1 and some of the relationships between them with emphasis on value added.

■ REMOTE SENSING

A perennial issue in performance measurement is interpretation of data when data collection remote from the source processes, or from the methods by which the data originated. If one has no direct experience with a process, the problem of interpretation is made more difficult. It's a little like astronomers trying to comprehend the universe from a paucity of data about it. Each new discovery adds to the perspective, and some are paradigm changing because newly observed data do not agree with prior theories. Then a debate begins—are the observation methods faulty, the data in error, or our theory wrong?

In manufacturing businesses the same kinds of debate take place daily. Only so much data can be absorbed and interpreted. It is far better to observe the process itself closely and follow a few well-chosen overall performance indicators.

■ TIME AND VALUE ADDED

➤ What Adds Value to the Customer?

The question "what adds value to the customer?" is tough because from a customer's viewpoint, satisfaction is based on their perception of their experience with a product or process. There's no way to avoid subjectivity, and customers need not be logical, consistent, sane, or civil. For instance, the value of a smile and banter from a server in a restaurant means nothing in accounting terms. Customers' reactions to a server's behavior is subjective, but if it makes them return, it contributes to results that an accountant can tally up, although gathering data and making a statistical case for the connection is a time-consuming chore.

Of course, if the dining area were noisy, the server might not make up for it. The noise subtracts from value. That judgment, too, is partly subjective. Within some range of decibel tolerance, "noisy" is an individual perception. Behavior and noise, however, are both process attributes directly sensed by the customer.

Customer satisfaction depends on whether expectations based on their prior experience are met, so bare minimum performance won't do. A person in dire circumstances, for example, will be delighted with any edible food, but a normal customer in a white-tablecloth restaurant has developed a much more comprehensive set of expectations.

➤ Hidden Processes

Restaurant customers judge results based on what they see, and they rarely see many hidden processes: food storage, kitchen cleaning, employee training, bill paying, and others. However, hidden processes, sometimes several stages removed from customers, should contribute to customer satisfaction.

In manufacturing almost all operations are hidden from customers, and customers might not understand them if they saw them. The value added by hidden operations has to be judged by their contribution to outcomes desired by customers, if they knew what was required to serve them. Unfortunately, to judge whether a hidden process adds value, we are often stuck imagining a customer we may not understand very well.

➤ Waste: Non-Value-Added

Fortunately, determining what does *not* add value is usually easier. Any process time that does not contribute to results a knowledgeable customer will pay for is a waste. Some secondary "customers" may be intermediaries, service people, employees (for health and safety), and the general public (for environmental issues, etc.). This complicates the assessment, but the end user is the primary customer, and anything that isn't done for *any* customer, primary or secondary, is definitely waste.

Fortunately, it isn't hard to get started. Much waste is easily spotted. Probably the most famous list of wastes is Shingo's list, shown again in modified from in Table 6.2.

Shingo's list in Table 6.2 is designed for production processes. A modification of the same list for service processes done in the customer's presence is shown in Table 6.3. Here assumptions about waste must be modified to allow for customer perception of the process. In addition, service processes such as hair styling can

---

Table 6.2. Shingo's List: Wastes in Manufacturing

---

1. **Overproduction**	Make only what is needed now.
2. **Waiting**	No value is added while something merely waits.
3. **Stocks and inventory**	Lots of things are waiting.
4. **Transportation**	Don't move anything further than necessary, or more often than necessary.
5. **Motion**	Excess motion of anything—man, machine, or material—is waste. Make every motion count.
6. **Processing itself**	The first question is why a part or assembly should be made at all, a design issue. Then, it's whether the conversion can be made with less work.
7. **Defects and rework**	No point doing something if the result can't be used. And no point doing it more than once.
8. **Information**	Figuring out what to do or when to do it should not take long, nor should it need double-checking.

The first seven wastes are from Shigeo Shingo, STUDY OF TOYOTA PRODUCTION SYSTEM (Portland, Oregon: Productivity Press, 1981). The eighth waste on information was added later. Shingo would probably approve.

The first seven wastes predate Shingo's book. They were commonly referred to by Taiichi Ohno and others back in the 1960s when Toyota was developing just-in-time production.

---

only be done with the customer present. A beauty shop cannot overproduce and store product in inventory unless it does wigs. Therefore, the waste is idle time of beauticians prepared to give service, but with no customer present. Conversely, customers sometimes wait to be served. Assuming that customers like the core beautification process when they receive it, this waste may be reducible by a better scheduling policy. Developing such a policy without offending customers also changes the total process.

Administrative processes that have no customers other than internal ones are great candidates for waste-busting kaizen. Any work that we do just for ourselves adds no value to any customer.

Shingo's list is a good starter for a Kaizen Blitz. People won't learn to recite the list, but they will get the idea and have no problem finding waste.

After that it becomes progressively more difficult. People reviewing flowcharts to check which steps are value-added (VA) and

Table 6.3. Shingo's List of Wastes Modified for Service Operations

1. **Service timing**	Do only what is needed when needed. (Ex: Food outside its desired temperature range is not as palatable.)
2. **Waiting**	No value is added while associates, material, or customers wait.
3. **Stocks and inventory**	Lots of things are waiting. (Some also deteriorate in value while waiting.)
4. **Transportation**	Don't move anything further than necessary, or more often than necessary.
5. **Motion**	Excess motion of anything—man, machine, or material—is waste. An exception: Some excess motion is to create an impression—show business.
6. **Processing itself**	Work that does not contribute to the desired effect.
7. **Defects and rework**	Doing it over is not only a delay; it's probably embarrassing.
8. **Information**	Figuring out what to do or when to do it should not take long, nor should it need double-checking. That includes both the freedom and the judgement to do what the customer really needs on the spot. Solve the customer's problem.

Adapted from Shigeo Shingo, STUDY OF TOYOTA PRODUCTION SYSTEM (Portland, Oregon: Productivity Press, 1981).

non-value-added (NVA) often want a third category, labeled something like "necessary evil"—shouldn't have to do it, but they see no way out of it. Beyond Shingo's lists, a couple of practical questions help identify NVA time:

1. *Would external customers pay for the activity if they knew its technical purpose?* If no linkage exists, it's waste. If the linkage to the customer is tenuous, either the purpose of the activity or the activity itself needs attention.

2. *Is this activity really done for ourselves, the bosses, the checkers, or "the system," rather than some kind of customer?* If so, it's probably waste. (Note that a customer might be a service person or others besides the end user.)

In assessing the second question, many companies have been caught in the well-meaning trap of working for an "internal customer," typically defined as someone whom anothers' work serves, perhaps the next person in a process flow. Without keeping the end-use customer or future life-of-product customers firmly in mind, the identification of waste can easily degenerate into Parkinson's Law ("Work expands to fill the time available in which to do it").

■ ELIMINATING NECESSARY EVILS AT GUIDANT-TEMECULA

Regulations of various kinds—necessary evils—are frequently excuses to tolerate waste. Guidant-Temecula (California) is an example of an organization that overcame many of the excuses. It makes medical devices such as heart catheters and stents, so Guidant-Temecula is subject to Good Manufacturing Practice (GMP) and other Food and Drug Administration regulations. It is easy to put much more work into these than is really needed.

When Guidant-Temecula workers began to examine process-flowcharts they found numerous instances of counting, count checking, recounting, rechecking, recording, backup recording, and so on. Some argued that all this was necessary for regulatory reasons. But, after reviewing GMP, in their case it covered mainly four requirements: cleanliness, sterility, product accuracy, and full traceablity of all material used. All these requirements have in mind the interest of doctors and patients—the real customers. The issue was how to accomplish what was truly necessary without waste.

Much of the identification of NVA was done by distinguishing whether a process was really just for Guidant themselves, such as a recount for their own peace of mind, or a contribution to external customer health and satisfaction. A big factor in killing this waste was to regard the process as a whole so that people along the process flow trusted each other's work.

Recounts were a big waste. The same items might be counted 10 to 20 times moving through different departments, just to be sure that the count was right. That custom was replaced by the following: Count it once. Count it right. Don't lose the count. (All the regulations require is an accurate count.)

Recounts are rework; checking is inspection. Rework and inspection were eliminated mostly by simple fail-safe methods. Within a year, NVA paperwork time dropped by over 90 percent. Guidant-Temecula continues to root out waste blamed on misguided regulatory compliance using a key slogan: "Sweat doesn't count; results do." And corporate policy can induce every bit as much wasted sweat as outside regulation.

➤ Evaluating Human Development to Improve Processes

Training and education is another tricky area to evaluate. Despite slogans that people are our most important asset, a training budget is an easy hit for a company short of cash. The necessity of technical training and on-the-job training is well understood, but the payoff for "soft-skill" and general training may seem to be long-term or nonexistent.

The effect of training on performance has been examined. According to *Industry Week's 1997 Census of Manufacturers,* the average U.S. plant has close to 20 hours per year of training for all employees, and 11 percent provide more than 40 hours per year. The correlation between training hours and the implementation of improvement initiatives, including kaizen, is strong.[1]

The value of soft-skill courses such as basic literacy, English as a Second Language (ESL), team skills, or problem solving is generally accepted by improvement-oriented companies but questioned by others. However, unless associates can communicate and problem-solve, work flows collapse into Taylorist station-by-station operations. Keeping a process flowing takes "soft" human skill and versatility.

Many studies show a positive correlation between education level and lifetime earnings for the total population, and at least one study has suggested that corporate soft-skills education for

---

[1] The *Industry Week Census of Manufacturers* is available from Industry Week, 1100 Superior Avenue, Cleveland, Ohio, 44114-2543 (Phone: 800/326-7000). Refer to pp. 3–15 and 3–16 of the 1997 report.

workers definitely has a payback.[2] Beyond that, specialists in complex fields spend a big fraction of their time just keeping up, and some kinds of research work are largely a matter of learning.

No process can develop beyond the human base to support it. However, whether and how a specific human development regimen will add value to customers is a knotty problem. Suppose an organization mandates that every associate must have at least 80 hours of training or education annually. Will all 80 hours eventually add value, or is some of it ineffective?

In any high-tech work, technical personnel can easily consume 80 hours a year and more keeping up. What about first-line personnel? To derive an answer, ask what people must be able to do not only to maintain process flow but to put themselves into the position of a customer and make sound value-adding decisions (called "skills needs and assessment" in human resources talk). Here is a brief list of capabilities needed for direct process personnel to maintain a flow of value-adding work:

➤ Team or group communication and participation

➤ Basic reading, math, and computer literacy

➤ Basic problem solving for both quality and flow problems

➤ Cross-training on a variety of tasks

➤ An understanding of how customers think

➤ How the company works (process flows, etc.)

➤ The performance indicators by which progress is measured

Some of the development may be classroom training. Some, like kaizen, is primarily learned by doing it. To save time and developmental cost, most companies contract or partner for some of the human development they need, but the major cost for human development is usually the time away from work of the people developed.[3]

---

[2] Norman L. McLinden, and Willis B. Perkins, "Hard Cash Returns on a Soft Skills Program," *Target* [publication of the Association for Manufacturing Excellence] 12 (November–December 1996): 7–13.

[3] Lea A. P. Tonkin, "Lean Training: How Companies Get the Most for Their Investment," *Target* [publication of the Association for Manufacturing Excellence] 14 (1998): 26–31.

Consider the time spent in human improvement as an investment. Companies with a long history of process improvement estimate that 10 percent or more of *all* associates' time is spent in improvement. Either they are improving processes or improving themselves. Sometimes the improvement just prevents processes from degenerating, but that, too, is important. The financially oriented may call it investing in human capital; the kaizen-oriented think of it as investing in people time to compress process time.

For primary-process personnel, the time for improvement breaks down something like this: Training totals around 5 percent, give or take, or about 40 hours a year. Two or 3 percent is spent in group improvement projects. On top of that, 3 to 5 percent of daily time is allowed for *jidoka*—keeping a process on track or making it better.

To keep a process working well, much less improve it, people need to think about what they are doing. They must learn how to see and solve problems, then take the time to do it when necessary. Stop and straighten out a mess when it happens. Better yet, stop and avoid a mess before it happens.

Mike Hall, now the proprietor of a steel construction design service, tells about learning basic *jidoka* when starting to fabricate stairs for construction. Their first day, he and a young cohort sweat profusely until noon to complete one stringer of stairs. "Old Man Ed," a wise, experienced workman, was building the same type of stairs. He sipped coffee, never broke a sweat, and seemed to be doing very little. By noon he had finished four stringers by himself.

They decided to watch Ed. The difference was that he studied the drawings ahead of time and mapped out what to do, then made every move count. That's *jidoka* coupled with development of standard work. The kids worked as though they were assembling Christmas toys without having read the directions.

Action-level people need to know about process indicators described here; in addition, they need to understand costs and financial statements. It takes time and patience for some action-level employees to get beyond the usual misconceptions about finance—believing that profit is at least 50 percent of sales, and so on. Although making cost and financial data available is controversial in a company if it has never been done, the inspiration for making a change can be found in discussions about open-book management.[4]

■ THE SYMBOLIC MARKERS OF VALUE ADDED

In a manufacturing company, value added (VA) is often presumed to be embodied in the products themselves—the hardware sold. However, a great deal of service and software is often bundled with the products in a total offering.

Many products (such as telephones and other communications equipment) have no intrinsic value unless they enable the customer to do something. Therefore, the flow of anything that contributes to customer satisfaction, not just hardware, adds primary value. Initially, it's easier to conceptualize VA and NVA applied to physical devices for which revenue is collected. Those can be easily seen, as can the processes to provide them.

However, the total offering to a customer may include instructions, ease of use, guarantees, software, regular upgrades, data, timeliness, backup, training, and other services. These flows may not be as easy to see as parts, and parts aren't always simple to track. Here is the Kaizen Blitz guide to identifying major value flows:

➤ Does it go to a customer? If so, it is VA, assuming that the customer thinks it is, which is another level of inquiry.

➤ Does it directly support a flow process for output going to customers? If so, it is VA. An example is equipment and tooling maintenance in production.

If it does neither of these, rigorously question whether it is VA. This questioning may be emotional, because everyone at first wants to think that their work must be VA, so minds work overtime to invent a logical association of their work to VA.

Kaizen is based on a customer-oriented view of the company and of a process. Two companies that have given considerable

---

[4] Jack Stack, and Bo Burlingham, *The Great Game of Business* (New York: Currency, Doubleday, 1994). A more extensive discussion of open-book management, including implications for compensation and profit sharing are in John P. Shuster, Jill Carpenter, and M. Patricia Kane, *The Power of Open Book Management* (New York: John Wiley, 1996.)

thought to this over several years are Deere & Company (John Deere) and Trane. Both have concluded that for almost any company, only four major processes are really value-adding processes, as shown in Figure 6.1. Everything else should be considered customer support.

The "eggs" shown in Figure 6.1 don't stir much controversy, but putting everything else in the support basket draws squawks. One contrivance is to simply presume that a process's output adds VA. For instance, accountants insist that customers cannot be served without a cost system. Production planners insist that nothing can be done without a schedule. Both are right, of course, but the customers for these processes are internal. The end customer doesn't give a hoot for cost systems or schedules. Both are support functions, and their objective is to enable others to make the prime VA flows move.

Another dodge is to refer to other stakeholders as customers. Finance supports the investment stakeholders, and indeed they are important. But they are not *the* customers. Human resource functions serve another stakeholder, the associates, many of whom take care of the eggs. Recognition can be morale boosting, and that is vital. Some time is spent in partying, and that, too, is important to

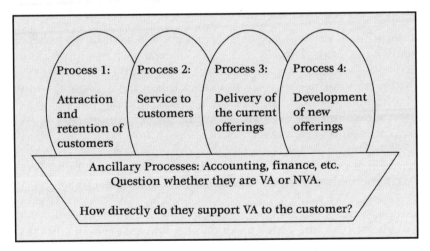

Figure 6.1. The Process Eggs in a Basket

This figure is adapted from material of C. Sean Battles of Deere & Company and Fred Shafer of Trane Unitary Products Division.

relieve tensions. But the associates are not *the* customers, either. Questioning how each person or process adds value to *the* customer is provocative.

Any time that does not directly contribute to one of the VA eggs is open to question, but not all that time will be declared waste. Stakeholders other than customers are important to the full process of serving the customers. However, the customer prefers to pay only for time that really counts. We can waste our own time.

➤ Primary Value-Added Flows

Flow diagrams can be constructed for people, material, equipment, and information. Sometimes, these four process elements are mixed in one diagram. Value-added ratios can be estimated for the flow of each type of element. If the product—composed of material—represents the key value to the customer, then developing a flow diagram for material is most important, and a prime objective is to reduce its flow time. If information was the key value to the customer, the primary objective would shift to reducing the duration of the time to provide that information.

➤ Value-Added Ratios

A VA ratio is an estimate of the fraction of available time that is spent in activity that adds value to the customer. Many VA ratios are very low. Suppose you drive five hours round-trip to fish in a prime lake. You spend three hours getting to the right spot in the lake and back. Add to that an hour to get ready and one more to put everything away after returning. But in one six-minute period, you land a six-pound bass. That's 6 minutes of unquestionable VA out of 600 minutes spent, a 1 percent ratio. The only other potential VA time are the parts of the story that you brag about over a beer; but if you hadn't landed the bass, you wouldn't bring them up.

Some NVA time is easy to see. Activity that positively adds value is harder to classify, so a VA ratio has some subjectivity to it, but once in use, the ratio is a valuable guide to action. Think of it as the fraction of time spent working for the customer—the end customer.

Some VA time is obvious, but all processes have steps that are dubious in adding value. For example, how much of the time used to dry paint should be considered value added? If a VA ratio is considered rigorously, instant-dying paint (with the same quality result) would be a marvelous technical advance.

A VA ratio can be estimated by developing a process-flow diagram and marking which steps of the process add value and which do not. If a process has not been studied for improvement before, big improvement is generally possible by eliminating unambiguous NVA. The first time around, don't fret over nuances of VA and NVA; just do it.

A VA ratio can be estimated for the process-duration times of people, machines, material, or information. Because of material movement, it is not possible for a strictly defined materials VA ratio to equal 1. But by focusing on one of these process elements, such as material processing, as the key to VA, one can work on combining the flow of all four elements to create VA with less time and waste. That tends to increase the fraction of time VA is being created from a total process—and for all direct and indirect investment associated with it.

Taylorist factories often attempt to simultaneously maximize both labor efficiency (output per person) and machine utilization (output per machine) workstation by workstation. The unresolved conflicts are left to smolder until near the end of the month when it's time to maximize dollar shipments. Then the drive for output takes over, resulting in the well-known "hockey stick" surge in end-of-month shipments. A kaizen plant attempts to organize around streamlining the flow of the highest value-adding element of the process—usually the material—and makes the VA flow constantly at the pace determined by the takt time needed to meet the current schedule.

In factories, material almost always sits a while before it enters production; then it continues through a process. Therefore a materials VA ratio can be calculated for material going all the way through a plant, until it enters process, while it is in process, or afterward. Considerable waste exists at each stage.

For example, consider an auto assembly plant running 60 jobs per hour, or takt time of one minute. If four hours of parts are in the plant on average (that's world class), and they enter the assembly process at various points along the line, only during the time each part is attached is value being added. The rest of the time potential value is merely sitting or moving. If it takes only one minute out of four hours to attach most parts to a car, then the VA ratio of material from receiving to the line would be 1 minute divided by 240 minutes, or 0.004. Even world class has a lot of potential left. The imaginary, and unattainable, ideal is for all parts to magically merge the instant after fabrication. But the reality is that we are stuck inching our way toward that idea. A calculation similar to this is shown in Figure 6.2.

In the same auto assembly plant, suppose that the time from sheet metal starting to be welded into a body until the finished vehicle off the line is 20 operating hours. Twenty hours of cars with a one-minute takt time equals 1,200 cars. Each car body has 1,200 available minutes for work to be done to it.

Value is not constantly added during each car body's 1,200-minute march through the plant. Often the car body is just moving on a conveyor. If workstations are spaced far apart, transit time is significant. Cars may also separate into multiple paint lines or be pulled out for special work, such as sun roof installation, and then reinserted in the line up. Adjusting the VA ratio calculation for the

---

The most common value-added (VA) ratio applies to material:

$$\text{VA ratio} = \frac{[\text{Time spent adding value to material}]}{[\text{Total time material is available}]}$$

Many VA ratios for assembly material are exceedingly small. For example, suppose one has a week's inventory of hose clamps, or 168 hours, in-house. It takes only one minute to install the clamp. So, for only 1 minute out of 10,080 minutes that the clamp is in house is it used to add value. That's a puny VA ratio of about 0.0001.

If the total time from fabricating the clamp at a supplier's location to installing it is considered, the ratio is even smaller. If a 99.4% reduction in in-house inventory is made so that only one hour of clamps are on hand, the VA ratio balloons to 0.017; that means nothing if the inventory is simply moved from in-house to out-house.

Trying to estimate with great precision the VA ratios of materials at line side for assembly has minimal value. The value is realizing that, for the vast majority of the time, nothing of value is happening and therefore much more potential exists for improvement.

Figure 6.2. Value-Added Ratios of Assembly Material

splits and side tracks can be done, but after all the adjustments, the key to performance is increasing the fraction of the 20 hours or so that value is really being added.

Figure 6.3 illustrates the calculation of VA ratios for the duration of processing time. One-piece flow with substantial VA in every progressive takt time increment is about as close as reality can come to the ideal. It is more approachable in some fabrication and subassembly cells than in the world's best auto assembly plants because current auto technology and material handling preclude packing the VA steps so densely. However, these obstacles are challenges for future improvement, and a big increase in a process-duration VA ratio indicates that major improvements have been achieved.

In the case of the auto plant, if the duration of a car on line can be decreased, the number of line stations can decrease. If in addition, the travel distance is decreased, the potential to reduce the space required goes up. Space is investment.

Figure 6.3 also shows that a VA ratio can be estimated for the work done at every line station. The interval during which a car (or any other product) occupies a station is usually one takt time or a multiple of it. So of the total time the product is in-station, what fraction of that time is value being added? If the dead transit time between stations can be eliminated using one-piece flow, then the VA ratio for the total sequence of stations is the sum of all VA times at each station divided by the takt time multiplied by the number of stations.

A common misperception by novices looking at a factory, or almost any other process, is to equate activity—lots of motion—with value being added. Taking advantage of this naïveté is one of the oldest ploys available to workers apprehensive about layoffs. A favorite way to stretch out dwindling work is to spend extra time handling tools or materials. During an impending cutback in the 1950s, one of the author's uncles described mostly moving tools and parts around his area for two weeks before anyone caught on. Sensitivity to the distinction between VA and NVA goes a long way toward overcoming the misperception that activity equals accomplishment.

Estimates of VA ratios are never as precise as one might like. As long as the estimates are made in a consistent manner, great precision is not necessary. An upward movement in consistently estimated ratios is a sufficient indicator of process improvement.

In this example, if work can be done in a sequence of stations, a VA ratio can be estimated from the takt time. As before:

$$\text{Takt time} = \frac{\text{Process work time available}}{\text{Number of units to be completed}}$$

Suppose 12 stations can be organized, and the takt time of the process is two minutes. Then the process throughput time should be: [12 stations] × [2 minutes per station] = 24 minutes.

Planned process sequence time: 24 minutes.

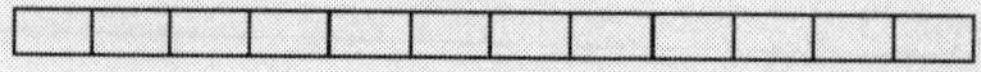

But suppose the actual process sequence time stretches to 29 minutes:

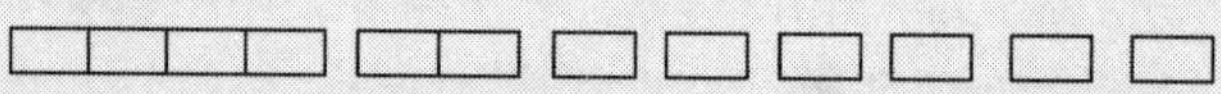

Then the VA ratio of throughput time on this basis is 24 ÷ 29 = 0.83, which quantifies that time is wasted in delays between stations. Such delays are marked by parts or units parked between stations (idle inventory). After achieving one-piece flow in a cell, those delays should be so small that they are incorporated in the planned work at each station, which is presumably containable within the takt time for each station.

A more rigorous calculation of VA time estimates the VA ratio at each station. Of the amount of planned work time available at each station, how much time is actually spent doing VA work? In this case, the VA time at station 1 might be estimated as 1.2 minutes. The VA ratio for station 1 would be [VA time/Takt time], or 1.2 ÷ 2 = 0.6 for this example.

Then the VA ratio of the cell, line, or sequence of 12 stations would be:

$$\text{Cell VA Ratio} = \left[\sum_{n=1}^{n=12} [\textit{VA time}]_n \right] \div \left[n \times [\textit{takt time}] \right]$$

Or in plain language, the VA ratio for the example sequence of 12 stations would be the sum of the VA times for each station; divided by 12 times the takt time. Suppose the ratio comes out to be 0.56. To reduce this VA ratio, we must work on removing waste from the detailed operations performed, station by station, in a one-piece flow process.

Figure 6.3. Value-Added Ratios
for Processing Duration Time of Units

■ SPACE RELATIONSHIPS

Both space reduction and travel distances are performance indicators related to space. Both are also time related. Shortening travel distances requires changing layouts to use less space. Space is consumed by the things sitting in it, so eliminating waste stocks of tools, materials, or anything else also frees space. And travel distances for people, machines, and material adds to transit time. (Great pride in "the size of the empire" is a dysfunctional emotion.)

The ultimate in minimizing factory space is to do everything in one spot. Because that is not possible, the real ideal is short, high VA flows. Physics, geometry, and time make that a tough challenge. A good exercise is to assess the fraction of floor space in which VA activity actually takes place. Don't be surprised if it's less than 10 percent.

Suppose one could machine a complex part in one place using a single, high-speed, multiaxis machine. If all the necessary operations can be completed within takt time, that will work. But it is more likely that moving all the tools and material through a confined area will either create a traffic jam or consume all the takt time, leaving none for VA. If the machine is designed to accommodate this with multiple stations, it starts to become a monster difficult to set up and to access for maintenance. It is better to develop a flow of operations through smaller, less complex, and, if possible, more flexible equipment.

Movement of people, tools, material, and even machines does not directly add value, but it is a necessary evil if work is to flow. Figuring out how to do everything within takt time is a problem of many variables. Simulation may be helpful, but modeling can be deceptive if relevant factors—such as awkward shapes, tough vision angles, and job instruction confusion—are not factored into the model. The workers wrestling the alligators on the spot are more likely to arrive, in due course, at a process that uses minimum space, minimum movement, and a maximum fraction of time adding value.

If possible, add value with every move of material. That's usually impossible, but two-moves-maximum is a good stretch goal for an assembly plant. The first move is receipt directly at line side. The next move is for attachment to the product. Then at least one of the two moves is associated with adding value.

The same is true for tooling. Move tools, as in a CNC (Computer Numerical Control) machine rack, only to use them or to maintain them. In machining, more time can spent moving tools than workpieces.

Doing spaghetti diagrams is a quick, useful way to document the number of moves and the distance moved. The total space required, which may also be called a process footprint, summarizes success in improving flow, minimizing movement, and shrinking distance. A well-developed process is quiet—devoid of clamor and useless motion.

Storage and movement are only two manifestations of just-in-case practices that consume space. A few others in factories are inflexible utilities so that equipment has to remain where it was originally located (flexible utilities allow frequent changes in layout), copious access space for maintenance and mess accommodation (takes some confidence building and equipment revision to get past that one), access routes for large material handling equipment (such as the space for a drive-in movie theater instead of a walk-in), and use of big containers instead of small ones.

Once the notion of space compression takes hold, ideas specific to a given workplace begin to germinate. From a financial view, if empty space is merely fenced off, it still must be paid for, so there's no cash gain from real estate. However, the big gains are from stopping the waste activities that consumed the space. If one needs to convert space measures to dollars, then revenue per square foot or gross margin per square foot will usually serve; to sense the progress, divide by the space actually used, not which is potentially available.

Externally, many manufacturers look at the spaceprints and timeprints of their suppliers in some fashion. A map shows where materials come from, with distances measured in both miles and time. As is known well to commuters, transit time depends on traffic and weather. Look at the miles and hours of transit time that logistics must manage daily.

■ RESOURCE USE

➤ Resource Use Ratios: Labor Productivity

Since the Middle Ages the most measured factor of production has probably been labor productivity. The basic idea is simple: Divide output by labor input. But what output by which input? If we make the question complicated enough, it will provide lifetime employment for accountants and economists.

To see how tangled the question can become, if a productivity ratio is inverted and dollarized, it becomes labor cost per unit. Even if units of output are easily agreed upon, a convoluted overhead allocation in the numerator of such a ratio is good for many meetings worth of confusion. What's included in overhead depends on whether one is trying to measure a process of limited scope or trying to estimate a cost roll-up to compare with unit price.

Whether one is interested in a straight labor productivity ratio or a labor cost ratio, it clarifies the issues to understand the purpose, scope, and nature of the processes for which they are computed, as well as the purpose of the ratio. When a factory cell is developed, divide a measure of cell output by the head count for cell operations. However, any gain is local if people are only shifted elsewhere. To see if total productivity is rising, monitor the productivity ratio of all processes in the total organization. Divide total output by a head count that factors in everyone, including sales force, temporaries, planners, support people, consultants, and executives.

Many complications arise because the process being measured is unclear in scope and nature. Finding an appropriate measure of output isn't always obvious. Same for the unintended consequences of relying on any single-spectrum indicator to drive performance. Almost everyone has heard of the old Soviet nail factory that was measured primarily by tons of output per person with no regard for customers. The organization made all spikes and no tacks.

Ask four questions about an indicator: (1) Do we understand the process being measured (flow diagrams)? (2) How will data be obtained? (3) How should the indicator be interpreted? (4) What other indicators are important to put it in context?

For example, most companies now recognize the futility of concentrating on *direct* labor productivity (or unit labor cost) if the production head count is a tiny fraction of the total. In that case, production is a fraction of all the processes that seem to be required to serve the customer. Attempts to interpret results are confounded if big pools of overhead (from various processes) are allocated. And used by itself, the indicator doesn't inspire ideas to improve the production process.

For a relatively meaningful productivity ratio, first assign to the numerator a measure of the output of the process of interest.

Then divide by the total head count or total work hours clearly associated with the same process. Where processes are highly interdependent, keep in mind that this indicator doesn't tell you everything you want to know. A productivity ratio covering a larger aggregation of processes might.

For a plantwide production process, use the total head count assigned to material conversion, including all support personnel. If the process is a product-line offering, use a head count associated with that offering, including people in the field. If the process is extended to cover an entire supply-chain organization, use that total head count. Most of the time, the process boundaries can't be untangled easily.

To see if a total set of processes is improving, create indicators that look at them as a whole. A troublesome legacy of Taylorism is the creation of subprocess indicators and either drawing too big an inference from them or simply adding them together.

➤ Performance Comparisons Are Imperfect; Ask Many "Whys"

The issues with use of productivity ratios are similar to those for many other performance indicators. Most of the comparisons simply track the same process over time—comparing it with itself. Even if the data for a process cannot be cleanly separated from others, an improvement is suggested if a productivity ratio is consistently calculated, and it goes up.

Using productivity ratios to compare similar processes (benchmarking) raises other issues, notably the similarity of the work content—and methods. Don't worry about it; ask lots of "why" questions. Those lead to improvement—to kaizen opportunities.

Suppose two different products perform the same function for the end user. If one has half as many parts as the other, its productivity ratios will likely be higher, both for fabrication and assembly. That may not be true, however, if the simpler product has a machined part functionally similar to the one with more parts, but it takes twice the time and twice the labor to fabricate. The machining productivity ratio is lower, and its unit cost is higher, but you still don't know anything useful. What's the cause? More faces to machine, more metal to remove, a slower removal process, higher scrap, or something not as obvious?

The value of making data comparisons is that it raises these questions. Process improvement is more important than a hopeless quest for "fairness" in performance comparisons. To really compare processes, have people intimately knowledgeable about them benchmark by comparing them directly with their own eyes. They see what others don't see.

➤ Machine Utilization versus Machine Readiness

Another bum legacy from Taylorism is the belief that every machine should be kept running. The premise is that the machinery is the core investment of a manufacturing company. Therefore, wringing the maximum possible output—assuming it will be sold—from each machine will maximize return on investment.

The performance indicator that corresponds to this is percentage of available time that each machine is performing VA work—machine-by-machine utilization. Like labor productivity, both the numerator and denominator of this ratio may contain flaky estimates. A machine that is running does not mean that it is creating value. Available time, or "its scheduled work time," can be creatively interpreted, and the same issues as with labor productivity apply.

The reality is that equipment is rarely utilized 100 percent. Most job shops that chart utilization find that it follows a Pareto pattern. A few pieces are used to excess while many are used only now and then. What is important is how the entire ensemble is used to create value for the customer.

Utilization has merit in heavy-investment process industries. For instance, oil refineries operate continuously except for major turnaround downtimes. Utilization is considered for the process as a whole. Where equipment has diverse purposes, the logic of utilization also diverges. A refrigerator should operate constantly. No one wants to operate a desktop computer constantly, although it may be booted up most of the time. And a fire extinguisher should function perfectly when needed, which one hopes is never.

A machine should properly do what is needed when it is needed. A measure corresponding to that is machine availability, the fraction of working time that the machine is capable of performing VA work, whether it is needed or not. When a flow of work stops because of a problem with any tool or machine in the path, value creation stops.

Strictly interpreted, value is added in a machine shop by tool-on-material time. As we have seen, the VA ratio for a total process depends on all elements of the process, not just the machines, but a stoppage of any machine can stop the entire flow. That risk is worrisome, so a machine availability ratio is often used as a driver for preventive and predictive maintenance.

Machine availability used as a driver as opposed to machine utilization also promotes another change in thinking. Extra equipment can be kept in storage in case it is needed. If it is not technically obsolete and has the capability to produce quality output, it can still add value if needed. So don't get rid of a machine just to raise the average utilization. Keeping old equipment out of the flow but available is also financially smart if it has long been written off. It's cheap capacity.

Spare equipment also makes a great sandbox for trying out new improvement ideas. A great Kaizen Blitz team is capable of doing a great deal to improve the use of their own equipment. They don't just "rearrange the furniture."

■ UNIT COSTS

Little that is new about cost accounting can be added here. Depending on how well accounting data correspond to the process of interest, cost figures have value. To estimate whether prices will bring in more cash than is spent, there is no alternative. But as an exclusive guide to process performance, costs are inadequate.[5]

Accounting models have numerous pathways than can add or subtract from profit. However, real processes add or subtract from profit, directly and indirectly, in ways that accounting models may not capture. No single process performance indicator, including cost, is self-sufficient.

Many cost measurements indirectly relate to time, space, or resources. For example, unit direct-labor costs and unit machine costs estimate the value of the resource time used to make one

---

[5] See H. Thomas Johnson, and Robert S. Kaplan *Relevance Lost: The Rise and Fall of Management Accounting* (Boston, Mass.: Harvard Business School Press, 1987). This book is still a classic in the history of trying to use cost systems designed to feed financial accounting for the monitoring of real processes. Johnson later wrote a sequel; *Relevance Regained* (New York: Free Press, 1992).

unit. However, costs do not capture the connections between different elements of a process (the interrelationship of the 4 Ms in a flow of work, sometimes captured with flow diagrams), much less the vital role of human initiative. Activity-Based Costing, sometimes expanded into Activity-Based Management, has been promoted in recent years to try to translate process changes into dollar models.

Those who are into process thinking, like production folk often are, may become impatient with people who need to see indicators dollarized for credibility. If it is necessary, do a translation, such as dollarizing a timeprint duration into a cash-flow timeline graph. Anyone into cash flow can readily accept a time-to-money indicator. The thing will be an approximation of course, but so are all financial pro formas and simulations.[6]

Most companies deep into process improvement don't burn a lot of time trying to refine cost measurement but rather try to make such cost indicators as they can capture available to more people. Improve the processes, and most cost indicators will go the right direction unless they are terribly warped by the process assumptions that have been built into the cost models—such as huge overhead pools allocated in various ways.

Regard unit costs, which are dollarized ratios, as any other indicator. Ask the same four questions about cost indicators that we asked about labor productivity: (1) Do we understand the process being measured (flow diagrams)? (2) How was data obtained? (3) How should the indicator be interpreted? (4) What other indicators are important to put it in context?

■ RESULTS

➤ Process Quality

"Quality is a given" has become a demand in major-league manufacturing, where conformance quality has become a basic qualifier

---

[6] In the 1980s the Westinghouse Quality and Productivity Center did a great deal of pioneering work developing cash-time profiles for processes. For a summary of this, see "Westinghouse OPTIM: Operating Profit through Time and Investment Management," *Target* [publication of the Association for Manufacturing Excellence] 3 (Spring 1987) 12–16. The article is based on a 1985 Westinghouse publication, *Achieving a Competitive Advantage*.

for admission to the league. Consequently, a Kaizen Blitz cannot afford to have an outcome in which there is regression in such standard indicators as defect rates, error rates, scrap, rework, or first-pass yield.

The usual Kaizen Blitz has an objective of reducing waste. Bad quality is a waste. If a workforce is not comfortable with basic quality problem solving, they may hang up on any tough quality issues lurking about. Ordinarily, attention to fast feedback, setup procedures, and fail-safe implementation will improve the quality indicators. Improving process capability in the technical sense may become part of a blitz; however, the techniques used to address it statistically are not covered in this book.

If reducing customer wait time is considered a quality improvement, then a Kaizen Blitz of a process such as a telephone answering system will focus directly on that objective. Identifying a time pattern of customer calls is a good challenge, too.

➤ Customer Satisfaction

If a Kaizen Blitz program is to be considered a success, the customer should start to appreciate some results from it sooner rather than later. Some should be seen directly and quickly: lead time, delivery, and perhaps, quality. When real costs—cash costs, which may be delayed in realization—drop dramatically, some can be passed on to the customer in the form of lower prices.

When a Kaizen Blitz initiative is beginning, there is enough to do to improve the delivery of the current offering, and the process improvement will yield some benefit to the customer. Over time, many companies want action-level people to become more familiar with customers and work more imaginatively on processes that give them better outcomes. Some teams have broad opportunities to contribute ideas for new product design. Where cross-company teams are formed to work out supply-chain processes, some associates who would never have done so before learn to work directly with customers and suppliers.

➤ Blitz Goals and Progress Indicators

The reality is that all Kaizen Blitz events look at a process of limited scope, and most have a few indicators that span the categories shown in Table 6.1. Most indicators used for a Kaizen Blitz are simple and easily understood by the team doing it. If they don't understand an indicator they're not going to pay attention to it. Some common types of performance indicators used for a Kaizen Blitz are shown in Table 6.4.

For example, The Wiremold Company is one of the best-known U.S. companies applying the Kaizen Blitz approach. Its history with the Blitz goes back six years, and its processes are still improving. Here are some typical indicators for a blitz in a production area: space saved, inventory reduced, duration time shortened, setup time reduction, defect-rate reduction, productivity increase, and cost reduction.

Sometimes other indicators may be used, depending on the case. A blitz may focus on ergonomic improvements, for instance. But basic changes that customers can appreciate are the bread-and-butter goals. Overall process performance at Wiremold is measured on the six parameters shown in Table 6.5. Because people

---

Table 6.4. Some Typical Performance Indicators for a Kaizen Blitz

1. Space required (process footprint)
2. Travel distances
3. Value-added ratios
4. Headcount (including direct support personnel)
5. Process duration (time to flow through process)
6. Time coverage of inventory associated with process
7. Linearity of time interval between completions (achievement of flow)

These assume that a relatively small process is to be improved.

Table 6.5. Wiremold's Overall Performance Parameters and Goals

- 100 percent customer service
- 50 percent reduction in defects per year
- 20 percent gain in productivity per year
- Inventory turns of 20
- Profit-sharing payouts equal to 20 percent of salary
- Establishing visual control and "5 S"

Taken from Art Byrne. "How Wiremold Reinvented Itself with Kaizen." TARGET. [publication of AME. 11 (1995): 13.]

can't get very excited about many performance measures at once, this total set is limited to only six "big hitters" for Wiremold, as is often the case in other high-performance organizations.

You can't measure it all, so don't. Pick some measures that cover the important process characteristics to improve and infer the rest. Then just do it.

Chapter

7

Uncovering the Flows: Establishing and Clarifying Process Flows

■ APPLYING BASIC PROCESS-IMPROVEMENT TOOLS

We can think of almost everything we do in a business in terms of flow—a series of actions or steps that move in a progression, building one upon another to ultimately satisfy a customer's need and, in return, fulfill the needs of the business by returning cash, a profit. Unfortunately, the common conditions of business, the prevailing environments, often disguise or obscure these flows. Consequently, decisions made and actions taken fail to match real needs or do so inefficiently, unreliably, and unpredictably. The movement of work (information, materials, effort) can therefore follow random or convoluted paths; flows can be restricted by unforeseen limitations (bottlenecks) or create conflicting demands on resources. Process-improvement efforts are frequently compartmentalized, focusing on local optimization, often without a consequential improvement in overall performance.

Clearly, establishing easily understood process flows and then clarifying or smoothing these flows is fundamental to creating a lean or just-in-time (JIT) business environment. The first stage in a kaizen improvement program focuses on familiarizing the organization with the process and demonstrating its value through a series of well-chosen projects. Then the real work begins, applying a range of improvement techniques through the kaizen process, to identify or create product or process flows and to clarify or smooth these flows by eliminating waste, streamlining bottle-necks, resolving conflicting demands, and providing simple, effective visual management tools to communicate status and signal actions needed.

The key to establishing and successfully clarifying flows is the application of several simple improvement techniques, many of which are probably already in use in your organization. Although not all of these tools should necessarily be applied through the kaizen process, kaizen provides a highly effective means to bring them to bear in a highly focused way that yields results quickly and visibly—and visibility is important. Seeing the stages of a process flow evolve helps to bring the whole organization into the process, a key factor in the later phases of establishing and sustaining the necessary process disciplines.

■ START WITH WHAT YOU KNOW: KAIZEN TOOLS

Beginners to lean manufacturing and the kaizen process often ask what tools need to be mastered to make kaizen a success. Remember, kaizen isn't an end unto itself; rather it's a tool of JIT or lean manufacturing for bringing about radical and remarkable changes in a highly focused fashion that lead to the achievement of the lean vision.

Kaizen is also a tool for employing other tools—from cell design to pull systems to *poka yoke,* the 5 Ss, and so on. The question most often asked is "What tools do we need to know; how many must we master before we begin?"

The answer is a simple one:

Start with what you know.

Virtually every organization employs a variety of improvement tools in its everyday pursuits. Many have experience building simple cells or working out innovative approaches to ease setups or in pull system concepts. Think of kaizen as a means of concentrating resources and driving improvement to unheard-of levels. Kaizen is an ideal vehicle for capitalizing on the skills that organizations and individuals in the organization *already* possess—for bringing these skills to action for immediate effect.

It's a mistake to take too broad or too scattered an approach, to try to employ too many improvement techniques simultaneously. The results may be superficial and worse yet, the hard part—sustaining the improvement—will be difficult.

The aim of initial projects, after all, is to encourage the organization to further action by achieving quick, highly visible, and sustainable success. How better to bring this about than by employing a few simple tools that people are familiar and comfortable with.

Because our objective is to move in the direction of a lean environment, the choice of tools is of some importance. Initially in this chapter, we will examine those that can be most useful in establishing and smoothing flows for products and processes. In applying them, our goal will be to establish the framework for pulling work through the business and for letting the customer's takt time dictate rates of flow through the system. This is the basis for moving toward a one-piece-flow concept.

Virtually all successful lean organizations, such as Wiremold and Lantech, began simply—concentrating on cell building, setup reduction, pull systems, the 5 Ss. They also started with tools they already knew—such as flowcharting, brainstorming, spaghetti diagrams, simple time and motion observations, ergonomics, and tool making.

The recipe is never the same. These companies are made up of different ingredients, but they all began by concentrating on applying what they knew. They leveraged their skills through the action-based kaizen process to build organic capabilities within the productive process itself to recognize opportunities and needs for improvement, apply the appropriate analytical and problem-solving tools, and constantly revise and improve processes.

Kaizen itself is a new and not easily mastered technique for most organizations. If you don't stick to a few simple tools, particularly at the outset, the degree of difficulty is dramatically increased. Kaizen's key principles and its potential as a rapid improvement tool may well be lost in the complication and difficulty of mastering several specific techniques at once.

■ WHAT IS IN YOUR TOOL KIT?

Think about the basic improvement tools your company uses every day. There are probably quite a few. Many of them can be put to work in the kaizen process. The key is to apply them in a simple and straightforward fashion. In the following pages we'll examine eight basic tools needed at various stages of the process: The Kaizen Blitz tool kit includes the following:

1. Flowcharting
2. Building cells
3. The 5 Ss
4. Simple pull systems
5. Kanban design
6. Value-added/non-value-added analysis
7. Setup reduction
8. Brainstorming

➤ Flowcharting

Flowcharting is a simple but very powerful technique that can be employed at many levels, at the initial stages and throughout on-going improvement processes. Prior to choosing initial Kaizen Blitz targets, flowcharting can be used to map the circuitous paths that materials take through a manufacturing process. The flow-chart will reveal points of constraint, conflicting demand, buildup of inventory, and so on. Often, in traditional functionally orga-nized environments, the real paths that products take are not ap-parent or not well understood by the people who do the work and manage it. Within the process itself, the flowchart is used to define and validate process-flow improvements as cells are constructed and refined to reduce process times, in-process materials and to in-crease agility.

Flowcharting exhibits many forms, from simple brown-paper maps to formal PERT diagrams to the many software based chart-ing systems. Generally the simplest, most easily accessible ap-proach for your organization is the best. Where a cross-functional range of associates such as a Kaizen Blitz team are to be involved in mapping real processes, a simple pencil-and-paper approach will usually prove to be the best.

There are three steps to successful flowcharting:

1. *Data gathering.* Collecting information about the process.
2. *Organization.* Categorizing and sequencing the information.

3. *Mapping.* Drawing the actual flows as a schematic or a representation of a physical flow.

From the standpoint of defining process flows, the key to an effective flowcharting process is to look at reality. Wherever possible, follow the physical paths taken by products and objectively record what's found. Along the way there will be opportunities to question associates on key issues. A checklist approach in a simple format such as the 4 Ms—man (person), machine, material, and method (including measurement and information)—can help to provide a framework for asking the key questions:

> What happens here?
> Where does the work come from? How often?
> Where does it go?
> Who does the work?
> How do you know what to do?
> How long does it take?

The aim of these and other questions is to collect the information that's needed to understand what *really* happens. Too often, formally documented routings or operations documents don't reflect the real situation.

But more important, these documents weren't developed to record all of the non-value-added actions, movements, information exchanges, and measurements that become the prime targets of a Kaizen Blitz team.

Also, during this fact-finding process, a team will often hear explanations of how the process is "supposed to be done" or "would be done, except." Although this may be interesting, what really matters is what is *being* done. The improvement process itself must start with how things *are* done, not how they ought to be done.

The next steps in a good flowcharting process involve organizing the information that's been gathered into a sequence of steps that can be used to literally map the process. Mapping various forms of time measurement, for example, can take as many forms as needed for the purpose at hand.

At the first stage, the need is generally for a simple schematic flowchart showing the sequence of activities, such as the underlying concept of a PERT chart that defines sequence and dependencies. You need to be very specific: for example, "First this must happen, then that."

Spaghetti Diagrams

As the improvement process progresses, define physical flows for materials, people, tools, information, and so on. Simple charts, named *spaghetti diagrams* after the convoluted tangles they illustrate, allow teams to recognize opportunities to reduce unneeded movements of materials, equipment, and people as part of streamlining or a clarifying process. They can also be used as powerful communications tools for building understanding across the organization and for tracking progress and improvements as they are implemented.

Classification of Activities

Another application of flowcharting techniques is to define the types of activities taking place along a process flow and to usefully categorize them. In the context of the Kaizen Blitz process, and fundamental to lean manufacturing and JIT concepts, there is a need to constantly evaluate the efforts of people and machines, the movements of materials and information, and measurement processes—everything that goes into delivering a product or service to the customer—and to group them into value-added (VA) and non-value-added (NVA) categories. These groupings, along with other pertinent information, reveal opportunities for improvement by eliminating or minimizing waste in the process.

Beginning with a clear set of criteria for these categorizations, the fact-finding phase of the flowcharting process gathers the basic information needed to appropriately represent VA and NVA activities. These VA and NVA steps and activities can then be easily represented in both schematic flowcharts and physical spaghetti diagrams (see Figure 7.1 and 7.2).

Flowcharting is a basic tool that can be constantly employed throughout the entire improvement process. Precision and elegance, however, are generally of little value, and striving for them will bog down the kaizen process. Simple, easily accessible and understood approaches are best suited to the needs of quick, highly focused, cross-functional Kaizen Blitz teams.

➤ Building Cells

Reorganizing functionally arranged operations or traditional assembly lines into one-piece-flow cells is a common objective of a kaizen team.

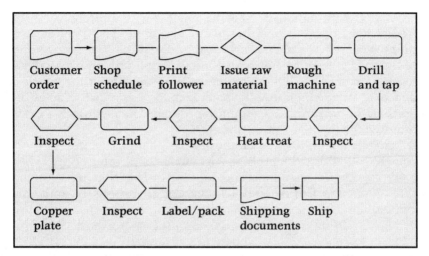

Figure 7.1. Schematic Flowchart

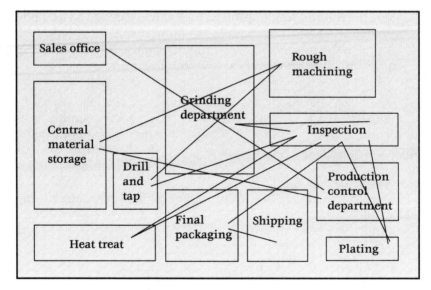

Figure 7.2. Spaghetti Diagram

Many team members view the process with apprehension. In traditional organizations the layout of a manufacturing department is viewed as a highly technical undertaking. It is seen as one best done by engineering professionals employing much analysis to prepare detailed layout drawings. Often months of preparation and planning, which usually include several approval/sign-off iterations, are required. Even then, a prolonged debugging process is required for the new arrangement.

A kaizen team composed mostly of "amateurs," however, is expected to examine the process, sort out the *real* value-added steps; bring together diverse machines and operations that are scattered throughout the facility and arrange the operations in a classic, right-to-left, U-shaped cell, balance the work among the associates, debug and formally document the new process, and be back in production—*in a week or less.* The team's advantage lies in being close to the reality of the situation, positioned to see the details of what really happens.

Clearly some prior planning and thought is required:

Can the equipment be moved by in-plant resources or should riggers be on call?

Is one of the processes a "monument," such as a heat treatment or chemical process that literally can't be moved?

Once these questions are resolved, however, the real work falls to the team. Again, the answer lies in applying a few simple tools in a commonsense fashion. After all, how realistic would it be to expect a temporary, cross-functional, multilevel construct, such as a kaizen team, to be able to effectively employ anything *but* a few simple tools?

The process can follow a number of paths, depending on the particular skills of the team members, but it breaks down into a few simple steps, for example:

➤ Calculate the takt time: At what rate does the cell need to produce to satisfy the customer's need?
➤ Diagram the process flow:
  How does the work flow now?
  What are the value-added steps?
➤ Identify the equipment and operations needed.

➤ Time the operations as necessary.

➤ Determine the bottleneck or pacing operation.

➤ Brainstorm to come up with an initial arrangement.

➤ Move some machines.

➤ Man it, run it, time it, move it again.

➤ Document the new standard practice.

Of course, this list is a superficial description. But the point is that the result comes not from a single flash of brilliance or from the application of highly complex formulae but from a simple step-by-step process that takes advantage of what the team members already know and what they know how to do.

Go with Your Team's Strengths

Each team and each organization has its own set of strengths and weaknesses. The kaizen process should be employed to capitalize on those skills already in place and proven. Of course, new skills and techniques must and will be learned, but begin with what you *already* know.

There are a few key principles to follow in building a manufacturing cell:

➤ **Build the process *around* the people.** Wherever possible, it's best to arrange equipment and materials in a U-shaped pattern with a right to left (counter-clockwise) flow, leaving as little room as possible between machines (see Figure 7.3).

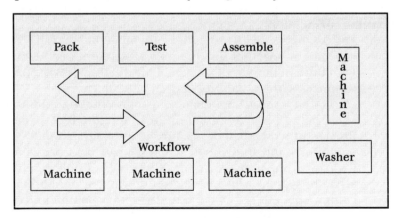

Figure 7.3. Cell Layout

The right-to-left flow acknowledges that up to 90 percent of people are right-handed and that they find this pattern of movement least fatiguing. Left-handed people have learned to function in a right-handed world and can generally accommodate themselves to this pattern.

Placing machines close together minimizes unnecessary movement of people and materials as well as minimizing opportunities for accumulation of unwanted work-in-process. Particularly in the early stages of a Kaizen Blitz–based improvement process, some planned work-in-process inventory quantities may be needed to help balance work flows and to accommodate long setup times. In this case, some space for this inventory should be deliberately set aside.

It's well to note at this point that although locating equipment to optimize flow is given primary weight at this stage, some consideration will have to be given to allowing access to the machines for setups and for maintenance. Access doors must be free to open, and so on. Figuring this out generally requires some trial and error, frequently meaning repeated adjustments in machine location until the team gets it right.

➤ Equipment selection. The selection of the specific pieces of equipment to be used in building a cell can be as simple as gathering typical examples of each type needed from existing functional departments.

Sometimes, additional equipment is required to fully outfit the cell for its intended use, whether it is dedicated to the manufacture of a complete product or the production of a complete subassembly or complex component. In either case, keep in mind these two important principles:

1. *Equipment reliability.* Because manufacturing cells link equipment together in an *almost* synchronous fashion, with little in the way of internal buffer stocks or WIP (work-in-process), the reliability of each piece of equipment has a direct and almost immediate impact on the overall output of the cell. Unlike the situation in a functionally organized process in which batches of inventory separate and buffer operations and individual machines can be scheduled to work overtime to make up for downtime, a whole cell literally stops when a machine goes down. The reliability of equipment selected must, therefore, be a paramount consideration. Think of it this way—a cell made up of 10 pieces

of equipment that each suffer 10 percent unplanned downtime might *never run*. This is an extreme example, perhaps, but it is one that helps bring home the point.

2. *Simplicity.* Another consideration in machine selection is simplicity. In a typical functional factory, operators, machine setters, and support personnel can be focused on a relatively narrow range of machine and process types and successfully meet their goals. When a wide range of machine types are gathered into a cell, however, the associates in the cell must learn to deal with all of them at once. This can represent an overwhelming challenge, particularly in situations in which frequent changeovers from one product configuration to another are needed, and it has caused many failed cell-manufacturing initiatives.

Maintenance and other support functions need to be considered, as well. Kaizen training early in the process helps to build a recognition of the kind of flexibility and rapid-response capability that these functions must develop to successfully provide support in a cellular manufacturing environment.

There are no hard and fast rules for the selection process, but a commonsense approach that emphasizes reliability and simplicity, putting reasonable limits on complexity, should be followed. It is better to err on the side of building a less-capable cell, or breaking operations down into two cells, than to take an overly ambitious approach that yields an excessively complex, unreliable result.

➤ The *pacing* operation or machine. Moving from a functional to a cellular arrangement of machines yields a process that is directly paced by the slowest process step. That is, the cell cannot produce products at a rate faster than that of the slowest machine or process step in the cell. *All* of the other equipment in the cell will be running at a pace less—sometimes considerably less—than its maximum capacity. This realization can be rather traumatic in environments where machine efficiency or machine utilization have been paramount institutional measures.

If the cell concept is being employed to focus operations on completing products as needed to meet real customer demand, as opposed to locally optimizing operations to satisfy some abstract and perhaps useless measure, and where sufficient equipment capacity is available to allow its dedication to a cell, this perceived waste of capacity is not a real one. Keep in mind, however, that this means that *all* productive demand on equipment must be considered when determining whether it can be assigned to a dedicated cell. In order to build cells with existing equipment, some surplus equipment capacity must already exist.

➤ **Balancing operations and flexible staffing.** The concept of balancing operations is used to distribute effort more or less equally among associates by examining the time required to perform each operation in the cell and trying various combinations of operator and task assignments to determine a best fit to meet takt time requirements.

Where fluctuating demand on the cell creates a need to operate to more than one takt time, this balancing process is used to determine the number of operators required and the tasks assigned to each for each takt time target. In this way the appropriate operating technique for each level of output is established. Output can then be adjusted as needed by changing the assignment and number of associates in the cell according to these predetermined patterns. In a self-directed environment, the cell associates can make these adjustments on their own as demand changes.

Initial cell-building goals typically focus on establishing flows and meeting output demands—takt time, with much reduced overall process times and inventories. As processes mature beyond the initial stages, improvements in productivity can be achieved through a more rigorous process involving the use of percent loading charts, changes in physical arrangements, and changeover time reduction efforts.

➤ The 5 Ss-Five Steps to Improvement

A set of five steps applied to organize and maintain the physical workplace are the so-called 5 Ss. The phrase "a place for everything and everything in its place" captures their spirit.

The origin of the 5 Ss is attributed to the "S" sounds of five Japanese words for these steps. While all echo a common theme, the 5 S concepts have evolved into a number of versions using English-language equivalents such as sustain, sort, or standardize and even an alphabet of company unique versions: 5 Cs—clean, categorize, and so on; 5 Os—organize, order, and so on.

The 5 Ss refer to a common series of five steps:

1. *Sort, clear.* Eliminate unneeded materials from the workplace. If it's not needed, throw it out; eliminate distraction and confusion.

2. *Organize.* Arrange everything in an orderly fashion and clearly designate its correct location. Make it easy to find and use things, information, and so on.

3. *Clean.* Put in place a system for regularly cleaning and inspecting the workplace, maintaining desired conditions, and inspecting for potential failure. This is a basis for preventive maintenance.

4. *Standardize.* Establish a routine or standard practice for the first three steps, including regular measures (grading) and feedback.

5. *Sustaining.* Maintain the whole process. Institutionalize the first four steps so that the process is sustained, measured, and enhanced on a permanent basis.

Sort

A Kaizen Blitz team on a 5 S assignment would begin by identifying needed and unneeded tools, materials, and information in a workplace—whether a single machine, cell, or department. Unneeded items would be discarded or recycled to other areas where they are needed, but definitely removed from the workplace. A heavy-handed "clean out the attic" or "when in doubt, throw it out" approach is in order.

Organize

The second phase of the team's effort is directed toward organizing the remaining needed materials by clearly identifying locations for everything in the area, from wastebaskets to hand tools to work instructions. The objective here is to create visual cues to locations, work flow, and so on.

Clean

The next step (often a team works on several steps concurrently) is to clean the workplace—really scrub it—and while cleaning, to inspect everything for flaws, defects, and impending failures, tagging items needing maintenance attention, and so on. This step is a precursor to developing a regular preventive/predictive maintenance process and a valuable step toward a formal TPM (total productive maintenance) program.

Standardize

The next step that the team must accomplish is to establish the routines and standard practices (well documented and displayed in the workplace) for regularly and systematically repeating the first three steps. Step 3—cleaning—in particular, must be emphasized as a regular (daily, weekly, monthly) process with clearly assigned responsibilities and procedures to be followed. Included in this step are procedures and forms for regularly evaluating (grading) the status of the process by inspecting the workplace and verifying compliance with procedures and standards.

Sustaining

As the final step, and this is one the team can't do on its own, the whole process must be institutionalized to ensure that it is sustained, maintained, and renewed to constantly strive for improvement. Management commitment is the key here. Because the 5 S process is a highly visible one, this step represents a significant opportunity for reinforcing or killing belief in management's true commitment to the kaizen continuous-improvement process.

➤ Simple Pull Systems

Once a process flow has been established, and initially identified constraints or bottlenecks have begun to be addressed, pull systems can come into play to simplify the management of flows and to directly signal customer demand throughout the process.

Pull system design is often viewed as a black art. Although many manufacturing professionals can articulate the basic concepts of a pull system, surprisingly few can actually build a working example. Enormous sums are spent annually on pull system education programs, seminars, and workshops. Yet actual implementation is often fraught with difficulty.

A kaizen team must keep it simple and approach the development of a pull system on a very basic level—focusing on a few key principles and desired functions.

Pull systems have three primary objectives:

1. Provide a *signal* for action
2. *Synchronize* flow through a process
3. *Limit* inventories

Signal

The first objective—signaling actions required to be taken—is by far, the most important. The pull system's primary objective must be to signal what, when, and how:

What to make

When to make it

How much to make

Consumption of product by the customer (internal or external) controls the process. Further, a properly designed system must provide these signals directly to the people who do the work, with no translation or interpretation necessary. Thus the need for simplicity.

Synchronize

Synchronization of operations should not, at least initially, be interpreted as meaning a hard-linked series of operations in lockstep, like an automated assembly line. Kanban container sizes and intermediate stock locations along a pull system should be sized to act as buffers to cushion the system from interruptions so that it can run reliably in the real world. Interruptions can be caused by breakdowns, long setup times, missed supplier deliveries, and so on.

As the kaizen process is applied repeatedly along a process flow to reduce setup times and improve process reliability and productivity, these buffer sizes can be reduced without penalty.

Limit

The third objective of the pull system, limiting inventories, is important, but it is often overemphasized at the early stages and frequently causes the pull system to fail.

Of course, it is important to physically limit the amount of inventory at each location. Stockless production, however, can't be brought about in a single step. We must first overcome the bottlenecks of changeover time, breakdowns, and unreliable sources to be able to reduce the size of buffers along the pull system. In fact, a premature emphasis on minimizing inventories is a common, perhaps the most common, cause of failure of pull system initiatives.

Stockless production may be our ultimate goal, but we must first identify and then gradually eliminate sources of interruption to gradually reduce the need for buffer inventories.

If we keep the above points in mind, we can overcome a key sticking point for many teams and simplify the process of building an initial pull system. The sticking point is the idea that kanban or buffer sizes must be based on some optimal mathematical calculation or algorithm. The experience of countless successful kaizen teams does not bear this out.

Start with a few simple steps. Ask:

➤ Where is the customer?

➤ How can the customer's signal be seen at the point of production?

➤ How long are the interruptions in flow likely to be? (setup times and frequencies, breakdown experience, etc.)?

Size the buffers (intermediate inventory points) to generously cover the interruptions. For example, if a machine takes four hours to change over (we can reduce this in a future kaizen) start with a six-to-eight-hour buffer, or more.

The point is to give the system enough cushioning or slack to let it start running. It can then be tuned and tightened (or loosened) as we gain experience and confidence in its operation.

Even the most vocal proponents of a more rigorous mathematical approach allow for a substantial contingency or "fudge factor" in their calculations. An inexpert kaizen team needs to start with a generous one.

Remember, the goal is to get the system to work, letting demand control production, to gradually improve synchronization; and finally, as experience is gained and bottlenecks overcome, to reduce required inventories. Once again, the *simple* straightforward approach is best.

Because the first use of a pull system in a manufacturing location will probably be to control the movement of materials through a physical process—ideally in a simple readily understood fashion—the physical characteristics of the system are of some importance.

➤ Kanban Design

The design of kanban containers and other devices should consider several factors: ergonomics, customers and suppliers, and visual management.

Ergonomics

Kanban containers are designed to be handled by associates throughout the manufacturing process. As such, the safety, comfort, and ease of doing the work need to be considered.

Wherever the size and weight of products allow, keep the weight of fully loaded containers to 30 pounds or less. This will ease lifting and movement by all employees and minimize the need for mechanized material-handling equipment. If possible, design kanban locations so that containers are located on waist-high racks or tables to eliminate bending or reaching. The containers themselves should have easily grasped handles, lips, or other devices to enhance safety and ease effort required in handling.

Customers and Suppliers

It is often possible to employ containers that can be used by your customer or for shipping products to the customer. Many reusable container types currently available incorporate features that facilitate their use in a kanban system. Similarly, a supplier's containers may be suitable for use in your manufacturing process or even for use all the way to the end user. Aside from the obvious benefits of reduced waste generation and cost, multiple handling and repackaging steps can often be eliminated.

Visual Management

Employ containers with features that make kanban quantities obvious or easily determined. A simple egg-crate-style cellular design is one example. Another is the use of a fill line for granular material. The kanban container should also be clearly marked as to its contents, either permanently or by providing a slot or window for an identification kanban. Simple and obvious are the key words.

➤ Value-Added versus Non-Value-Added Analysis

At the core of the Kaizen Blitz process is the concept of defining activities according to whether they add value to the product and categorizing those that do not as waste. The fundamental means of improvement, therefore, is the elimination or minimization of this waste.

In the flowcharting process all of the actions taken and the time spent along a process flow or within a specific process step are noted, recorded, and categorized in a number of ways according to need. Perhaps the most important categorization from the standpoint of the Kaizen Blitz process is value-added versus non-value-added status.

A simple approach to determining this categorization starts with a simple definition:

> *Any action that changes the physical state of the product to move it closer to the form desired by the customer adds value. Anything else does not.*

For example, cutting a metal part on a lathe or installing an electronic component on a circuit board are VA activities. Storing these same materials or moving them around the factory or setting up the process machinery, however, does not add value. Nor does inspecting, counting, or reporting on the status of their production. This may seem like a harsh and simplistic definition, but it provides a clear, easily understood basis for identifying opportunities for improving processes by eliminating waste in a variety of forms.

Clearly, most time and, often, most effort in typical manufacturing processes is spent on NVA activities. A simple mechanical product that takes several days or even weeks to move through the required range of operations may actually spend only a few minutes or *seconds* in actual value-adding steps.

The ratio of total time spent in process to actual VA time is often several thousand or *tens-of-thousands* to one. The opportunity for improvement in process times, inventories, needless handling, and repetitive reporting can be enormous.

Most organizations have concentrated improvement efforts, their human and financial capital, on reducing these VA minutes and seconds. The Kaizen Blitz focuses on the NVA hours, days, and weeks to achieve rapid and dramatic results. Therefore, the identification of the various types of NVA activities in a process is a key step in any kaizen project.

Once the real VA activities have been identified, group NVA activities into categories that can be targeted for improvement. These may be in the form of the traditional principle wastes of part travel, walking, waiting, and so on, or into more detailed categories—such as loading and unloading parts on a machine, visual examination, repositioning during a process. The specific categorizations that will be useful to a Kaizen Blitz team will normally be easily derived from the project objectives.

> *It is nearly impossible to eliminate all NVA activities. In fact, a further categorization into avoidable versus unavoidable NVA activities is often useful. An example of an unavoidable NVA process might be the need to move materials to a central processing point where physical size constraints, costs, environmental considerations, or the limits of technology make it impossible to do otherwise. It is sometimes useful to check off the unavoidables in the flowchart to help the team to focus on those areas where real progress can be made.*

➤ Setup Reduction

Setup reductions are perhaps the most common initial project selections. They have the advantage of being simple to measure—the results are obvious to all—and of offering perhaps the most dramatic short-term improvement opportunities: A 90 percent reduction goal is standard operating procedure in many companies.

The key to setup reduction is separating the internal and external elements of the setup process—that is, those that must be performed while the equipment is stopped (internal) versus those that can be performed while production is still going on.

By borrowing a few simple project management techniques, the team can categorize the steps into a work breakdown structure. It can then brainstorm various ways that the steps can be combined, simplified, sequenced, or eliminated to ease the setup process.

Do some simple time observations with a stopwatch. If you're a runner, your sports watch will work just fine. If it's a long and complex process, videotape it for more detailed study.

Make a simple flowchart of the steps that can be done in parallel rather than in series.

If you have a skilled toolmaker or mechanic on the team, or even a clever basement handyman, their talents can be put to work developing simple fixturing or shadow boards to keep needed tools readily at hand.

Setup reduction efforts commonly address needs in the following areas:

➤ **Workplace organization**

Thoroughly clean and eliminate unneeded materials, tools, and equipment from the area.

Establish point-of-use storage for tooling and other needed material within or as close to the workplace as possible to minimize or eliminate search, walking, and transportation time.

Identify hand and small power tools needed by setters and locate them conveniently at hand where needed. Simple shadow boards within painted outlines that provide locations for tools are often mounted directly on the machines where they are used.

Locate measuring devices and gauging at or near machines for rapid validation during the setup process.

Stage raw materials and product components at the workplace in advance of the setup to eliminate search and material movement time.

➤ **Methods**

Develop and document uniform setup procedures, a "best-practice" sequence of steps to be followed for each setup, and display them in the workplace.

Preset or prepare tooling and gauging elements in advance of the setup either by setters themselves or by support personnel.

Develop and implement procedures for examination, repair, and storage of tooling and gauging after use to ensure availability when needed.

Adopt team setup concepts where two or more associates work together in a defined process to hasten setups.

Prioritize support services to eliminate waiting delays during a setup. Some support services—special laboratory measurements, for example—may be required to perform periodic checks on ongoing production. If this same equipment and staff must also validate a setup "first article," setup pieces should be given top priority for these services.

Use lifting devices, rollers, and other mechanical aids to reduce operator effort and enhance safety.

Incorporate "positive stop" concepts in the design of tooling to minimize or eliminate adjustments in setups—often the source of the bulk of total setup time.

Poka-yoke: mistake proofing to eliminate chances for error.

➤ **Information flow**

Locate all needed information, prints, specs, work instructions at the workplace to eliminate wasted gathering time.

Provide complete instruction information packets and schedules to support functions in advance of need to allow for timely preparation of needed materials.

Simplify or eliminate record keeping or reporting requirements for setters.

It is primarily the application of a few simple techniques, in a disciplined results-oriented process, that brings results—not the mastery of some new and highly complex technology.

Of course, as an organization gains experience in the kaizen process, the potential benefits of learning and applying newer and more sophisticated techniques will become clear, as successes fuel a drive to constantly hone existing skills and add new ones to achieve even greater results.

➤ Brainstorming

Brainstorming is a widely used, well-understood tool. Whether it is employed as a free-form idea session or in a formally structured and focused session it is an excellent tool for getting a new team together to quickly surface ideas for change.

In a kaizen project, where action is the key, a few brief brainstorming sessions (don't spend too much time in the conference room) can help get a team "out of the box" quickly and be a catalyst for actually *trying* new ideas.

Because kaizen challenges participants to achieve what seems to most to be radical change, it is important to start making or trying real changes early in the process. Brainstorming is a simple device for sparking ideas that can be tried immediately.

The only caution is that many will have used this tool only as part of deliberative processes where the expected result is only a plan or proposal. In kaizen, brainstorming needs to be used as a breakthrough tool, to clear away the old thinking and get to something *new* that can be tried *now!*

Chapter

Forms, Charts, and Measurements

Information flow—the collection, organization, and dissemination of information—is critical to the operation and improvement of an enterprise. Measurement choices, both what is measured and how it is measured, dictate to a great extent the behaviors of organizations and they drive decision making from the upper echelons of management to the factory floor. The philosophies of lean manufacturing, just-in-time (JIT), and the Kaizen Blitz reflect an understanding of the power of the right measures—simple, consistent, and easily understood measures that reveal the true status of the work and point clearly to needed actions.

"You get what you measure." If you need a certain output per day, then measure pieces per day, not indirect products such as "earned standard hours." But it is also true that *the best measures are direct measures,* those that can be taken directly, especially by those who do the work.

Powerful improvement techniques such as AME's Kaizen Blitz can deliver dramatic results, but they cannot do so without the right sets of measures, the right way of looking at problems and gauging solutions. Similarly, organizations will find great difficulty sustaining these dramatic improvements unless the right measures are in place and employed at all levels of the organization to measure performance, drive appropriate actions, and gauge results.

A few simple charts and forms are used in a broad range of applications to develop and carry out a Kaizen Blitz project. They direct and organize the collection of information and facilitate the development and evaluation of the team's improvement innovations. Other forms derived from the same concepts provide the simple and clear ongoing measures needed for these improvement innovations to be sustained and to yield real improvement in day-to-day operations.

■ KAIZEN BLITZ FORMS

The number of different formats used for Kaizen Blitz–style improvement project forms is almost as great as the range of businesses that employ these techniques. In fact, over time most organizations develop their own variants to suit a particular corporate style, emphasize ownership or commitment to the process, or reflect a focus on a particular environment or technology. Although they may go by a number of different names depending on where they are found, all follow a similar pattern and adhere more or less to the same basic principles of simplicity and direct measurement. The set presented here is a generic representation.

➤ Kaizen Work Sheet

The kaizen work sheet is used to describe and set the goals for the project itself (see Figure 8.1). It provides the basic background information the team needs:

Where is the project?

What processes are involved?

What is the customers demand?

What problems must be overcome?

What are the specific goals of the team?

It also serves as a focal point for reviews with management during the project. A typical form includes the following:

Location and description of the site

Details of the operation—equipment types and processes.

Organizational information—staffing, work shifts, etc.

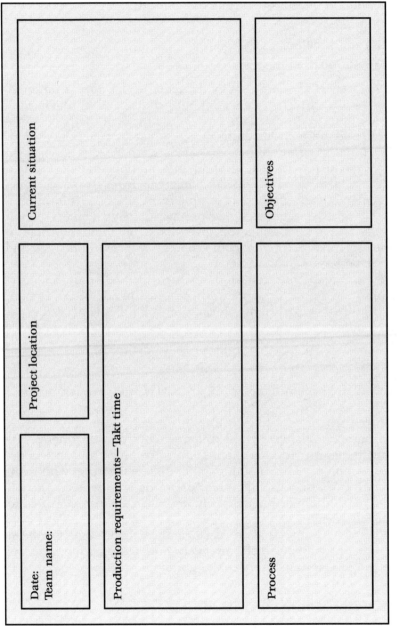

Figure 8.1. Kaizen Work Sheet

Production needs—takt time calculation

Customer requirements

Current problems

Specific goals of the team

The work sheet is completed by the team leader after a thorough investigation at the site, collecting needed data, often in consultation with the facilitator. This form is the focus of the team introduction and presentation at the meeting that launches the project.

Figure 8.2 is an example of a kaizen work sheet that has been completed to provide background information and goals for a team tasked to build a one-piece-flow cell from dispersed functional elements. It presents in simple form all of the information the team needs to get started. The production requirements section with its takt time calculation gives basic demand information needed in constructing the cell. Problems are clearly defined and specific targets or goals are set.

Teams are discouraged from wasting time and energy creating elaborate or formal presentations. A quick, hand-written version that captures the pertinent information is all that is needed to get the job done.

➤ Daily Performance Report

The daily performance report (Figure 8.3) is used to report progress and discuss actions taken and planned at the daily team leaders' meeting. It helps the Kaizen Blitz team and management track performance and make needed course corrections. Progress, or lack of it, against improvement goals is recorded and the report serves as a point of discussion in daily update meetings with management. It is also a useful tool for planning out the week's activities so that sufficient progress is being made against each goal to ensure success.

Figure 8.4 shows a daily performance report that has been filled out by the valve cell, one-piece-flow team as they tracked their progress through the weeklong project.

➤ Kaizen Reporting Sheet

The kaizen reporting sheet (Figure 8.5) is used by the team to report the specific problems addressed, actions taken, and results

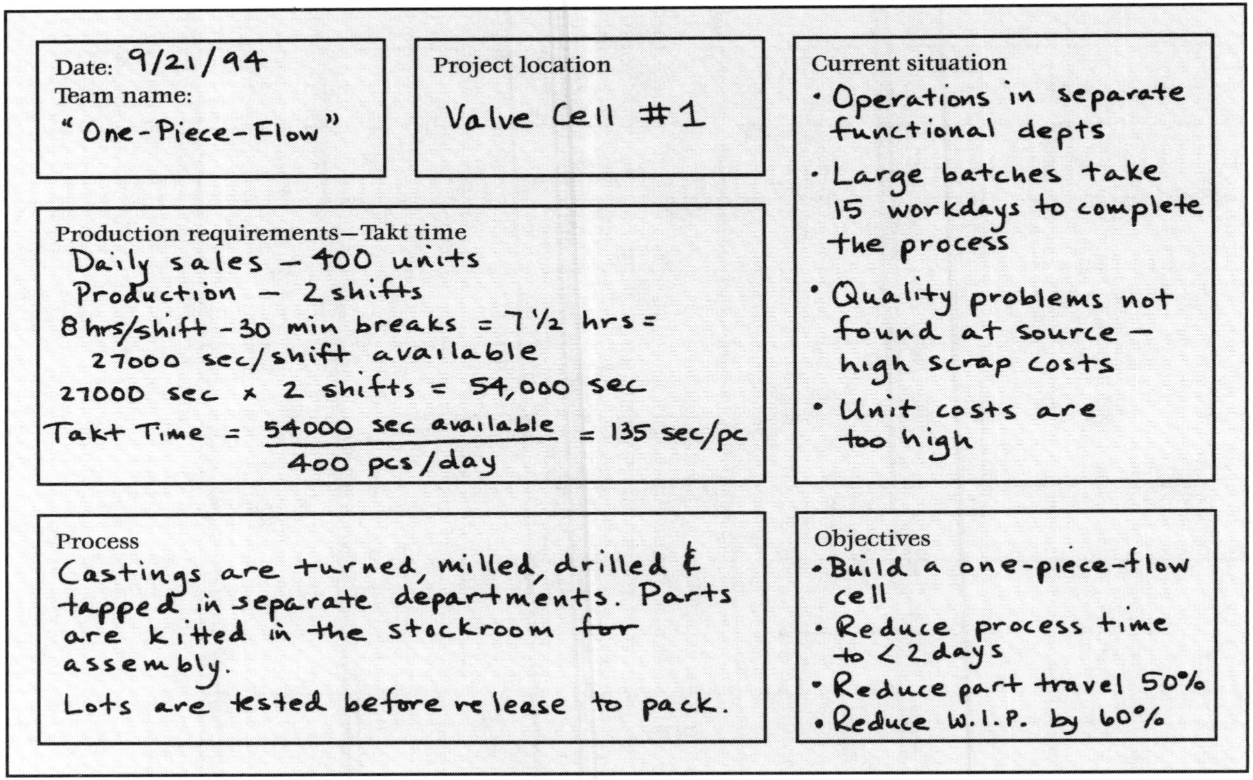

| Date: 9/21/94 | Project location |
| Team name: "One-Piece-Flow" | Valve Cell #1 |

Current situation

- Operations in separate functional depts
- Large batches take 15 workdays to complete the process
- Quality problems not found at source — high scrap costs
- Unit costs are too high

Production requirements—Takt time

Daily sales — 400 units

Production — 2 shifts

8 hrs/shift - 30 min breaks = 7½ hrs =
27000 sec/shift available

27000 sec × 2 shifts = 54,000 sec

$$\text{Takt Time} = \frac{54000 \text{ sec available}}{400 \text{ pcs/day}} = 135 \text{ sec/pc}$$

Objectives

- Build a one-piece-flow cell
- Reduce process time to < 2 days
- Reduce part travel 50%
- Reduce W.I.P. by 60%

Process

Castings are turned, milled, drilled & tapped in separate departments. Parts are kitted in the stockroom for assembly.

Lots are tested before release to pack.

Figure 8.2. Kaizen Work Sheet: Example

197

Date _____

Team name _____

	Goal	Start	Mon.	Tues.	Wed.	Thur.	Fri.	Total change
Space (square feet)								
Inventory (number of pieces)								
Walking distance (feet)								
Parts travel distance (feet)								
Lead time								
Number of people								
Productivity								
Setup time								

Figure 8.3. Daily Performance Report

Date 9/21/94

Team name One-piece-flow Valve Cell #1

	Goal	Start	Mon.	Tues.	Wed.	Thur.	Fri.	Total change
Space (square feet)								
Inventory (number of pieces)	4,080	10,200	8,400	8,400	600	218	218	Reduced 97.8%
Walking distance (feet)								
Parts travel distance (feet)	545	1,090	1,090	680	600	490	411	Reduced 62.2%
Lead time	<2 days	15 days	15 days	15 days	3 days	<1 day	<1 day	Reduced 93.3%
Number of people								
Productivity								
Setup time								

Figure 8.4. Daily Performance Report: Example

Date _____

Team name _____

Problem	Actions taken	Results

Before	After

Figure 8.5. Kaizen Reporting Sheet

200

achieved. A team may use several of these to present a clear and concise "before and after" picture of their work.

Often, the sheets are used to report ongoing actions and results during the daily management update meetings. They serve as an effective means to flesh out the data on the daily performance report.

Figure 8.6 shows one of the kaizen reporting sheets that the valve cell team has prepared. This example addresses a wide range of issues, from inventory to quality to travel distances. For clarity, many teams would prepare a separate sheet for each topic. This would also make it easier to allow more of the team members to actively participate in the presentation of final results. Look for opportunities of recognition for all team members. The focus of Kaizen Blitz efforts is on real hands-on improvement, not on polished presentation skills. The forms employed and the style of presentation used should emphasize a simple, commonsense approach shared by all of the team members.

➤ Time Observation Form

The time observation form (Figure 8.7) is a tool used by the team to determine the time required for each major step in the process, to identify opportunities, and to validate the final process design.

The team conducts simple stopwatch timing exercises (usually at least 10 repetitions) to establish a realistic time. A typical approach is to use the second-best time for each step—this takes away the effect that "flyers" (unusually high or low times) have on the average.

In observing an operation or series of operations, the team must break the activities observed into a series of steps. Usually, several easily observed points in the process, typically transitions from one activity to another, are chosen as timing points. These points are entered in the "Points Timed" column on the right side of the form.

The observation points divide the operation into a series of steps that are entered in the "Operation" column of the form. The complete operating cycle is timed up to 10 times and the results were recorded in the appropriate columns. The result is a set of typical times for each step and for the overall cycle. Based on this and other observed information, the team can direct its efforts toward meeting its particular improvement goals. In the cell-building example, the time required to perform each step must be known to

Date _9/25/94_

Team name _One-piece flow Valve Cell #1_

Problem	Actions taken	Results
• Operations in separate depts, long travel distance, many stockroom transactions req'd. • Quality problems not found until late in process. Whole lots rejected at final test. • Excessive inventory and material handling required.	Moved equipment to single cell eliminating repeated trips to stockroom. Provided gauging and training at all operations in cell. Built one piece test station into cell. Minimal "standard work in progress" allowed in cell. Machines closely spaced to minimize handling of material.	Part travel distance reduced 62.2%, lead time to <1 day Operator checks are effective-feedback comes in minutes. No queuing for final test. No outside material handling effort needed in cell, < 1 day total W.I.P., W.I.P. reduced over 97%

Before	After
Large batches traveled throughout the plant and back and forth to the stockroom — 15 day lead time Quality checks by audit many defects not found until final test = high scrap costs. Excessive inventory and material handling costs.	One piece flow cell performs all operations. All req'd components are at the cell and operators can check their own work. Valves are tested and packed one at a time. Only a few parts can be made before defects are discovered. Operators are in control!

Figure 8.6. Kaizen Reporting Sheet: Example

Time Observation Form

Operation	1	2	3	4	5	6	7	8	9	10	Operation Time	Points Timed
Total Cycle Time												

Date ___ Time ___

Figure 8.7. Time Observation Form

appropriately balance effort among the operators to achieve the target output or efficiency. As the team progresses, changes or new ideas are validated by repeating the timing process.

Traditional industrial engineering approaches and some management practices have engendered a healthy mistrust of the time observation process in many organizations. In the Kaizen Blitz, the tools and techniques of time observation are in the hands of the people who do the work. They are encouraged to use this valuable tool to study their own work, develop the skills that can help them bring about needed improvements on their own, and decide for themselves the best way to do the work. Used in this way, "ownership" of the results, helps to sustain improvements long after the team's work is completed.

When teams face prolonged operations or nonrepetitive phenomena (things that don't happen every process cycle), it is often useful to videotape the process and then time the steps from the tape. Studying a prolonged setup process is a good example of this type of problem. However, because some associates may be sensitive to being videotaped, this should be approached with some caution. It is always a good practice to let the team members tape themselves and to build trust by assuring them that the tape is for their use only.

Figure 8.8 is a time observation form completed by the valve cell team to study the process steps in their one-piece-flow machining and assembly cell. This a good example of how a simple tool that can be quickly mastered by a team of "amateurs" will yield considerable insight into what a casual observer would conclude is a complex process. The ability to break down complicated tasks or sequences into simple elements for study with simple tools is fundamental to the success of the kaizen concept.

Figure 8.8 shows the major steps of the process, the points that were used for timing, and individual times for each cycle. The "operation time" shown is the second-best time observed, not the average.

➤ Standard Work Sheet

A standard work sheet (Figure 8.9) is used to diagram the production process or process flow. It is also used to provide an initial picture of the process for the team, a "spaghetti diagram," and then to document the new process. It becomes part of the documentation left in the workplace as part of the visual management system.

Time Observation Form

	Date	Time
	9/24/94	2:00 PM

Operation	1	2	3	4	5	6	7	8	9	10	Operation Time	Points Timed
Pick up/load	6.1	6.0	6.3	5.8	6.3	6.0	5.9	6.2	5.8	6.1	5.9	Chuck lever
Mill flat	16.6	16.4	16.4	15.9	16.1	16.0	16.2	16.2	16.0	16.1	16.0	Start mill (button)
Drill for lever	12.0	12.0	11.4	11.5	11.8	11.6	11.6	11.8	11.7	11.7	11.5	Load
Tap for lever	10.9	10.9	10.7	10.4	10.9	10.6	10.6	10.5	10.7	10.8	10.5	Pick up part
Wash	15.5	15.4	15.1	14.8	15.6	15.0	15.2	15.3	15.0	15.1	15.0	Check
Install piston	10.1	10.1	9.9	9.8	10.0	10.0	9.7	9.7	10.0	9.9	9.8	Twist
Install seals & end cap	12.9	13.4	13.3	13.3	13.4	13.2	13.1	13.5	13.4	13.7	13.1	Wrench
Install lever assy	17.0	16.0	16.6	16.9	16.3	16.3	16.4	16.2	16.7	16.5	16.2	Pick up washer
Pressure test	10.4	10.4	10.0	10.1	10.1	9.5	9.9	10.2	10.0	10.1	9.9	Switch on
Label	13.9	13.4	12.6	13.4	13.3	13.6	13.2	13.6	13.4	13.3	13.2	Reset button
Pack	12.1	12.1	12.4	12.2	12.3	12.0	12.4	12.1	11.5	12.0	12.0	Close box
Total Cycle Time	137.5	136.1	134.9	134.1	136.1	133.8	134.2	135.3	134.2	135.3	133.1	

Figure 8.8. Time Observation Form: Example

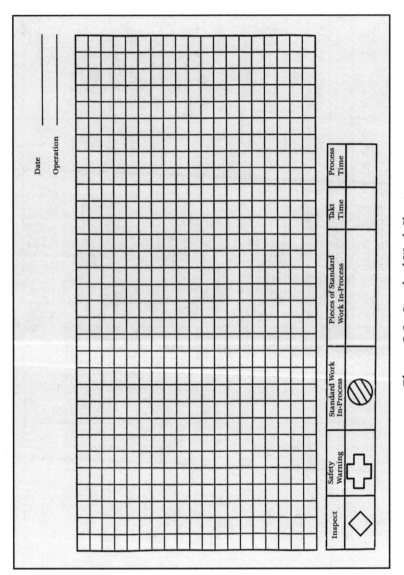

Figure 8.9. Standard Work Sheet

206

The symbols along the bottom of the sheet indicate quality checks, safety precautions, and the locations of planned or allowable work-in-process. Because the standard work sheet is used to display needed information throughout a facility, standard symbols support a common understanding throughout.

Normally, this form is filled out by team members who do not have formal drawing or drafting skills. Primary emphasis is on a clear and understandable representation of how the workplace and work flow are supposed to look. Once again, emphasis is on ownership by the team and the people who will do the work once the team is gone.

As with the kaizen reporting form, the standard work sheet is employed by teams to sketch out ideas and report on progress in daily updates. It is a working tool as well as a formal reporting and documentation format.

Figure 8.10 is a standard work sheet filled out to show a sketch of the cell built by the valve cell team. The locations of equipment, materials, hazards (in this case a pinch point in a fixture), and people are clearly shown. Takt times and process times are shown from the kaizen work sheet and the time observation form. If the way in which the work is to be done is changed by a Kaizen Blitz team or any other method, the standard work sheet that is posted in the workplace, must be changed.

Figure 8.11 shows a spaghetti diagram prepared by the team to show the flow of work among the functional operations that were in place as they began their cell-building exercise. Again, a team may use this technique repeatedly to map out its path to completion.

➤ Standard Work Combination Sheet

The standard work combination sheet (Figure 8.12) graphically shows the relationship between takt time (the rate of customer demand) and cycle time (the pace at which operations are performed). The steps and data shown on the time observation form are used to complete this form.

The graph also shows the relationships between manual and machine operations and walking (people movement) time. It is maintained in the workplace and displayed along with the standard work sheet to document the process.

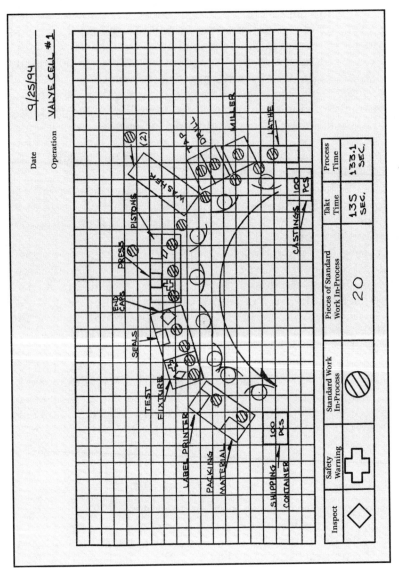

Figure 8.10. Standard Work Sheet: Example

208

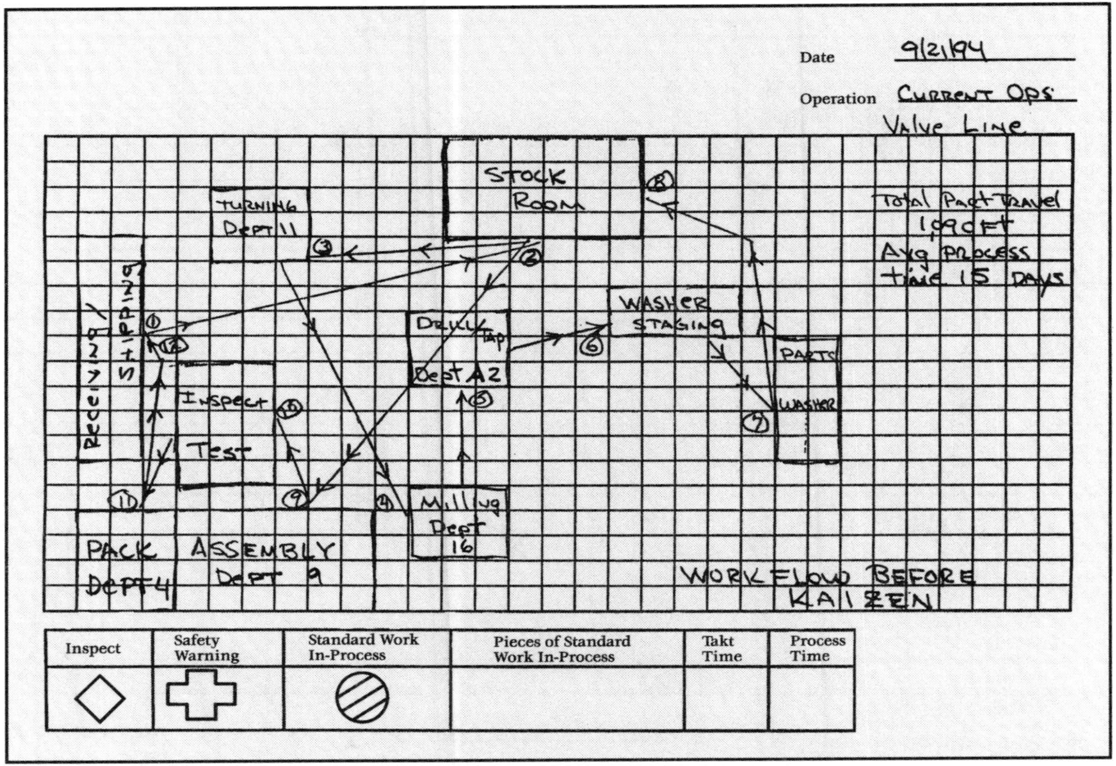

Figure 8.11. Spaghetti Diagram Example

Figure 8.11. Spaghetti Diagram Example

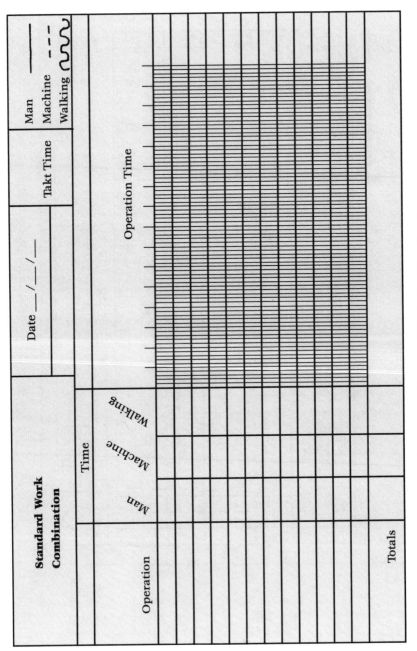

Figure 8.12. Standard Work Combination Form

Figure 8.13 shows the standard work combination sheet prepared for the valve cell. It shows the time required for each step and breaks that time down into manual effort, automatic machine effort, and walking or people movement time. The relationship between takt time and cycle time is clearly shown.

➤ Kaizen Follow-up List

The kaizen follow-up form (Figure 8.14) is used to list future enhancements or simple follow-up actions recommended by the team. Usually the duration is limited to 30 days. Items may include "hardening" some temporary wiring or plumbing or acquiring some small purchased items.

Items on this list should *not* be required to achieve team goals—that is, they are not required to be done during the project period itself.

Figure 8.15 shows a follow-up list for the valve team. No major actions are required, only some cleanup items. It is best to limit this list to a few items. Management should follow up on the progress of these items for a month or so after the project is completed. Anything not done by then probably won't be getting done. Perhaps it should be saved for the next project.

➤ 5 S Checklist

The 5 S checklist (Figure 8.16) provides a simple means of scoring or evaluating the status of a workplace with respect to cleanliness, orderliness, visual management, and discipline. The standard work documents normally displayed in the workplace are a part of the visual environment that the 5 Ss strive to create.

■ PERFORMANCE MEASUREMENT

After the Kaizen Blitz project has been completed, the primary objective is to sustain the gains achieved in a meaningful way, to show real performance improvement. Some simple measures, ones often put in place as part of the project itself, can be used to maintain the focus started by the team. We've already discussed the stan-

Standard Work Combination		Date 9 / 25 / 94		Takt Time		Man ———
		Valve Cell #1		135		Machine − − − Walking ⌇⌇⌇

Operation	Time		
	Man	Machine	Walking
Pick up/load	5.9	12.0	
Mill flat	16.0	12.0	
Drill for lever	11.5	8.0	
Tap for lever	10.5	14.0	
Wash	15.0	29.0	
Install piston	9.8		
Install seals, end cap	13.1		
Install lever assy	16.2		
Pressure test	9.9		
Label	13.2		
Pack	12.0		
Totals	133.1	75.0	

Figure 8.13. Standard Work Combination Form: Example

212

Item	Problem	Action Required	Person Responsible	Due Date

Date _____

Team name _____

Figure 8.14. Kaizen Follow-up List

Date _____9/25/94_____

Team name _____One-piece-flow_____

Item	Problem	Action Required	Person Responsible	Due Date
1	Kanban location taped on floor	Remove tape & paint	WFB	10/1/94
2	Temporary hoses for water line	Hard plumbing	"	10/4/94
3	Handwritten signs	Purchase painted signs	CRM	10/8/94

Figure 8.15. Kaizen Follow-up List: Example

	1 Poor	2	Level 3	4 Excellent
Step 1 Sorting	A cluttered workplace with many unneeded items in random locations. Haphazard.	Some unneeded items remain. Somewhat easier to find needed items.	Only needed items remain, but quantities required are not defined.	Only the bare essentials remain. Only defined quantities of items evident.
Step 2 Organizing	No organization. Essential items are lost in the clutter.	Some organization of items. All locations not dedicated. Some visual cues.	All items neatly arranged. Dedicated locations and visual cues.	A visual work environment. "A place for everything and everything in its place."
Step 3 Cleaning	Dirty area with no evidence of systematic cleaning.	Area is generally clean. Routine not in evidence. Inspection not part of routine.	Cleaning and inspection of equipment clearly in evidence.	A spotless, inviting environment. Attention to detail is obvious.

(continued)

Figure 8.16. Simple 5 Ss Checklist

215

	1 Poor	2	Level 3	4 Excellent
Step 4 Standardizing	No evidence of a documented routine.	Procedures exist but not evident in workplace. Inconsistently applied.	Procedures clearly in place and beginning to be practiced.	Clearly defined, effective cleaning process is in constant use.
Step 5 Sustaining	No evidence of management monitoring or support.	Visual measures of 5 S performance posted.	Continuous improvement process in place. Evidence of management follow-up.	Primary focus is prevention. Standards constantly being upgraded.

Figure 8.16. (continued)

dard work documents that should become a part of the workplace to show how the work is to be done. Measurements of how well or successfully it is being done are needed as well.

A few simple tools can be employed in a variety of environments to provide feedback to associates and management on day-to-day performance. They can also be used to gather data for ongoing problem solving and improvement efforts or to help choose future Kaizen Blitz targets. The most useful types are setup charts and daily production charts.

➤ Setup Charts

When a Kaizen Blitz team has completed a project aimed at reducing the time needed to change a machine or process over from one product to another, further steps must be taken to ensure that the benefit of their efforts continues into the future. Work instructions, standard work, and so on provide the how-to. What's needed is feedback for the associates and management as to how well the process is working, and if it is not, what needs to be done to correct it. A setup chart is used to record and display, for all to see, the time required for each setup performed. The form shown in Figure 8.17 is a typical example. The horizontal axis shows the days of the month, and the vertical axis shows the time required for the setup—"last good piece to first good piece."

In practice, the person doing the setup, often using a clock installed for that purpose, records the time taken for each setup. The legend on the chart shows how times for each shift are displayed.

Figure 8.18 is a completed chart. By observing the distribution of points, one can determine the average time required versus the standard set by the team or versus a new goal. Comments can be handwritten onto the chart to indicate the source of problems or to explain flyers. If needed, statistical trends can be derived from X-bar charts built from this data.

A key principle in charting of this sort is that the charts should be visible to all and that the data must be entered by the people who do the work. This self-measurement, self-improvement philosophy is the long-term goal of the kaizen process.

➤ Production and Output Charting

Clearly, one of the primary reasons for conducting a Kaizen Blitz or using other improvement tools is to enhance output or increase

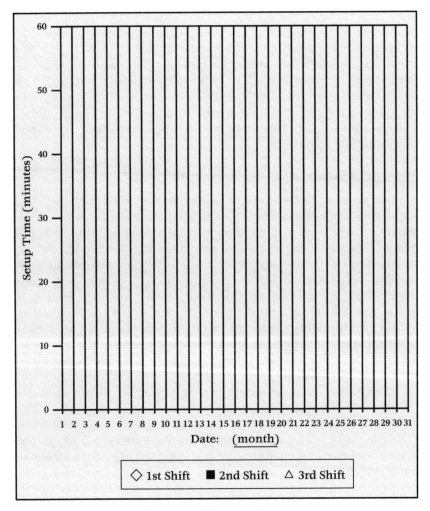

Figure 8.17. Setup Chart

production efficiency. Effectively sustaining such improvements requires constant and current feedback at all levels. Traditionally employed production reporting schemes, more often than not based on the perceived needs of accountants, have many limitations. Many provide indirect data, such as standard hours earned, and do it too late, showing what happened yesterday, last week, or last month.

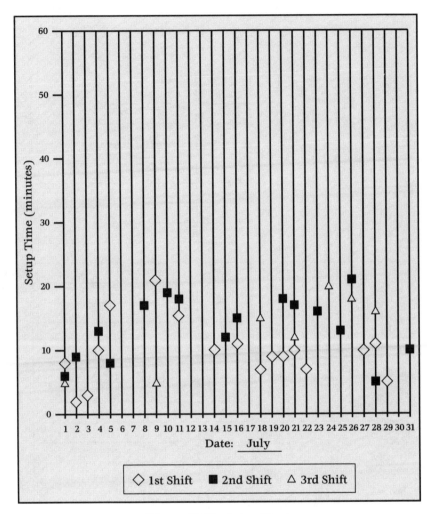

Figure 8.18. Setup Chart

A great deficiency commonly shared is the usual focus up the management chain. Consolidated reports are produced for higher-level review. They are generally inaccessible or not understandable by those who do the work. (They are often not understood by management, as well.)

Another deficiency is that data is often gathered remotely or without the direct involvement of the workers, leading to skepticism and lack of ownership of the results.

		Target Output	Actual Output	Comments
Date: Cell: Item:				
	1:00			
	2:00			
	3:00			
Shift 3	4:00			
	5:00			
12:00 A.M.–8:00 A.M.	6:00			
	7:00			
	8:00			
	9:00			
	10:00			
	11:00			
Shift 1	12:00			
	1:00			
8:00 A.M.–4:00 P.M.	2:00			
	3:00			
	4:00			
	5:00			
	6:00			
	7:00			
Shift 2	8:00			
	9:00			
4:00 P.M.–12:00 A.M.	10:00			
	11:00			
	12:00			

Figure 8.19. Daily Production Chart

Date: 7/14/98
Cell: Valve #2

		Target Output	Actual Output	Comments
Item: PRH-9	1:00	42	0	Setup
	2:00	42	41	
	3:00	42	38	
Shift 3	4:00	42	44	
	5:00	42	24	Broken bit
12:00 A.M.–8:00 A.M.	6:00	42	40	
	7:00	42	28	Oversized bores
	8:00	42	0	Scheduled P.M.
Item: PRH-9	9:00	42	15	Minor setup
	10:00	42	42	
	11:00	42	43	
Shift 1	12:00	42	10	Team meeting
	1:00	42	41	
8:00 A.M.–4:00 P.M.	2:00	42	44	
	3:00	42	33	Part shortage
	4:00	42	0	Out of spacers
Item: PRH-12	5:00	26	9	Setup–12's
	6:00	26	25	
	7:00	26	6	Team meeting
Shift 2	8:00	26	28	
	9:00	26	24	
4:00 P.M.–12:00 A.M.	10:00	26	26	
	11:00	26	20	Adjust hones
	12:00	26	29	

Figure 8.20. Daily Production Chart: Example

One easy solution to these problems is a simple daily production chart. It can be set up to show hour-by-hour results and causes of shortfalls (another interval may make sense in your organization) and focuses on direct measures of what is wanted—output per hour, for example. Based in the workplace, they provide current information to everyone involved in the process so that actions can then be undertaken immediately to remedy problems. With regular analysis recurring patterns can also be discerned and future improvement projects planned. Because the charts are filled out and maintained by operators themselves, credibility and ownership are strong.

An almost infinite variety of such charts can be developed as the needs of the work dictate. The basic principle is to show what is being done, targets for output, and actual performance. Space for comments and observations is critical. Figure 8.19 is a typical example of such a chart.

Figure 8.20 is an example of a daily production chart that has been filled out to show hourly performance with comments explaining shortfalls. Products being run and changeovers needed can be clearly seen and the information is available to all spark actions as needed.

In some cases it will be useful to use the daily production chart concept as the basis for charts to track cumulative production to target through the day. These can take a number of forms, but simplicity and immediacy remain the keys to effectiveness.

Whatever tools are chosen to monitor the progress of work, they should be chosen and applied in accordance with the themes of *simplicity*, *immediacy*, and *consistency*.

Chapter 9

Sustaining the Gain

This chapter looks at what happens *after* the initial investment in education, training, team building, and project execution has begun to achieve some remarkable results. Maintaining the new and improved version of the process the Kaizen Blitz team has so skillfully created—sustaining the gain—is perhaps the most difficult discipline an organization must learn. Just as kaizen achieves its remarkable results through the application of commonsense methods in a highly focused and disciplined fashion, so too, the follow-up, support, and lasting changes in work habits that are needed to sustain the improvements it brings depend on acquiring a new set of disciplines. Incorporating new lasting disciplines has proven for many to be far more difficult to master than the disciplines of the Kaizen Blitz itself.

Many of the leading lights in the kaizen firmament report that their early efforts, although blessed with strong management support and mentored by real experts in the field, turned out to be mere softening-up exercises. Many months of initial project results withered away or failed to yield meaningful results in terms of real business performance improvement.

Gathering and focusing teams on challenging problems and having them meet or even stretch beyond their goals can invigorate an organization. It is easy to find advocates for this new and powerful tool of change and to see it applied to an ever-broadening spectrum of applications and processes, across a plant or even a whole business. Unfortunately, in the enthusiasm for the kaizen process itself and the celebration of its individual successes, organizations fail to see the deeper, more fundamental changes that are needed before real sustained process improvement can be realized. Integration of immediate successes with long-term objectives and focused management attention is critical.

■ REALISTIC EXPECTATIONS

➤ Wiremold Sustains the Gain

The Wiremold Company is widely recognized as a world leader in lean manufacturing. Arnold J. Sargis headed Wiremold's just-in-time (JIT) promotion office during its widely reported and spectacularly successful implementation of JIT principles through kaizen. During his tenure. Sargis and his team carried out over 800 kaizen projects within the Wiremold operation and with scores of suppliers. He relates the following story:

> From the outset, Wiremold's management, led by Art Byrne, its dynamic new president, wholeheartedly embraced a rapid implementation of JIT principles through kaizen. Byrne led by example.
>
> He personally taught kaizen classes. His staff served as team members in every imaginable type of project, visibly supporting the difficult changes they were asking the organization to bring about. World class consulting services were constantly in evidence, at not inconsiderable expense. They trained, coached, and critiqued, always raising the bar.
>
> Staff members, as well as a number of shop-floor associates, were sent to Japan to learn about the Toyota production system at its roots, in the factories where it was developed. Facilitators had the chance to work on production lines and on kaizen teams in Japan to experience the process first-hand and to learn from true masters with decades of real experience. Management spared little expense and did everything it could to follow best practices and give real support throughout the implementation.
>
> Despite these efforts and the success of initial projects, the first six to eight months of achievement were hard to see in

terms of real change in the way the business worked. Many projects that had yielded spectacular results quickly faded, and much momentum was lost. Old practices reemerged and erased some of the new ways the teams had developed. The age-old problem of people under stress reverting to what they knew and felt comfortable with was hard to overcome. Sargis emphasizes: "It's so easy to go back to the old way."

To Byrne's credit, he had anticipated the difficulties they would encounter and was prepared for the long road ahead. Changing the physical part of a process, building a cell for example, is simple. The cell remains because the machines were moved and are in a new place; the old structure isn't visible any longer. But changing the way people behave, how they go about their work in setting up a machine, is another matter. This kind of human change requires commitment, perseverance, and discipline.

As Sargis puts it, "If you don't have top management commitment, with a capital "C," bold and underlined, it won't work."

■ LESSONS LEARNED

Organizations must learn how to sustain gains before real business process improvements can be realized.

Learning how to change, how to achieve radical improvements with highly focused kaizen teams in narrowly targeted areas, is only a first step. Overall change in business performance requires repeated application of the kaizen process to link a series of projects until whole product or process flows are clarified or streamlined. This is the first point or level at which real improvement in the performance of a plant or business unit is likely to be discernable, and this point is not easily reached.

Once competence is achieved in the selection of projects, the organization of kaizen teams, and successful execution, the next step is to learn how to apply this powerful technique in the right place, in the right sequence, and at the right time. The organization must learn to select projects that link together to overcome constraints and interruptions to establish a uniform flow from one step to another in producing a product. Chapter 6 outlines the basic phases of this process, but in practice most organizations must still spend considerable time in trial-and-error effort developing their own competence.

But, even this level of achievement, and it is certainly a real achievement, is not enough.

Unless individual gains can be substantially sustained, linking together projects to improve whole product or process flows doesn't work.

Even if we consider only a 50 percent long-term retention of the improvements achieved by a kaizen team as substantial, most companies will find great difficulty in meeting this standard. The problem then, is in learning how to sustain the gain, to make the new methods developed by the kaizen team the ongoing, everyday practice.

■ CHANGING THE CULTURE

The transition to a JIT, lean, flow-based (you pick the term) philosophy of operation should be seen as an evolutionary process composed of three basic steps or phases (see Figure 9.1). The first phase brings the concept of change itself and validates it for the organization. The next refers to developing and institutionalizing improvement skills across the organization, making them part of the job for everyone. The last, standard work, requires the creation of the disciplined workplace that makes it possible to sustain the gains in a broad sense, yielding real improvement in overall business performance. These last, difficult to accomplish, phases require real changes to the basic culture of the organization. The effort required is great, and the potential reward is in proportion to that effort.

■ CHANGE: KAIZEN BLITZ AS A CATALYST OF CHANGE

At the outset, kaizen is a powerful tool for bringing change to the workplace. Highly visible teams, focusing intently on change and

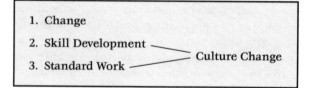

1. Change

2. Skill Development

3. Standard Work — Culture Change

Figure 9.1. Changing the Culture

seemingly working outside all the traditional constraints, rules, and norms of the organization, achieve what appear to be unbelievable results, in the blink of an eye. Emphasis is on the shop floor, the people who do the work. Their voices are heard; their suggestions are implemented. As a matter of fact, they *do* the implementing. Management praises their accomplishments. Change is in the air.

All of this can certainly have a salutary effect on the spirit of an organization, opening up channels of communication across all levels and disciplines, building mutual respect, and more; new leaders and experts appear where before there were none. In truth, this is often as far as many companies will go or want to go. They use a Kaizen Blitz as a catalyst, as a way of demonstrating that rapid change can happen and that all employees have potential for contribution far beyond and outside their traditional roles. A new tool is validated that can become a useful part of the repertoire of improvement techniques an operation can bring to bear when needed.

At this level, the kinds of improvements that are most likely to be maintained are those that involve a significant physical change in the workplace. Building cells is a classic example. Once machinery has been brought together from former functional locations and grouped tightly into a cell, reverting to the old batch-and-queue, large-lot philosophy can't be done. The change in the physical structure of the workplace, in this case, largely dictates how the work must be done. The time taken to do a setup, or the number of people in the cell, or its output may deteriorate from results demonstrated by the original team, but the workflow concept cannot change.

Similarly, if the kaizen team, by eliminating non-value-adding activities, does away with redundant forms or meaningless reporting steps, the steps should not spontaneously return. The principle behind sustaining a part of the improvement here lies in eliminating the old path, or making it invisible or impossible to follow again.

➤ Taking the First Step

This first step, preparing for and conducting a Kaizen Blitz, bringing and demonstrating real change, is a needed one, a foundation stone of the changes that must follow if a truly broad-scale improvement campaign that takes full advantages of kaizen's potential is to be pursued.

This first phase of bringing change itself to the organization demonstrates that things can and *will* change and that the process can be a positive one in which all levels of the organization participate. Kaizen, by its dramatic nature, is an excellent tool for this task. In this first phase, however, no real commitment to changing the culture of the organization is needed. To move forward to the next levels, where changing the *way* people work is fundamental to the gain, the hard work of changing the culture must begin.

■ DEVELOPING NEW SKILLS

Serving as a member of a kaizen team doesn't really change what one does for a living. The assignment is temporary, the experience may be intense, but the temporary change and empowerment it brings is often seen as a refreshing departure from the day-to-day routine of a regular job, the *real* job.

Developing the skills to apply kaizen as a regular improvement tool for all or most of the associates and staff in an organization is the second phase of the change process and the first major cultural change that must take place. If kaizen is to be an effective tool for change and the direction of change and momentum of change is to be maintained, the skills needed to apply kaizen must be developed and honed across a broad spectrum of the organization. Learning and applying these skills and techniques then becomes part of the job for many, if not all employees. Engineers, customer service specialists, administration, traffic, and purchasing professionals are all part of the team.

The long-term objective of kaizen is to put the tools of improvement directly in the hands of the organization, the people who do and support the work. They can then learn to recognize the need and opportunity for improvement and take the actions needed to get there. This, for most, is a radical departure from the narrowly proscribed, "get the work out" assignments typical in the workplace.

➤ Visibility Helps

As an organization evolves and moves toward a JIT environment, people can more easily see for themselves what needs to be done through pull signals and other visual management cues. Over time they will also gradually equip themselves with the tools to *do* what needs to be done. This whole process of change de-emphasizes traditional supervisory roles and changes the ways in which a host of supporting disciplines interact and provide their services. The workplace becomes more inherently self-directed, perhaps not through a formal articulated process designed to develop self-directed teams, but as a direct consequence of the process of wringing out waste, leaving only the bare minimum of information, equipment, and process in the workplace, in the hands of the people who do the work.

➤ Career Change Hurts

Changing the culture to accept and embrace new concepts and roles is difficult at best, particularly when change begins to strike directly at the heart of what people do and have done throughout their careers. Many will find the path uncomfortable or unwanted. There are many examples of organizations in which numbers of individuals have opted out or even been forced out because they were unwilling or unable to adapt to new roles. The new roles include the mastery and application of improvement techniques and particularly for first-line and middle management, the changes can be profound. The old supervisory roles with their heavy emphasis on deciding what needs to be done and getting people to do it become less and less pertinent or needed. This creates demands for the development of new skills, a real need for coaches, guides, and facilitators. These are roles for which many, particularly in the traditional supervisory hierarchy, find themselves ill equipped.

➤ New Roles, New Measures

Moving through this transition to the next level is for many organizations a watershed. This is where some of the hard decision making and soul searching begins. If the real objective of the organization is to build a truly JIT environment, then the roles of a major proportion of both shop floor and management associates must change, in some cases profoundly. It is commonly reported that the adaptation of associates on the factory floor poses far fewer difficulties than the adjustments needed at the first and second level of management. This problem has its roots in the composition of traditional supervisory jobs, the selection, processes by which they are filled, and the behaviors that are rewarded.

In a typical manufacturing operation, a "push" environment, a large part of a first-line supervisor's time may be spent determining what needs to be done next—tracking down the next job, finding the materials, filling out the shop orders, and so on. Another major element of the job is to tell his or her associates what to do, often how to do it, and to make sure that it gets done—within the rates or other measured parameters set for the work. A third, and often the most highly recognized role, is that of expeditor—making sure that the rush order gets through on time, especially on the last Friday of the month. People who prove themselves adept at this kind of impromptu organizing and direction under fire, while meeting the numbers by which performance is traditionally measured (earned hours or the like), are often seen as ideal models of the resourceful supervisor. The selection and reward process naturally reinforces the importance of these roles and behaviors, and the promotional ladder is commonly filled by those who have earned their stripes by these measures.

In consequence, when the demands of a JIT environment begin to call for a completely different skill set and when new more direct measures such as "customer orders filled on time" displace the old, many find themselves ill prepared for the change.

➤ Reskilling

Dealing with this transition is never easy. Frequently, several levels of management and a variety of functions must face the challenges of change. Clearly, opportunities for training or reskilling should be offered. Look for alternative functions for those who struggle with the transition. Almost inevitably, however, some will fall out or opt out of the process. The ways in which your organization can deal with their situations will color the perceptions of the overall process for all. One thing that stands out again and again is the need for commitment, integrity, and trust in the process. Getting people to change their behavior, and that's what we're asking them to do, particularly after years, even decades of reinforcement, can be traumatic. How we manage their transitions speaks volumes about true commitment and trust.

In dwelling on the problems the transition poses for many, we shouldn't overlook those who see opportunity in change. Some see the opportunity for personal growth and professional advancement. Others see opportunity to break out of tired routines. Some see change as a risk, but a lesser risk than continuing on old paths that no longer work and seem only to lead to failure. An organization intent on change and improvement needs to identify, nuture, and encourage these risk takers and potential leaders. They can become the scouts and pioneers who blaze the new trails and help remap the processes and ultimately the enterprise itself. The kinds of change that are needed are difficult to achieve, and the more who can and will help, the better!

■ STANDARD WORK

Standard work is the foundation of improvement. It has been said that there can be no improvement without it. Simply stated, standard work is the combined set of instructions that define and clearly illustrate how every aspect of the work is to be performed. They include the simple mechanics of what is to be done, as found in a typical shop routing: "Drive the screw, apply the label." But they go far beyond these in detailing how almost everything is done and *how everyone* works. There are, as described in Chapters 2, 6 and 8, a number of more-or-less standardized ways of assembling and displaying this needed information in the workplace. One of the key responsibilities of a Kaizen Blitz team is to prepare standard work diagrams and instructions and to leave them in the workplace as a guide to how the work should be performed from then on. The principle of standard work is that the work will only be performed in the way and at the rates in which it is described and documented in the standard work instructions. If this discipline is followed, then the measured performance achieved by a Kaizen Blitz team can be substantially replicated on an ongoing basis.

Developing and institutionalizing the disciplines of standard work is perhaps the most difficult phase of transition for an organization to master. It is also generally a later phase of transition, as other adjustments in behavior and approach that have gone before must have been reasonably well absorbed before this challenge can be seriously undertaken.

➤ Discipline

Kaizen is a disciplined process, a framework within which improvement steps are taken to reach a goal. But kaizen is also an innovative process through which a variety of unique and creative solutions are developed and applied. This dichotomy between innovation and discipline is a basic characteristic of the kaizen process. Kaizen is in some ways a liberating and empowering process that leads to the creation of a highly disciplined environment. It is this disciplined environment that must be realized in order for standard work disciplines to become the norm and the basis for sustaining improvement throughout the operation.

We can think of the kaizen experience as leading two waves of cultural change. The first gives emphasis to process improvement and begins the transitions necessary to make it part of everyone's daily responsibilities.

This then leads to a second, deeper change, the creation of a disciplined environment. Without this second cultural change, the disciplines necessary for sustaining real improvement and the baselines from which to move ahead to the next level of improvement cannot be established. Recognizing the need for this change and major actions needed to bring it about are critical to success.

➤ Denial or "Not Invented Here"

Perceiving the reality of the current environment is the first step toward understanding the kind and magnitude of change that is needed. Many business leaders will argue that their organizations, their factories, are already well disciplined. They will point out that there are rules, procedures, and policies that describe and mandate how work is to be performed and how transactions are conducted. They will also point out that discipline is really at the core of their management systems, with measurements in place to ensure that performance does not vary considerably from the norm or standard that has been set for it. (Variance accounting and management long ago reached the level of religion in many firms.) The question may legitimately be asked: "How many of these rules and regulations are visible to or even known to the people who do the work?"

Another emphasis on discipline often cited is the current zeal for quality system or process "certification." The manufacture and marketing of "ISO9000" and "QS9000" banners, flags, jackets, and more must be an enormous business. The consulting and certification and audit groups that support these and other similar initiatives seem to grow almost daily, as well. European and U.S. industries spend substantial sums and dedicate significant resources to certification processes such as these. Isn't this evidence of a real commitment to discipline?

➤ Documentation

The most-often-heard simple, and overly simplified, statement of the philosophy behind these initiatives is "Say what you do and do what you say." In other words, document your processes and make sure that you follow the process you've documented. It is the level of detail in the documentation here and the kinds of actions that are documented that are the issue with respect to standard work.

Depending on the industry in question—the semiconductor industry is a good example—internal documentation and control of difficult technical processes may go to extremes to ensure the production of quality products at predictable costs. In other cases there is the issue of compliance with safety certification and regulatory agency standards to be met in the production of products. Underwriters Laboratories, Canadian Standards Association, IEC, VDE, the Federal Aviation Administration, and many other groups publish detailed regulations that cover process documentation and specific required testing steps. Many also audit periodically for conformance of product as well as of process documentation and control systems. Again, an argument can be made that disciplines inherent in these businesses are sound, but the focus is generally on what is done and not on the circumstances that surround its being done—that is, how people go about their work. Again, this is what sets this kind of discipline apart from standard work disciplines.

Of course, there are many ways in which disciplines are applied in businesses today. There are, as well, many differences in the level and rigor with which disciplines are applied in various work environments, even within a single company. The concept of standard work incorporates many elements of the disciplines discussed above but goes considerably beyond them.

Standard work instructions normally include the "mechanics" of how a process is to be performed:

1.1. Install screw with air driver to 10-inch oz. torque.

1.2. Conduct ground continuity test.

1.3. Apply inspection stamp.

1.4. Install label.

1.5. Etc, etc.

These may be the same or even be in the same form an organization already employs routinely. Where standard work documentation and discipline go far beyond what is normally found in the workplace is in defining the organization of the workplace and the detailed methods that people use to conduct their work.

In comparing what is found in a typical manufacturing environment with that found in a standard work environment, one can quickly conclude that typical work environments are relatively undisciplined. That is, rather than defining in detail much of how each worker does his or her job, we grant considerable latitude to individuals in how they carry out their work.

The concept of finding a best way of doing the job and having everyone conform to that way, until a better one is found and agreed to is not the operative rule in most workplaces. It is perhaps best to explain this fundamental difference through examples.

➤ Standard Work for Setups

Setup reduction projects are a common first focus of kaizen teams because setups are usually an obvious source of much waste. Time spent changing machines over from one product to another is lost to production. Lengthy machine setup times are often real bottlenecks and impediments to a continuous flow of production. And the results that can be achieved by well-run teams are dramatic, with 80 to 90 percent reductions in changeover time almost commonplace.

When gathering baseline data in preparation for a Kaizen Blitz event, the team leader is charged with determining the current setup time, the starting point. Invariably, particularly in multiple-shift operations, a fairly broad range of answers can be found. Some of the differences depend on who is asked, or which set of performance measurement data is referenced. (It is almost axiomatic that generally the time required becomes greater the closer one gets to the people who do the actual work.) But some of the variation comes from real differences in how the work is done, either by one shift versus another or by one operator versus another. There may be written procedures, but generally they only define the major steps of bolting on the tools, making adjustments, getting the work inspected, and so forth.

The dramatic improvements the kaizen team develops come from analyzing the process at a much more detailed level, step by step, from beginning to end. Nothing is taken for granted:

How far does the setter walk to get a tool?

How much time is spent rummaging through a tool box to find a socket, for example?

How long does it take to get a set of prints or specs?

The team's solutions are based on eliminating as much waste as possible from the process.

The kaizen team literally choreographs the setup. The team completely documents the way the work should be done from then on. It leaves behind complete and detailed instructions on every aspect of the setup. If these procedures are followed, the old 60-minute setup can indeed be replaced by one performed in 10 or 15 minutes. We know it can because the team demonstrated seven- or eight-minute setups.

Following those instructions to the letter, every time the job is done and by everyone who does the job, is the essence of standard work.

SOME PRINCIPLES OF SETUP REDUCTION

➤ Only needed items are left at the machine.

➤ All unneeded materials are removed.

➤ Specific hand tools are mounted on tool boards close at hand, not left in a tool chest.

➤ A key principle is that the setup person should not leave the machine once the changeover has begun.

➤ A second operator may assist at particular points during the setup.

Displaying, using, and reacting to charts that show the time required for each setup is another fundamental of the standard work philosophy. The key measurement in the workplace is the new one, set by the Kaizen Blitz team. The usual simple measure is the time in minutes spent to make the change from one part to the next. The objective for the worker is to do the work the same way every time and to get the same result every time. Management's role is to monitor the process, using the same simple measure, and to reinforce the disciplines to maintain the process. (See the discussion of performance measurement in Chapter 8 and Figures 8.17 and 8.18.)

➤ A New Level of Discipline

The problem faced by most organizations is that the concept of discipline and the forms of work instruction and oversight used have never been applied at this level of detail before. Further, the human aspects of applying this level of discipline can be challenging. If it is normal for each machine setter to have his or her own (locked) tool box, and to use the tools and approach that is most comfortable, the whole concept of a standardized process such as this will be hard to swallow.

That is one of the reasons why setup reduction teams like to involve as many associates as possible, particularly members from off-shifts who may not ordinarily be exposed to other improvement processes. The hope is that their involvement will bring with it ownership of the solution—the new process—and along with that the feeling that this new process is indeed the easiest way to get the job done. However, even if everyone could be on the team—and they can't—an underlying discipline is still needed.

➤ Productivity: Staffing the Cell

Another common assignment for kaizen teams is to build manufacturing cells from separate functional process steps and equipment. Their work differs from that of the setup reduction team in that they first create a new arrangement of operations and bring together groups of operators in the new environment they've created for the first time. This brings some new dynamics into the equation that make their analysis and structuring of the work more difficult and their subsequent documentation of the new process more critical.

As with the setup teams, a great deal of attention is paid to timing operation steps. A basic flow concept is established, and through a trial-and-error process, the team tries various arrangements of equipment and people to meet their goals of productivity or process time. Balancing the work among the associates to equalize effort and make sure it can be performed without fatigue or risk of injuries is a major part of what they do.

The standard work documentation that a cell-building team develops defines the configuration of the cell and the complement of associates who will operate it. In some cases, where a cell is intended to operate at more than one output level—to meet seasonal demand for example—the complement of workers for each level is defined.

Ordinarily, the standard work documentation also shows how the individual operators fit into the cell, that is, where they stand or sit and what operations each performs. In some cases, where a few people move around within a relatively large cell, the standard work sheet indeed resembles a choreographer's diagram, with footprints on the charts showing their movement from place to place.

Once the cell is in operation, formal time observations establish the range of time needed to perform each step in the operation and give the overall cycle time of the cell versus its takt time target. In the case of cells designed for multiple output levels, this documentation is repeated for each level. As in the setup reduction example, careful attention is paid to the placement of tools and location of materials.

Performance measures typically consist of simple output charts that show output at hourly (or sometimes other) intervals versus targets and track daily variations. As with setups, management's attention to these measures, common measures that everyone understands, and reinforcement of the standard work disciplines is an imperative. (See the discussion of the daily production chart in Chapter 8 and Figures 8.19 and 8.20.)

As in our other example, getting the workforce—and supervision—to understand the importance of everyone doing the work in exactly the same way takes effort and real commitment.

From these examples it should be clear that the kind of discipline we refer to in the context of standard work has quite a different definition than that we normally apply. Achieving the kind of disciplined behavior described above may seem challenging indeed. But how much more challenging must it be to reach this level of consistent adherence to norms across a whole plant or company? This is the real challenge that must be recognized by management, because *standard work sustains the gain.*

■ TAKE IT FROM THE TOP

Changing the culture of an organization so that it accepts and practices standard work is difficult. The need for a simple, universally understandable, and easy-to-follow approach has to be understood by everyone from top management to the kaizen teams who are developing the process improvements themselves.

Every organization should have its own set of basics that defines the general expectations of the workforce. It includes overarching work rules that everyone understands and follows and the common technologies that everyone is expected to understand and master.

Developing the skills in the organization to create the kind of documentation of process steps and techniques needed is hard to do. The process of practice, observation, repetition, and refinement becomes an endless cycle. The first step may be to learn how to clearly describe how one goes about his or her own work in sufficient detail so that someone else can do it from the instruction alone. It soon becomes clear from this exercise that a common language is needed—everyone looking at and breaking down tasks in the same way, using a common approach to describe how they are done.

Instructions for operators should be simple and self-created, and over time they should evolve to a common, easily understood pattern. If they are developed and written by the operators themselves, they are more likely to be simple, direct, and usable. Stick with simple declarative statements; there is no room for technical jargon or abstract concepts here. Try reading a regulation or spec form from one of the regulatory agencies that looks in on your business. Is this the kind of instruction that will be crystal clear to an operator on the third shift at 3 A.M.? Is it clear to you now?

We have described the work of a setup reduction team as choreographing the setup process. As choreographers, they must keep in mind the talent and skills of the performers. Complex, hard-to-execute steps may work for a few seasoned and talented professionals, but the average performer will be plagued by missteps and failure. That kind of performance won't be repeated willingly. Cross-training associates so that they can demonstrate a common skill set helps not only in giving flexibility to the workforce but in establishing a mutual understanding of the skills inherent in the workplace. This makes knowing what makes up an understandable and executable standard work document easier in the long run.

Reinforce instructions by making sure that the kaizen teams, and everyone for that matter, focus on developing easier ways to do things—ergonomics matter. New ways of working will tend to stick if they are seen as easing the effort required. When the old way seems easier, backsliding happens.

Documentation can take many forms. Often, critical instructions are hard to convey quickly and unambiguously in words alone. Visual aids of all kinds are often employed to enhance understanding. Actual pieces of hardware may be used to clarify good/bad conditions; videotapes may give a clear description, and even computer displays (be sure that you know what "user friendly" really means) may be used to visually break down a complex process.

Fail safing operations—arranging things or steps so that they can only be done one way, the right way—is a powerful way to help cement a standard work process. This takes some learning and development of skills, but many simple techniques can be used to good effect. *Poka yoke* techniques should become part of the improvement repertoire as the organization advances.

■ MEETING THE CHALLENGE

Arnie Sargis puts it succinctly when he relates a conversation he had with a Japanese expert. He asked him why he and others from Japan were willing to share many of the secrets of their success in kaizen with U.S. companies, many of whom are strong competitors. The Japanese expert replied that U.S. companies don't have the self-discipline to sustain real improvements for the long term. That may have once been the common wisdom. But more and more, companies are demonstrating that disciplines such as we describe here can be successfully established. There are few, to be sure, who have traveled the whole road, but the message is clear; With conviction, commitment, and perseverance, success can be achieved.

■ PLANNING FOR FAILURE

The kind and magnitude of cultural change needed to establish a successful standard work environment requires a real commitment and understanding on the part of top management. It also requires a realistic understanding of the length of the road to be traveled. Change like this cannot come overnight, and the prospect for failure along the way is real.

Launching teams, building cells, changing traditional measures, and establishing new standards of performance are all actions that focus on, and depend on, people. An organization cannot bring about such dramatic changes in the ways that people work and interact with each other without suffering some failures along the way. Planning for such failures, sharing realistic expectations about the difficulty of the path with the rest of the organization, is essential.

One of the objectives of the benchmarking and expert mentoring recommended in earlier chapters is to help to establish a clear understanding of the kinds of change that can be required and to learn how others have dealt with them; both what has worked and what hasn't. Keep in mind, however, that each organization has its own unique culture that grows from the business it is in and from the backgrounds and personalities of the people who make it up. Solutions to problems of change must therefore, be uniquely developed for each organization.

We can learn what others have done, but we cannot always directly apply their lessons to our own problems. What is important is that the magnitude of change required is recognized and that management is prepared to make the kind of real and lasting commitments required to see them through. That in the end is the only way to sustain the gains.

Chapter 10

Lean Leadership

Any successful organization, particularly one based on lean principles, needs the right kind of leadership.

Leaders of powerful continuous improvement initiatives such as AME's Kaizen Blitz are a new and special breed. They understand that the demands of a typical Kaizen Blitz require the leader to know how to encourage and facilitate, to know when to direct and when not to manage. Very often, the biggest challenge for the lean organization's leader is to learn and try to adopt the appropriate level and style of management for this new process.

Too much direction, and kaizen teams never break free to form their own processes; they never trust the work or feel real ownership. Too little direction, and the change may be misdirected or not fulfill the overall need. Learning to manage in a lean environment, driving change through the kaizen process, takes a whole new management mind-set, and for some, the challenge is too difficult.

Kaizen leaders understand the overwhelming importance of their role as guide, cheerleader, mentor, and above all, leader. They understand that the Kaizen Blitz event is first a learning process—not all results are intended to flow directly to the bottom line. Beyond the specific improvement needs they fill, employees' kaizen experiences are intended to teach problem solving and a way of thinking about production; a good kaizen event creates a path for more worker involvement, for real participation in the business. From suggestion systems to redesigning product and process flows to redefining their own jobs.

Successful kaizen leaders look for the learning as well as the results.
The learning is a part of the development of the whole organization, for indeed, the long-term goal is to change the thinking of all of the associates about the business and to engage them in improving the business.

Any successful organization, particularly one based on lean principles, needs the right kind of leadership. Kaizen is one of the tools of lean manufacturing, the primary implementation tool for converting a business to one that focuses on driving out waste of all kinds in pursuit of perfection in customer satisfaction.

Because the primary role of kaizen is to bring about change, radical change, leadership for change is an absolute essential to sustained success. Moreover, the demands of lean organizations are special because lean organizations need flexibility and the ability to change, they need to be philosophy or principle driven, and they need to value people as well as machines and processes.

■ LEAN MANUFACTURING

Lean manufacturing is an approach to production, to the whole enterprise, that aims to quickly and efficiently satisfy customer needs by reducing the production process to its core value-adding elements, eliminating waste in all forms throughout the enterprise.

A lean organization's goal is to provide products or services *as needed, when needed, without waste, and without flaw.*

Lean operations are driven by simple customer demand, a pull-versus-push strategy. Customer demand, ideally, is immediately translated to appropriate actions, pulling materials from suppliers and adding value continuously until the final form needed by the customer is achieved. Rapid, lean processes emphasize speed and responsiveness, driving out backlogs and minimizing dependence on forecasts—sources of waiting time for the customer, a major waste.

Lean organizations tend to be team-based both in organization for production and as the operative basis for all improvement initiatives. Teams build flexibility and emphasize information sharing. Learning, therefore, becomes an underlying strategy and a core competence for the workforce of the lean organization.

Learning takes place at many levels and in many forms, whether it is planned hours per month in the classroom, developing specific technical skills, or cross-training for greater flexibility. Learning happens in classrooms, on the factory floor, or even at other sites, on benchmarking expeditions.

The emphasis on continuously adding value (one-piece flow) is a hallmark of the lean enterprise. On the manufacturing floor, one sees machines dedicated to specific functions—cutting, grinding, assembly—arranged in cells to allow workers to complete a customer order without shuffling parts around the entire plant; teams of workers meeting to review schedules and quietly disbursing to complete the job; visual management signals—painted kanban squares on the floor, color-coded line-side parts storage; housekeeping and plant maintenance that suggests careful attention to detail and the standards of a laboratory; above all, clearly visible, simple, and easily understood performance measures.

■ LEADERSHIP TYPES

As we have observed in hundreds of very different teams employing the Kaizen Blitz process, the qualities of an ideal leader have emerged. Other management styles can derail the process, undermine workers' confidence, or so dilute the benefits that focus and momentum are lost. The kaizen process depends on trust, individual initiative, and a real drive to succeed. Inappropriate leadership approaches can quickly destroy its effectiveness as a tool for implementing lean manufacturing principles and thereby destroy the effectiveness of lean manufacturing itself.

There are three identified leadership types, each of which we can view in a production environment: the results-oriented leader, the process-oriented leader, and the lean leader (see Figure 10.1).

➤ The Results-Oriented Leader

The results-oriented, or "get-it-done-at-all-costs," leader is focused purely on a goal; "Just get it done." Sometimes the more rules you break, the better. This hard-charging leader is not seeking answers about how to improve the process; indeed, bad news about process capabilities often elicit a "shoot-the-messenger" response. Production workers and lower echelon management learn to play this leadership game by being politically tough and smart; they always hold back some critical information.

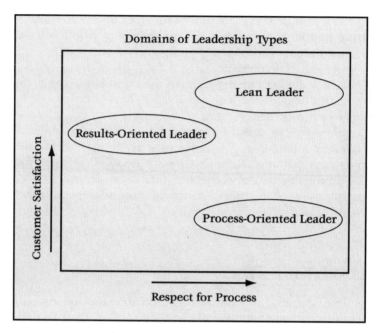

Figure 10.1. Leadership Types

➤ The Process-Oriented Leader

The slogan of the process-oriented, or "trust-the-system," leader is "Don't violate the process." He or she believes that strict adherence to process alone will bring success, maybe not now, but eventually. Hesitant to make real and radical change, this leader is unwilling to stretch or stress the process to meet the *real* needs of the business. Frequently, process improvements and understanding of how to flex and improve processes are buried by this dogmatic approach to maintaining the status quo.

➤ The Lean Leader

There are times during the kaizen process when the leader must pull, or motivate the associates to move ahead, but there are also times when the leader's job is to stand by, cheer at the successes, and silently witness the near failures. An experienced kaizen champion can read the flow of the project, as well as the strengths and weaknesses of the team, and knows when to intervene. The lean leader has a balanced leadership style—not merely a blend of the first two leader types, but a balanced combination of the positive attributes of both.

From a kaizen standpoint, the lean leader is the champion of the team's process, a leader who insists on and rewards getting things done the *right* way—the right way being one that adheres to lean-manufacturing principles and follows the processes that the team's have built.

A consistent, measured leadership style is appreciated by kaizen practitioners. Even when teams and their leaders "make mistakes," the strong support and guidance of an enlightened leader allow participants to move on, maintaining their momentum. Effective leadership is needed if lean manufacturing is to be a sustaining philosophy of the business rather than just a demonstration.

■ LEADERSHIP WITH INTEGRITY

No effective leadership styles work without integrity because so much of the success of each project or phase depends on trust. Workers and managers must trust their ability to examine all possible causes of waste, for example, and be empowered to proceed with its elimination.

To successfully lead an organization through what is clearly a radical change a leader needs to be *trusted*.

■ LEADERSHIP CHARACTERISTICS

Let's look at the characteristics of the three leader types we've described.

➤ Type 1: The Goal or Results-Oriented Leader

How does the results-oriented leader behave? This leader's mottoes are "Take the hill at all costs," "Break all the rules if you need to," and "The greater the crisis, the greater the reward." This type of leader doesn't respect the process or the structure.

Although this leader verbally supports the process, his or her actions destroy the message and reinforce the feeling that "rule breaking is okay."

Type 1 leaders justify their actions by expedients—the external "beyond our control" situations that make rule breaking excusable:

The customer

The end of the month/quarter/year

The Type 1 leaders are telling their colleagues, the whole organization, that the process or system *can't* get the job done, that they you can't trust it in a crisis.

This also says that crises, situations the *system* can't handle, are to be expected, that they are unavoidable. In other words, we can't build a system that deals with the randomness of the real world and the argument is that it is unreasonable to expect to be able to do so.

When words and actions don't match, there is an integrity gap.

Another common Type 1 behavior is to impose solutions. This is particularly damaging in the lean environment. A typical example is to second guess a kaizen team—"This would be better" (unsaid: "Better do it my way"). A consistent set of beliefs is not apparent—it may be articulated, but opportunistically chosen actions don't follow a consistent theme. The words don't go with the music. Type 1 leaders don't demonstrate by their actions that they have a long view (of the lean manufacturing process) or are committed to a long-term vision.

This type of leader may do well during a Kaizen event, supporting the innovations and approaches taken by the team during the project period itself, but not in following up and sustaining the gain—that's where support *really* counts.

➤ Type 2: The Process-Oriented Leader

Now let's look at what we call the process-oriented leader. Type 2's motto is "Trust the process; eventually things will work out." This behavior reveals a mixed message: The words say "Radical change is what we *want*, not "Radical change is what we *must have*."

Change tends to be compartmentalized under this type of leadership; effects are contained so as not to disrupt the system and are brought about through a gradual, methodical process. Initiatives are often limited to changing how things are done, not *what* is done: for example, in an administrative process, finding ways to handle all of the forms more quickly, not eliminating most of them altogether!

Although the process is respected and procedures perhaps religiously maintained, the system is protected from stress. It's not put to the test.

These leaders talk about the customer all of the time, but the customer doesn't *really* enter into the equation. Often, the customer never visits and employees don't go off-site to see real product applications. Type 2 leaders don't push the system to it's limits to serve the customer and therefore never find that weak link or bottleneck that needs to be the next target for improvement. Continuous improvement becomes discontinuous or has a predefined slope rather than being driven by the real needs or opportunities of the business.

In the environment a process-oriented leader creates, standards for improvement tend to slip over time, often in the name of teamwork: "The team isn't ready to change this just yet; it makes them uncomfortable. Let's look at it again in a few months" (or never).

Kaizen teams are not challenged to excel: "Reducing setup times by 90 percent would be great, but 50 percent is a more reasonable goal; good job guys!"

➤ Type 3: The Lean Leader

Finally, we'll examine the leader who is goal *and* process oriented, Type 3. The Lean Leader's message is "We'll get it done and we'll do it the *right* way."

This leader *demands* change, a *real* result, and having achieved the result, is the champion of the new process: "We'll do it because the team decided it was the best way to proceed," "We'll do it until we decide there's a better way."

This leader's objective is to take the hill through the process; there are no excuses that justify breaking the rules. In other words, the organization will satisfy the customer's need—do whatever it takes—but they will use the system to do it.

This approach puts the system under stress. It finds the weak spots and drives continuous improvement. For example, whenever we find that the current process struggles with a particular form of customer demand, we *need* to change the process to overcome this limitation and enhance service.

Another characteristic behavior of this type is to demand that all of the processes respect and adapt to the system. For example, sales learns to level sell. Rather than fighting for a 10,000 piece order now, a salesman works with the customer to establish the *real* weekly or daily need and communicate that need directly to the factory.

Lean leaders show respect for the team by respecting, in a real sense, the process they've built: "It's not perfect, never will be, but we'll follow it until we develop something better."

These leaders don't impose their own solutions on the team, directly or indirectly. They show they value both the results and how they are obtained. They show respect for the process.

Above all, these leaders are consistent, calm, and secure in their beliefs. Beliefs are clear and consistently articulated over time: Action is consistent with rhetoric.

Beliefs are not the same as "actions needed" at a particular time; beliefs underlie action decisions. These leaders demonstrate by action *and* word a commitment to a long-term path: *how* to achieve the vision.

■ DEVELOPING PEOPLE

As we view the characteristic behaviors of each of the three leader types, and their influence on the behavior of their organizations, we must also consider the development of individuals within these organizations. The success of the organization, after all, does not depend solely on the behavior of the leader but on that of the organization as a whole, and that is in turn influenced by the skills and developed behaviors of the individuals who make it up. What does each type of leader strive for, nurture, mentor for, and *reinforce*. The answers should not come as a surprise, conforming for the most part to the demonstrated behaviors of the leaders.

What stands out is the need to develop and select among all employees leadership skills that are shown by the Type 3, lean, leader. Successful lean organizations must constantly grow and evolve. That growth and evolution must be fueled in part from within, from a strong core of individuals with the right stuff—the skills, vision, commitment, and integrity to move to the next level.

No individual leader can long sustain the path to success in an increasingly competitive and constantly leaner world without developing others who can, with their fellows, ever more independently shoulder the load in moving the enterprise forward.

In addition to the skills, commitment, and integrity of the business leader, success requires the development of the supporting resources who will work at the cutting edge of change. Kaizen is a facilitated process; that is, it is carried out with the guidance and direction of expert resources who work to ensure that key principles are maintained. They also help teams overcome the difficulties, frustrations, and uncertainties they will doubtless encounter along the way.

The facilitator and team leader, the characters Steve and Frank in the Universal Valve story in Chapter 1, play key roles in the success of individual projects and in building the pattern and tone for the overall kaizen-based improvement program.

■ THE FACILITATOR

The facilitator is often the key protagonist or individual who personifies kaizen or lean manufacturing in the organization. His or her skills include fluency in the whole range of improvement tools teams may employ in their work, but most important are the facilitator's people management or mentoring skills. They come into play as the facilitator guides the team and its leader through the inevitable difficulties and personality conflicts that arise during an intense kaizen project period.

A facilitator's skills can only be developed through experience—real practice with real teams. As a consequence, choosing candidates who will be successful in this role is difficult at best. There is no archetype of the ideal facilitator. Successful facilitators come from a variety of backgrounds: engineering, manufacturing supervision, human resources specialists, shop floor associates. What they have in common is their ability to guide a team through the process, recognizing the stresses and conflicts as they build, knowing when to press, when to back away, when to coach. Experience is both the best teacher and the best screening process for the facilitator.

A skilled facilitator will have served as a member of several kaizen teams, gaining first-hand experience in the day-to-day activities and personal interplay of the team. Then comes team leadership. The team leader's role is considerably more stressful than that of a team member. Some would argue that the pressures the team leader faces are greater than those of the facilitator. The team leader is accountable for the success or failure of the team, keeping them on track to find and implement the solutions needed to reach their goals. Guiding and mentoring the team leader is one of the key responsibilities of the facilitator. Experience as a team leader in several environments helps to build a real understanding of the stresses, uncertainties, and conflicts faced in that role and is an indispensable element of the facilitator's development.

Successful team leaders are then given the opportunity to co-facilitate and team teach alongside an experienced facilitator, a real mentor and guide. Eventually, the process culminates with the candidate independently developing a series of kaizen projects. With input from management, project sites are selected and goals set. Team leaders and members are chosen and training programs delivered. Finally, the actual projects are carried out under the guidance of the facilitator candidate.

The team's success is the facilitator's success, for, in truth, the failure of a team is seen as a failure of facilitation and of management. Some aspect of the project selection, training, or critical guidance during the project fell short of what was needed for success. This is a high standard, but the one successful practitioners set for themselves. It is also one that helps build the kind of confidence that an organization needs to go forward with such a challenging and daring approach to improvement.

This "certification" process is necessarily time consuming (six to eight months of full-time effort for a beginner is not uncommon) and prone to false starts, with candidates falling or opting out along the way. A serious kaizen improvement program requires experienced guides developed through a rigorous process such as this for success.

■ THE TEAM LEADER

The team leader's role, as discussed above, is one of transition, often transition from the status quo that he himself may be charged with maintaining. The team leader feels the weight of responsibility for the success or failure of the team. He or she has to bring together the often-disparate members of the team into a cohesive group that can quickly apply its collective skills to developing and implementing creative solutions to challenging problems. In addition, within the short, time-compressed, working life of a kaizen team, periods of confusion, frustration, and sometimes frantic effort combine to heighten the pressures the team leader faces.

A team leader ideally will have served as a member on one or more teams and therefore, has some sense of the routines and pressures of the kaizen process. Individuals who demonstrate a bias toward change, an open-minded attitude, and who can perform well under pressure are obviously preferred, but these attributes are not absolute predictors of success. The kaizen process is unique, and some adapt more readily to it than others.

The role of the team leader is not to supervise the team or to apply his or her own solutions, but to draw out the talents of the team and *lead* it to its goals.

■ ENSURING SUCCESS: ADVOCACY VERSUS SPONSORSHIP

Another critical element of an effective leadership picture is true sponsorship. Change agents aren't enough. Kaizen cannot become an effective tool for change within an organization unless it is strongly sponsored from the top. Don't confuse sponsorship with advocacy.

To sponsor means to give support in a real sense, not merely as a cheerleader. The sponsor of the kaizen initiative, the senior manager who "owns the business," must demonstrate in tangible ways his or her commitment to the process. The manager must not only suggest change but be prepared to describe it as an imperative so that the whole organization can clearly see its direction and need.

For a kaizen team to be successful, it must be seen as carrying out the actions needed, or better yet, demanded by management for the success of the business. Because the changes are radical, the need for clear top management support is all the more acute.

■ INTEGRITY

The successful lean-manufacturing leader demonstrates a high level of personal integrity.

Creating a lean-manufacturing environment means asking people to make radical change, to follow what seems an uncharted path, to take risk, and to take personal responsibility for a broader range of actions and results than ever. This must be based on *trust*. To a great extent, trust comes from consistency and predictability. Measures are a good example. Trusted leaders say what they want clearly and unambiguously and don't change that measure without reason or without explanation. Their motto might be "I do what I say."

No organization successfully transforms itself without taking risks—individual risks and risks taken as a group. Kaizen teams epitomize risk-taking groups that depart radically from the known in search of dramatic improvement. The results are not always what were envisioned, but radical change requires real risk taking—the kind of risk taking that can only take place in an environment of trust and support. The integrity of the leader allows him or her to credibly encourage risks and to support the right risk-taking actions—those that adhere to core principles or underlying beliefs. The words *always* go with the music.

Chapter

Never Look Back

"Never look back; something might be gaining on you" is the best-known saying of the legendary pitcher Satchel Paige. Paige's description of athletic speed was to "turn out the light and be in bed before the room gets dark." He is estimated to have pitched at least part of 2,500 baseball games as a starter (60 games or so a season), and he hurled three innings in his last major-league game at the age of 59. In his younger days with the old Kansas City Monarchs, Satchel Paige *was* the strategy. He "made something happen."

Championship sports analogies to business can be overdone, but they are powerful. Many managers—male ones anyway—don't seem to tire of them. Whether they are true or highly embellished, the common theme of championship stories is *winning*. They may extol a champion's humble beginnings, brilliance of strategy, pain of preparation, or grace under pressure, but unless the outcome was *winning*, there is no punch to the story. And in the end winning depends on execution. Baseball is a game of execution. The better your execution, the tougher the league you can play in.

■ THE NAME OF THE GAME IS EXECUTION

The Kaizen Blitz is also about execution—making something happen. Kaizen Blitz seems simple. On the surface, baseball is simple too; young children can understand the basic rules well enough to play. At the major-league level, the rules are extensive, keenly studied, and occasionally the subject of bitter dispute. But when a player is on the field, what he actually does—or tries to do—comes from well-honed instinct. A major-league player makes difficult execution look easy.

In any kind of business, people would like to execute better. Learning the basics of process improvement is like picking up the basic rules of baseball; they aren't hard to understand. However, both in baseball and in business, few aspirants can execute at the major-league level.

Major-league baseball is laden with statistics. Records kept on every conceivable achievement, glorious and inglorious, fuel the announcers with gas during a dull game. Statistically, half of all players and half of all teams must be below average, and only one team can win the World Series. However, players of major-league caliber have spent a lifetime of practice—eating, sleeping, and breathing baseball—to learn how to execute better than the rest of us. With today's science-based training, batters even have exercises to train their eyes to follow a pitch that most of us would only hear pop in the mitt.

■ OVERCOMING WEAKNESS OF EXECUTION

The Association for Manufacturing Excellence has a Champions Club. From time to time, a few of its members meet to learn more about a topic of interest and share ideas. One of their recurring themes is that knotty issues must be resolved to put simple concepts of process flow and quality into practice, so "getting it all together" for great execution isn't as simple as it seems. But paradoxically, those whose organizations have made substantial progress acclaim in retrospect how simple it seemed.

The paradox is that putting it all together in execution goes much faster in some settings than others, and much faster with some leaders than others. Execution isn't knowing all about the subject; it's putting what you know all together. When that happens, execution appears to be easy, just as superb fielders make a diving catch look so easy that you have to have played to appreciate the feat.

Nobody learned to play major-league baseball in a day. Nobody reaches the major leagues in process improvement in a day either. But if they are going to get there, they start playing and stay with it—usually for a lifetime.

■ THE FUNDAMENTALS: ONE MORE TIME

Even professional ballplayers regularly practice the fundamentals. After a few days off, fundamentals that should be automatic start to become rusty. Here are the encapsulated fundamentals of the Kaizen Blitz that need to be regularly practiced:

1. Assess where the organization (processes) are.
2. Look ahead: What's changing in our environment? What do we have to do really well? Size up the players and the skills that must be further developed.
3. Pick a process, or several processes. Make sure that the people working them know what is going to happen.
4. Commission a Kaizen Blitz event—or a series of them. Let the imagination rip. You'll need some experienced facilitators for events until your own have gained experience.
5. Study the demonstrated results. Stimulate support personnel to study the results.
6. Follow up until the process can regularly function as well as, or better than, the demonstration. Here real leadership makes the difference in sustaining the gain. Not standardizing the new method and supporting it is usually the downfall of improvement by Kaizen Blitz.
7. Repeat points 3–6 again and again; as much as the organization has the capacity to do. Develop people to expand the organizational capacity to streamline processes by Kaizen Blitz.
8. Monitor the improvement of processes to be sure that changes are making a difference where it counts—in the processes and with customers, then with associates and investors. Keep the total program herded in the right direction.

That's it—details excluded—in sales-job format. Unless you try to play over your head too soon, an enthusiastic group of players will soon get their kicks from victories in process improvement.

When you dig into the details, improvement programs with Kaizen Blitz explode into the kinds of stories and advice that aficionados tell about baseball. As with sports, there are numerous perspectives from which to describe kaizen adventures, and infinite varieties of them. It isn't possible to describe them comprehensively, just as it isn't possible to be totally comprehensive in sports publications—even in the statistics-laden ones.

Work up confidence and start. Use simple tools you already know or can pick up quickly. Add to the tool list as you get better. When projects flop, analyze why and go at it again. Toyota didn't get it right the first time, and neither has anyone else. After a process appears to be well refined, or even before, look for a breakthrough concept to serve the customer in a totally new way. Always challenge existing practice. Start refining the breakthrough process too. Once started, don't look back.

■ FUNDAMENTALS DON'T FADE

High-tech or low-tech, continuous improvement is becoming fundamental to operational competitiveness. In tough competition, companies fall out before they get so flabby that a turnaround artist can save them by whacking half the payroll and letting the survivors figure out how to do whatever work truly needs to be done. (That's the original kaizen in the United States.)

The ideas and tools used are not new; they are proven and making their way into mainstream operating practice. Forget becoming a champion just because your processes are kept fit. Everybody of consequence is getting fit; it's fundamental, a base on which to build.

The garden-variety Kaizen Blitz takes out "silly" waste, the activity that, if people had been conditioned to lean processes, would not have accumulated, but which did because attention was directed to other goals or perhaps to staying occupied. A more ambitious Kaizen Blitz strives to create a capability that no one else is known to have—such as being able to regularly deliver custom-engineered pneumatics systems within 24 hours. (This is a well-known ambition of several competitors in that industry, which are "competing on timeprint.")

Like physical fitness, the ability to keep processes trim takes constant attention. It makes no difference whether the processes build cruise ships or enter orders off the Internet. If we are not paying attention, we assume that fitness has not deteriorated until we need to call on it and it's no longer there. Maintaining attention on fundamentals is as hard as keeping fit year in and year out.

So, what is fundamental to process health and fitness? And what is merely a fad? A technique is not a fad if it is reasonable to implement and if it improves a process as indicated by quality, timeprint, space, customer satisfaction, resource use, and of course, profitability. If it promises weight loss without dieting, performance improvement without practice, or physical fitness without effort, it should be regarded with healthy skepticism.

If a change is real, it is visible by some kind of indicator. If we noticeably change our physical fitness, we have changed ourselves. If we noticeably change the process fitness of a working organization, we have also changed its work habits—or work culture—to some extent. That's why implementation of anything truly effective takes leadership.

Creating process excellence has attracted numerous "fitness coaches" with an endless variety of improvement regimens and recipes. Some are promoted much more heavily than others. No one can sort out the promotions even if they work at it full time. Anyone with a real job doesn't bother to open all the mail. None of the recipes and regimens will develop a champion if there's no time or will for implementation.

Furthermore, fitness does not prevent one from being run over by a beer truck or dying of pneumonia. Promotions tend to exaggerate the benefits of process fitness for most organizations. Percentage changes are particularly misleading. For instance, if an assembly operation drops inventory by 90 percent—from 10 months to one—it just transitioned from dead to breathing. It may still be too fat and slow to be competitive.

From Materials Requirements Planning (MRP) packages onward, industry press stories about changes actually adopted by many companies start with enthusiastic acceptance, then stories of failed implementation, and followed by stories of "what it really takes." Following these stories from a distance, it's hard to tell early on whether the concept to be implemented is poor or whether the stories represent a "normal casualty rate" from poor implementation.

Can an organization pay too much attention to process fitness? Yes, just as an athlete can be in top condition but ineffective in a real game: a golfer with a 300-yard drive that can't sink a pressure putt; a hunter great on the practice range who panics when faced with a real bear. Fitness just gets you in the game—or in the hunt.

This book has concentrated on process fitness. In a manufacturing company, that's often narrowly construed as efficient shop-floor operations or, a little more broadly, as efficient materials pipelines. Concentrating on material flows assumes that value is added only by the product, which is another legacy ghost from Taylorism. In U.S. companies classified as manufacturers by the SIC codes, a high percentage of people are engaged not in either product development or production but in service. Of course, most of the U.S. economy now is also service.

The shift to service has opened a different perspective on business, and it opens a new arena to Kaizen Blitz. Physics-and-geometry production projects are training exercises. When designing or revising service processes, the objective is to positively add value as well as to eliminate the obvious NVA waste. Start where people can readily learn alligator fighting, keep going, and don't look back.

■ PRODUCT DEVELOPMENT KAIZEN: LANTECH

In manufacturing it is obvious that product design strongly influences the processes to make it. Fixed designs inhibit radical ideas to transform the process, so they become barriers to cost reduction and performance improvement. Once concepts of fast-flow production have become actionable, one can design products to fit a production process—and for all other processes later in its lifetime as well. In technique speak, this is called DFX—design for everything. Doing so greatly speeds product introduction too. At its ultimate, DFX allows customer engineering for each order to be done within a total process duration time acceptable to the customer, and with the capacity to complete the engineering for different custom orders at planned takt time intervals.

Here's how one company, Lantech, Inc., got started in 1992. Lantech had 320 associates at the time. Its business is material handling and packaging machines, primarily stretch wrappers. Most orders call for customer options or customer engineering.

The first shop-floor Kaizen Blitz was in the spring of 1992. The culture for it was ripe, so the first blitz was rapidly followed by others that converted a job shop system to cells. Pat Lancaster, Lantech's founder, is an inventor, entrepreneur, and believer in pushing real responsibility to the working level. Within months, duration times to build a machine dropped from five weeks to two days.

Previously, Lantech kept huge inventories of popular models and modules on hand. To fill a customer order, they pulled these from stock and configured them to the order, with considerable variance in the amount of time required to do it. A machine often had to be stripped and substantially rebuilt, so in effect, it was assembled twice. With a two-day production time, Lantech filled orders from production faster than they had by reconfiguring modules pulled from stock.

Around mid 1992 Lantech was also working on the design of a new machine—the Q series semiautomatic, intended to be easily customizable and highly flexible in adapting to different customer needs for size, volume, and speed. Lantech had also studied its customers' processes. For the Q to meet its market objectives, it was clear that the design had to be manufacturable in two days or less, same as the current models, but Lantech had never designed for produceability before.

The time was short and the pressure was on. Lantech assembled a cross-functional team for a 12-hour design blitz of the Q. Many team members had never before been involved in design and were skeptical. The blitz began with the lead design engineer and a marketing team member presenting the design objective and the sales objective. Their mission was to maintain those objectives while also making the Q design compatible with one-piece flow.

As a learning experience, it was a rip snorter. In 12 hours the design blitz team repeatedly assembled and disassembled the prototype and made about 200 design changes and enhancements. At the end they knew that they could easily build the Q and that it would be a market winner besides. Furthermore, the design of the Q now belonged to everyone; it wasn't an unwanted orphan thrown over the wall from design engineering. The box copy shows a few excerpts from the day's work.

As soon as design engineering locked down the changes that had been made, a second one-week factory blitz was held to design a new production process for the Q. Most of the team had already participated in the blitz to convert to cells. They started with the revised design, a blank flip chart, and the objective of producing 10 machines a shift using one one-piece flow in a one-shift duration process. They sited the processes, selected the equipment, laid out the flow and cells, and determined how to integrate it all into a work flow paced with a takt time. The flip chart became the blueprint to develop the production system for the Q.

The Q factory was designed for 20 percent of the cost that Lantech would have incurred by using an outside designer. Before start-up, they tuned the process with another blitz, then tried it out

MAKING 200 DESIGN CHANGES IN 12 INTENSE HOURS AT LANTECH

When Steve DeGrasse's team reached the shop floor the morning of the design kaizen for the Q semiautomatic, they found themselves staring at large pile of unpainted fabrication parts. "We didn't know where to start," said Steve, so they started at the bottom, the base of the Q. The machine has two major parts: the base—a five-foot wide turntable that rotates the pallet to be wrapped; and the tower with the control panel and the roll carriage that dispenses plastic film.

One Idea Yields Another

The four support bars for the center bearing in the base were made of 3/8-inch by 2-inch flat stock; most other pieces of the upright were cut from 2-inch channel. Why not use all one stock?

They quickly jumped to a bigger opportunity. The four bars in an H-shape were all of different length and different hole pattern. If they could make every bar identical, they would save time cutting and machining. Within a few minutes the team had generated an alternate design with uniform support bars in a polar array. Rather than stand around jawing about it, they got some stock and immediately tested it out. It worked, cutting material cost by half and machining time per base by 12 minutes.

No Sacred Cows

Some modifications challenged long-established practice, such as welding the top cap to the tower, which had been done for 13 years. With a welded top cap, the roll carriage had to be inserted without its guide wheels, which meant lifting it into place with a hoist, then walking around it to bolt everything together. Why not bolt the cap instead of welding it so the roll carriage could slide into the tower while still on its side and with the wheels on the carriage? A hue and cry arose on why that might not be such a good idea, so they tried that one too. It worked. It saved 20 minutes of assembly time and presented a much-reduced safety hazard besides.

"We made a paradigm shift that day—from handed-down to hands-on," explained DeGrasse. Now commonsense things happen regularly at Lantech.

and fought alligators for a week. On the first full day of production, they finished eight machines. Reaching the goal of 10 machines a shift took several more months, but it was still the best start-up that they had ever had up to that time. The project also reinforced the principle of do-it-yourself process design and revision.

That was six years ago. Today many companies—perhaps most of them—design for assembly and design for production, but possibly not with the concurrent pizzazz and speed of Lantech's short, intense blitz sessions. At Lantech, Kaizen Blitz has become a part of life—part of the work culture. A new product or service is conceptualized in a blitz. Others follow as the new offering is prepared for market and delivered. They imagineer, decide, and execute. And they don't look back.[1]

Companies such as Lantech use Kaizen Blitz imaginatively. Organizations that just clean out the waste from existing processes make a great start, but they will stagnate if they believe that there is a golden future in being like the Japanese artists who paint the same picture again every day of their life until they get it perfect. The discipline of perfectionism combined with innovation is where the future is.

■ PRODUCT CLINIC

A key element of Kaizen Blitz is self-discovery. People execute—make something happen—when they discover for themselves why it is necessary. That characteristic is also present in a longer, more comprehensive version of kaizen that has been stirring change in German industry, where high costs remain a huge concern. The Germans call it *Produktklinik,* or Product Clinic.

Product Clinic is used by Mercedes Benz, Volkswagen, Thysson (steel), and numerous small-to medium-sized companies. A few results from a sample of these companies is shown in Table 11.1. Very few Product Clinics, perhaps 1 in 20, have gone offtrack without an ingenious course of action rolling out, which is a remarkable im-

---

[1] Pat Lancaster, and Ron Hicks, "Using Kaizen to Improve Designs and to Speed Development: How Lantech Kaizened a Problem Product," *Target* [Publication of the Association for Manufacturing Excellence] 11, (September–October 1995): 24–29.

Table 11.1. Examples of Company Improvements from Product Clinic

Company	Improvements
BTR (Argus Ball Valves)	Reduced production cost an average of 60%. Reduced throughput time by 78%.
Kuka (robotics)	Reduced cost by 55% in four years. Improved performance specifications in same time.
Schmitz (semitrailers)	Reduced total production cost by 50% in two years. Increased labor productivity by 100%. Doubled plant capacity.

plementation record for anything. One of the more instructive cases is Peter Schmitz, a manufacturer of semitrailers.

Product Clinic takes on all the processes associated with a product or product line at once, unlike a process-focused Kaizen Blitz, so the core part of a Product Clinic takes several months, not a week or less. First, senior management assigns a team of 10 to 20 persons to analyze a product versus the competition, look at the strategy for it, and propose a workable breakthrough solution, to be immediately implemented. Senior management, the leaders at the top, do not take part directly. The objective is for action leaders in the company to discover for themselves what must be done.

The central part of a Product Clinic is a carefully planned comparative disassembly of the company's products versus those of competitors. The disassembly exercise is carefully planned to go well beyond the usual reverse engineering. It not only compares product functions and features but also examines the processes by which they are probably deviled, made, distributed, serviced, and salvaged. This results in a table of benchmark ideas and comparative costs. The team can cherry pick these and try to improve on them.

The core of a Product Clinic is preceded by a marketing study that compares different competitors' offerings with their own. A typical conclusion is "We don't really know much." Then the scope of the Product Clinic is thrown wide open. The team can review any process: supplier management, production, field service, and so on.

As this exercise proceeds, the results are typically posted in a "war-room" area to which other people have access, so they too can track what is being discovered. Other persons may be called in to work with the core team from time to time.

Within the core Product Clinic team, the focus has to be kept on discovering the facts because as "stupid stuff" and horrible legacy monsters are discovered, emotions can run high. For this reason, most meetings are neutrally facilitated. After several months of this, the usual outcome is that the grassroots personnel cannot be held back much longer from tearing off on a revolutionary plan.

Product Clinic is a concept very similar to Kaizen Blitz, but more comprehensive. The intent is to use it more imaginatively and more broadly than to grub out the Parkinson's Law sclerosis from existing processes. As with Kaizen Blitz, all Product Clinics have similarities, but each one is a unique experience depending on the situation of that company. A few companies, such as Kuka, have now conducted Product Clinics more than once on the same product line. Product Clinics are also starting to be used for software and service products as well as manufactured ones.

■ PETER SCHMITZ

Schmitz produces trailers for semitrucks. Its forte is special-purpose ones, particularly refrigerated trailers. Three years ago, plagued by Germany's cost demons, the chief executive officer heard of product clinic and attended a two-day introductory seminar. A week later he arranged for the Technical University of Munich to facilitate a Product Clinic at Schmitz.

The Schmitz team reviewed the market, compared their trailer's on-the-road performance with those from competitors, reviewed strategy, and then disassembled several competitors' trailers along with one of their own, analyzing differences and the reasons for them. They quickly concluded that action should proceed on two fronts: simplifying designs and streamlining production—both at once.

Redesign yielded the most startling changes. Schmitz had long given each customer what they asked for, so tailored designs had ballooned the proliferation of part numbers. The key to simplifying designs was a strategic change. Make the top-of-the-line features standard on all trailers, but at a price lower than the plain versions had been previously. Another strategic move planned by management before the Product Clinic was also beneficial. Schmitz trailers are now sold exclusively for Benz tractors, which minimizes the types of connects. The companies formed a marketing alliance.

The part-number database for new trailers shrank to an anorexic level. For example, Schmitz had accumulated 136 different designs for parking stands (to hold up the front of the trailer when disconnected from the tractor). These were reduced to two types: one for the right side and one for the left.

Parts were reconfigured for easy modification. For example, light cluster mounts were filled with holes like Swiss cheese, so lights were easily arranged (and changed) in any pattern a customer might want.

The redesign was also done with a much smoother flow process in mind. By the time they finished, the new Schmitz processes greatly simplified customizing, planning, and manufacturing. Then they kaizen blitzed these processes from end to end.

In a little over a year Schmitz cut costs by half and doubled factory capacity with the same workforce, and all with a minimum of investment. The takt time for trailers dropped by half, from 40 minutes to 20.

Aside from product clinic, Schmitz also brought out a breakthrough idea from research and development, a nonabsorptive insulation for refrigerated trailers. All the competitors' trailers are still using the kind that absorbs a couple of tons of dead weight in water over its lifetime, which saps fuel economy. Schmitz's bottom line looks pretty good too, and they aren't looking back.[2]

Schmitz has yet to do a second Product Clinic. What do you suppose they could do with a design breakthrough blitz that included some customers and suppliers?

■ DISTRACTION AND THE TOYOTA DILEMMA

In the United States, Germany, Japan, or anywhere else in the world in which disciplined process improvement has taken hold in the past few decades, its methodological roots go back to one com-

---

[2] Horst Wildemann, "Produktklinik: Getting It All Together in Germany," *Target* [Publication of the Association for Manufacturing Excellence] 13, (November–December 1997): 22–29.

pany: Toyota Motor Company. In the latter half of the twentieth century, Toyota became for manufacturing management what Frederick Taylor had been in the first half.

Today some of Toyota's suppliers possibly "out-Toyota" them, and other companies may be more imaginative, but basic kaizen and Plan-Do-Check-Act (the Deming Circle) still endure there. Toyota itself faces new challenges.

When talk of the "Japanese miracle" began around 1980, Toyota was still a homeland-bound company that exported. It had very few foreign plants. Aside from the manufacturers who had been pushed to the wall in Japan, few Japanese had ever heard of the Toyota Production System, much less understood it. (There's no reason for most Americans to understand the Ford Production System either.) Western learning about Japanese work methods was still in the curiosity stage.

That began to change quickly. By the early 1980s the impetus to learn about all things Japanese held sway. A few Western pioneer companies cranked up a fledgling version of JIT production. Omark, Black & Decker, Harley-Davidson, John Deere, and Hewlett-Packard began chugging while most U.S. companies were still scratching their heads. However, the quality movement really took off. U.S. companies began some serious shaping up. By 1988 the United States had inaugurated the Baldrige Award.

About this same time Toyota was occupied with much more than the fundamental advancement of waste-chopping production improvement. Overseas expansion had begun. Toyota's operating philosophy went abroad with it, encountering a variety of alien work cultures. Riding global expansion is a far different management challenge from perfecting production processes for export goods.

However, to expand their global market share, Toyota had to regularly roll out new models. By the mid 1980s, Toyota kept the production processes ultralean but concentrated more on improving the product development process, keeping designs simple and part counts down. Both inside the company and with suppliers, the Toyota design process was efficient but dependent on "peopleware," or close communication among people. Among the ways that Toyota and its suppliers promoted such relationships was by placing young "comers" on kaizen teams so that they got to know each other, thus forming working relationships for a lifetime. The company is acknowledged to have achieved the fastest product launch time to date for a major vehicle—18 months—and that too has received recognition.[3]

Toyota learned a great deal from the *gaijins* of different working cultures that it has encountered. For instance, Westerners are not as keen about process improvement if the work doesn't physically ease as well, so ergonomics is more important to them. Westerners (and now many younger Japanese) do not prize the Japanese work culture discipline that endures 1,000-fungo baseball drills (shag 1,000 batted balls, or until you drop, whichever comes first). They prefer to concentrate improvement on winning the games. Americans work hard in bursts and prefer to have fun doing it; Japanese focus intently on work and long persist at it.

Another important lesson, still not fully absorbed, was the importance of "packaging" techniques and management philosophy for export. The working culture was sometimes coded in Japanese cultural analogies, so different stories were needed. Within Toyota the documentation of standardized process elements was done in excruciating detail, but how to arrive at the methods and how to actually do the standardization is a far more difficult skill to explain. It is still not fully explainable in any language and simply has to be learned by doing it.

At present Toyota still "out-Toyotas" almost everyone else, but the competitive advantage is not what it used to be. As the Japanese put it, conventional kaizen in Japan is mature. The biggest bites have been taken from the apple of waste; flattened learning curves depict only little nibbles from the apple core.

Toyota's break-even points are low. For years, an objective of process design has been to break even at 30 percent of capacity, so the company is well positioned to weather the economic setbacks in Asia. Their exceptional fitness has bought them time, but the clock is ticking. Time for a new breakthrough. Time for a new process platform.

Today Toyota is dedicated to transforming into a truly global company, with people from all countries in senior positions. As

---

[3] Allen Ward, Jeffrey K. Liker, John J. Cristiano, and Durward K. Sobek, II, "The Second Toyota Paradox: How Delaying Decisions Can Make Better Cars Faster," *Sloan Management Review* 36, (Spring 1995): 43–61. The authors dwell on the practice of making many design proposals, part by part, sifting through them to find the best one from several points of view, then running rapidly through the prototype–tooling–trial run process. It's a grand-scale kaizen approach.

can be seen from their recent technical advances, Toyota's people are not shabby in creativity, but CEO Okuda thinks that they need to emphasize it more.[4]

The globalization is distracting to top management. Precise direction for future operational development is yet to be clearly articulated, and both for Toyota and much of Japan it is a big dilemma. Will it be possible for Toyota to retain a spot at the top of the benchmarking pyramid? Moreover, how important is it to be there? Along with the rest of Japan, Toyota is groping for a new fundamental direction.

A number of Japanese future scenarios have been developed. Some have had impact. One developed outside Toyota was called "Manufacturing 21" in the United States.[5] That study noted that in the advanced economies, the era of Henry Ford–style mass production was passing quickly, and calls were now for smaller, highly decentralized, but highly communicative work organizations (dubbed "holonic" organizations) to replace hierarchy by seniority. It proposed customer-unique problem solutions implemented through short-duration, high-flexibility operations called "holonic manufacturing."

A similar idea was named "agile manufacturing" in the United States.[6] Companies have already pursued agile manufacturing—or think that they have. For example, the *1997 Industry Week Census of Manufacturers* reported that 53 percent of all responding plants had to some degree adopted agile manufacturing practices—whatever the respondents interpreted them to be. It's almost as if manufacturers wanted to provide instant customer satisfaction over the Internet, as can sometimes be done with service. However, if customer satisfaction requires a physical product, digitization allows many wonderful tricks, but it cannot yet e-mail a truck.

Both of these projections have now aged. Toyota, along with almost everyone else who has been busy streamlining processes, is

---

[4] Tanya Clark, "Destructive Force: Toyota's Okuda Speaks Out," *Industry Week*, July 6, 1998, pp. 38–42.

[5] *Manufacturing 21 Report* (Wheeling, Ill,: Association for Manufacturing Excellence, 1990). This is a summary in English of the Japanese projection done by a Japanese industry group working out of Waseda University.

[6] *Twenty-first Century Manufacturing Enterprise Strategy,* (Bethlehem, Pa.: Agility Forum, 1991). This is a U.S. counterpart proposal for agile manufacturing akin to "holonic" manufacturing concepts in Japan and Europe.

struggling with where to head next with this capability. Developing economies are still well served by lean mass production—when they are economically healthy.

Elsewhere expectations are different; mass-produced goods are less acceptable or less satisfying to jaded people weary of their sameness—or even their feature-laden ease of use. For example, it has been noted that amateur photographers like point-and-shoot, artificial-intelligence cameras. Serious photographers prefer to twiddle the knobs themselves. Therefore, are mass production, mass service, and mass media really just a stage in which we are amateur customers?

Most of the crystal-balling leads toward improvement of processes in which customers participate, and in which solutions for *their specific* problems are customized for them and quickly implemented. More problems may also be environmental. In that case, a grand process kaizen would examine a full life cycle of a product, from birth through multiple use/recycle/remanufacturing phases to final disposition.

Many futurist scenarios depict the twenty-first century as an era of biology, complexity, and human exploration of our own capabilities—of kaizen applied to genetic codes. In this environment, mass production would only create "platforms." Smaller-scale, highly flexible, closely connected "boutique" manufacturing would support customized solutions. Others would tend to the management of materials life cycles.[7]

In other words, our interests could easily wander from those that are supported by a twentieth-century industrial base, Toyota-style or otherwise. Something analogous happened in the United States after World War II. By that time Taylorism was mature, and people began to neglect basic process development until the likes of Toyota jolted them back into it. The same kinds of distractions could happen again, but they shouldn't.

■ IMAGINATION AND THE KAIZEN BLITZ

Properly used, the power of the Kaizen Blitz comes from combining imagination and discipline in a short period of time. Do something different. Do it right. Set it up to do it again and again. And

---

[7] To pick up on this, one has only to track articles in *The Futurist,* a publication of the World Future Society, Washington, DC.

make the change quickly—hands-on at the point of action. Kaizen Blitz is about making something happen—execution.

Sure, there are many ifs, ands, or buts. Swing at every pitch and you're strike-out bait; never swing at a pitch and your batting average is zero. Batters have to think—maybe even have a strategy. But unless batters swing sometime, there isn't much point to the whole game.

The AME Kaizen Blitz is also about trying new ideas. To try them, you must first get them. In the right setting, getting ideas isn't hard; it's usually fun. Most of us like creativity exercises, and the world is full of creativity stimulants. One of the more elaborate ones for technical problem solving is TRIZ (the Russian acronym for theory of inventive problem solving), which migrated from the former Soviet Union.[8]

The more difficult part of process improvement is the discipline of standardization. Concepts of standard work began with Frederick Taylor, but it took the perfectionism of Toyota to show how people doing the work could develop their own standardization instead of having their work standardized for them.

Finally, a few examples have hinted at what can really be done. As always, no one knows what twenty first-century business or manufacturing processes will really be like until they are here. Super Kaizen Blitz breakthoughs could well speed the development of radical new process ideas. Used in entrepreneurial fashion, it might even create from a blank page the platform for a new company with new offerings and totally different processes for supplying them. But the need for disciplined imagination should be promoted to implement such ventures.

Just start and never look back.

---

[8] Victor Fey, and Eugene Riven, "TRIZ: A New Approach to Innovative Engineering and Problem Solving," *Target* [Publication of the Association for Manufacturing Excellence] 12 (September–October 1996): 7–13.

Index

Page numbers referring to figures or tables appear in italics. Page numbers referring to footnotes are followed by n.

Anthony C. Laraia has over twenty-five years experience in engineering and operations management, and as a Director of the Association for Manufacturing Excellence was instrumental in developing and promoting the AME Kaizen Blitz program. While Manager of Manufacturing Engineering for the Fafnir Bearings Division of the Torrington Company, a subsidiary of Ingersoll-Rand, he directed over 200 kaizen projects bringing dramatic improvement to a broad range of business processes.

Patricia E. Moody is a manufacturing management consultant and author with more than 25 years of industry and consulting experience working with companies such as Motorola, Solectron, Mead, and Johnson and Johnson, and seven books to her credit, including *Leading Manufacturing Excellence, Breakthrough Partnering, Powered by Honda, The Technology Machine,* and *Ten Best;* her eighth book, an industrial thriller titled *Mill Town,* will be out next year. For eight years she was the editor of AME's *Target* magazine. She can be reached at *PEMoody@aol.com.*

Robert W. Hall, one of the founders of AME, is currently editor-in-chief of *Target* magazine. He has authored or coauthored five books related to lean manufacturing including one of the original ones, *Zero Inventories.* He is the Professor of Operations Management, Kelly School of Business, Indiana University.